Economic History of India

Ancient to Present Day

Second Revised and Enlarged Edition

N. Jayapalan

ATLANTIC
PUBLISHERS & DISTRIBUTORS (P) LTD

ATLANTIC
PUBLISHERS & DISTRIBUTORS (P) LTD
7/22, Ansari Road, Darya Ganj, New Delhi
Tel.: +91-11-4077 5252, 2327 3880
E-mail: orders@atlanticbooks.com
Web: www.atlanticbooks.com

Reprint 2026

Published by Atlantic Publishers & Distributors (P) Ltd.

Printed & bound in India by Atlantic Print Services

Preface to the Second Edition

It gives me great pleasure to place in the hands of the readers the second edition of the book *Economic History of India—Ancient to Present Day*. The overwhelming response received to the first edition of the book has encouraged me to bring out this new edition. It has also given me the opportunity to update some chapters adding latest developments wherever required, for the benefit of the readers.

India's economic history spans nearly 5000 years and dates back to Indus Vally Civilisation which flourished around 2500 B.C. Many objects discovered from the archaeological sites of Mohanjodaro and Harappa bear testimony that they were big industrial centres having trade relations with central, west and south India, west Asia and other parts of the world.

From Vedic literature we get a detailed description of the economic condition of early Aryans who were quite familiar with cultivation of crops, as well as indulged in various manufacturing activities besides doing commerce with Babylone, Sumeria and some other countries. A glimpse of the economic life during the later Vedic period can be had from *Atharva Veda*. Agriculture, trade, commerce and industry marked the economic life of people living in the epic age of *Ramayana* and *Mahabharata*.

From the Buddhist literature, particularly Jatakas and Tripitaka we get abundant information regarding the economic condition of India from 650 to 321 B.C. when every village was a self-sufficient unit. The merchant ships laden with a variety of articles like silk, muslin, ivory-works, gold and silver jewellery sailed to Burma, Siam and Ceylone. The barter system had ended and the new system with its standard and token coins had come into existence.

Kautilya's *Arthasastra*, Megasthenes' *Indica* and Vishakhadatta's *Mudrarakshasa* describe in detail the economic systems of the Mauryan period. The accounts of Chinese travellers Fa-hien and It-sing serve as reliable sources to know the socio-economic condition of the Gupta period, which many scholars have described as the golden era of Indian history.

The economic life of people during the Mughal period was satisfactory. Sher Shah and Akbar did a lot to improve the economic condition of the people. Some economic reforms were undertaken through Revenue System of Todar Mal and Mansabdari System. To use the words of Manucci "All things were in great plenty...fruits, pulses, grains, muslin cloth, gold and silver."

The British came to India as traders but succeeded in carving out their empire in the country. During their rule of over two centuries, they drained India of its wealth and destroyed the self-sufficient character of its villages. The British economic policies increased agricultural indebtedness, undermined village and cottage industries and gave rise to a capitalist class in India with the growth of new urban centres. When India achieved independence in 1947, the economy was in shambles. The industrial base was weak, agriculture was backward and poverty was widespread. Our leaders had a gigantic task of nation-building. The Planning Commission was established in 1950 to prepare the blueprint for development, taking an overall view of the needs and available resources of the country. The economic planning envisaged a growing public sector with massive investments in the basic and heavy industries. With the liberalisation of Indian economy in 1990s the country has been put on a high growth path and is making rapid strides in different sectors of the economy.

The book captures all the significant elements of India's economic history till date in a lucid manner. It will fulfil the needs of students and teachers of this subject and prove immensely helpful to the aspirants of Civil Services and other competitive examinations.

I am thankful to Atlantic Publishers and Distributors (P) Ltd., New Delhi for publishing the revised and enlarged edition of the book.

N. JAYAPALAN

Preface to the First Edition

It gives me great pleasure to place this book in the hands of the reader. The book is quite comprehensive and covers all aspects. It covers the entire syllabus prescribed by several universities. I have narrated all the events chronologically from the beginning to the end. I have also made a serious attempt to present the matter in a simple manner.

There is a plethora of books on the "Economic History of India". Most of them are bulky. Hence, I have written this book in a sizable Volume, *i.e.* neither too small nor too big. In addition to this, I have given importance to the Economic History of Modern Period, *i.e.* from Nehru period to the present time.

My experience of teaching the subject at the college level for several years has prompted me to write this book for the students of our universities mainly to meet their requirements. In addition to this, it has been designed to meet the requirements of the examinees of Civil Services Examination in History. I hope that the present book will prove to be more useful to the students than any other book on the subject available in the market.

I am thankful to the M/s Atlantic Publishers and Distributors (P) Ltd., New Delhi, for readily agreeing to publish this book and bringing it out expeditiously and efficiently.

Suggestions, if any, for the improvement of the book in the next edition will be highly appreciated.

N. JAYAPALAN

Contents

Introduction

1

The Indian subcontinent extends from the great Himalayas to the grand sea. It is known as Bharatavarsha. In other words it is called the land of Bharata.

According to the Puranic legend, Bharatavarsha was named after the legendary emperor Bharata.

After the early invasions of the Persians and Greeks our country acquired new name—India or Hindustan. In fact, these invaders could not go beyond the Indus river or Sindhu.

The Persians pronounced the word 's' as 'h' in those days of their invasions. It began to be pronounced as Hindu.

Similarly, the word 'India' is derived from the word 'Indus'.

After the Muslim occupation of India the rulers started designating the country as 'Hind' or 'Hindustan' and its inhabitants came to be known as Hindus.

Thus, it is very obvious that the present name 'Hindustan' is an Indo-Iranian hybrid.

The subcontinent of India is a very vast peninsula with the shape of an irregular quadrilateral. It has an area of 32,76,441 sq. km. Its length is 3,119 km. and breadth is 2,977 km.

According to 1971 census, the population of India stands at 54,79,49,809. Now it has crossed 100 crore. In terms of population, it is the second biggest country in the world.

India is a geographical unit bounded on the North, North-East and North-West by the mighty Himalayan Mountain chain and on the other sides by the Sea, *i.e.* the Bay of Bengal on the East, the Arabian sea on the West and the Indian Ocean on the South. This geographical unity has enabled the growth of cultural unity within the country.

Geographically, India has been divided into the following four units:

(i) Mountainous Ranges in the North
(ii) Great Indo-Gangetic Plain
(iii) The Deccan Plateau
(iv) Coastal ghats.

(i) Mountainous Ranges in the North. Physically and intellectually, India has been greatly influenced by the Himalayas. These are spread over about 1,500 miles in length and 200 miles in breadth. In the past the Himalayas was inaccessible: but today it requires national defence. It has many passes which give way to invaders. Many rivers flow from here which have made our northern plains prosperous.

The Aryans, Persians, Greeks, Kushans, Parthians, Huns, Turks and Mughals came to India through the North-Western passes. The Himalayas give life to the three great rivers, the Indus, the Ganges and the Brahmaputra.

(ii) Great Indo-Gangetic Plain. This is a very prosperous plain and has been the centre of foreign invasions. All important empires, trade, art, architecture and cities have developed in this plain. This plain has made India rich and a centre of knowledge. This plain contains alluvial soil and hence the lands are very fertile. Here, the people are easily able to get almost all their requirements and enjoy leisure. Further they are able to think of the problems of life and rise high in civilisation.

(iii) The Deccan Plateau. Though India has a geographical unity, there are two national divisions, namely, Aryavartha or Uttarapatha or North India and Daksinpada or the Deccan or South India. The Vindhyas and Satpura Mountain are the dividing ranges between North India and South India. It is isolated from the rest of the world. But it had its own advantages as well. In ancient times, the culture of North India could take shelter in the South. For example, when Buddhism was attaining popularity in the north, Hinduism took shelter in the South and thereafter re-established its supremacy even in North India. The rulers of the southern dynasties such as Andhras, the Cholas, the Chalukyas and the Hoysalas welcomed the literature and civilisation of the North. It was due to this isolation that true ancient Indian civilisation could be found in this part of the country, long after the north had been influenced by the culture and civilisation of its invaders. This region was calm when there was looting and plundering in North by the invaders.

(iv) Coastal Ghats. On the East and the West in South India are situated large sea belts which comprise the deltas of Godavari, Krishna and Cauvery. It also possesses two parts, Malabar and Konkan. On the Western coast, there are Hill ranges about 700 miles long with Arabian Sea. These ranges are 3000 feet to 8000 feet long. The lands in the Eastern Ghats are low. The inhabitants of both these Ghats maintained relations with Eastern countries like Java, Sumatra, Burma, Siam and Indo-China.

Effects on Political History. Geographical conditions deeply influence the political history of any nation and India is no exception to that. The effects are as follows:

(1) The vast Himalayan mountains and its western and eastern ranges in the north have separated India from the rest of Asia.

(2) The passes have given way to many invaders like the Aryans, the Iranians, the Greeks, the Sakas, the Huns, the Turks, the Mughals and others.

(3) Due to Himalayas we have ignored the defence of our country. It serves as a great defence to the people of India.

(4) It has divided the country into various territorial divisions.

(5) Many of our rivers flow from Himalayas. They have brought us prosperity.

(6) Vindhya mountains have divided India into two parts.

(7) Indo-Gangetic plains are the most prosperous region of the world.

(8) Due to prosperity people of the plains loved peace and ease.

(9) Many empires have developed in our plains.

Effects on Cultural History. Geography of India not only influenced the political but also the cultural history of India. It is evident from the following points:

(1) In the field of culture the contribution of North India is supreme. The wealth and plenty of this region made the people peace and ease-loving. Free from the worries of livelihood, they had enough time for the cultivation of art and literature. The Vedic Literature is the most valuable treasure of our country. The art and architecture under Mauryas and Guptas, the Gandhara Art under Kushans, the establishment of Nalanda and Texila universities are considered as cultural effect of Geography on History.

(2) Life in the South was safe and secure as compared to the North. As a result, South proved to be the defence of Indian Civilisation and Culture at a time when the North had to face the attacks of foreign invaders.

(3) The absence of transport and communication created many difficulties in those days in India. So trade and commerce dwindled considerably. During the Gupta period, Indian trade and commerce was at its prime and it was due to the establishment of certain colonies abroad that India was termed as "Greater India".

Unity in Diversity

India has been described as an ethnological (racial) museum in which a number of races of mankind are found. This diversity is found in the climate, races, languages, religion, etc. But despite this diversity India has enjoyed a sense of unity in various spheres which is a very peculiar feature of this country. Let us examine the various facts of this diversity as well as unity prevailing in India.

1. Geographical Diversity. India is a vast country with great diversity of physical features. Certain parts in India are so fertile that they are counted amongst the most fertile regions of the world while others are so unproductive and barren that hardly anything can be grown there. The regions of Indo-Gangetic valley belong to the first category while certain areas of Rajasthan fall under the latter category. From the point of view of climate, there are sharp contrasts. As Minoo Masani has said that, "India has every variety of climate from the blazing heat of the plains, as hot in places as hottest Africa-Jacobabad in South—to freezing point—the Arctic cold of the Himalayas". The Himalayan ranges which are always covered with snow are very cold while the deserts of Rajasthan are well-known for their heat. The country also does not get uniform rainfall. There are certain areas like Cherrapunji in Assam which get almost 460″ of rainfall per year which is considered to be the highest in the world. On the other hand, Sindh and Rajasthan get hardly 3″ of rainfall per year. This variety in climate has also contributed to a variety of flora and fauna. In fact, India possesses richest variety of plants and animals known in the world.

2. Racial Diversity. India possesses a rich variety of races. In view of this variety Prof. V.A. Smith says, "From the human point of view India has been often described as an ethnological (or racial) museum in which numberless races of mankind may be studied". The vast population of India consists of the jungles tribe (like Bhils, Kols, Santhals), the Greeks, the Sakas, the Kushans, the Hunas, the Mongolians, the Arabs, the Turks, the Afghans, etc. The physical features and the colour of the Indian people also differ from region to region. While the people of Kashmir are handsome and fair in complexion, these qualities are missing among the habitants of Assam.

3. Linguistic Diversity. India not only possesses racial diversity but also linguistic diversity. It is said that almost 400 languages are spoken in India. Some of the prominent languages recognised by the Constitution include, Assamese, Bengali, Gujarati, Hindi, Kannada, Kashmiri, Malayalam, Marathi, Oriya, Punjabi, Sanskrit, Sindhi, Tamil, Telugu and Urdu. In fact, it is commonly believed that in India the language changes after every four *kos*. There is not only variety of languages but also variety of scripts in India. Some of the popular scripts in ancient times were Pali, Kharosti, Devnagri, etc. What is really striking is that almost all these languages possess their own literatures which differ a great deal from one another.

4. Religious and Social Diversity. In the religious sphere also India possesses great diversity. Almost all the principal religions of the world like Brahmanism, Buddhism, Jainism, Islam and Christianity are found here. Most of these religions are further subdivided into various sects and divisions. For example, Buddhism is divided into Hinayana and Mahayana; the Jainism is divided into Digambaras and Swetambaras and the Brahmanism is divided in the Vaishnavas, Saivas, Shakts, Brahmo Samaj, Arya Samaj, etc. In addition, the primitive men have their own peculiar cults which are quite distinct from these major religions. Thus, we can say India possesses complete diversity in religions sphere.

In the social sphere also the general customs and manners of the people greatly differ. People of different regions use different types of dresses. Their eating habits and customs are also quite different. They are quite civilised while others are still backward in their customs. Thus, we find as Radha Kumud Mukherjee has put it, "India is a museum of cults and customs, creeds and cultures, faiths and tongues, racial types and social systems."

5. Political Diversity. The diversity in culture, races, languages, religion, etc. greatly stood in the way of political unity in India. As a result, from the earliest times India has been divided into several independent principalities. The rulers of these principalities were always engaged in wars with each other for supremacy. The disunity and friction was fully exploited by the foreign invaders to bring India under their subjugation. No doubt certain rulers like Chandra Gupta Maurya, Ashoka, Samudra Gupta, Ala-ud-din Khilji and Akbar had subjugated these principalities and established strong empire but they were only handful of the rulers who could accomplish it. For most of the time India presented the spectacle of a divided country. Even under these mighty rulers a real unity could not be established both due to the lack of means of communication and transportation as well as national consciousness. In short, we can say that really speaking India could never be united politically.

Unity

In view of the above diversity certain people have formed the impression that India was never a united country. But this view is not fully correct because under the façade of diversity India has always enjoyed a deep note of fundamental unity. Dr. Radha Kumud Mukherjee says that a superficial observer fails to discover this unity. To quote him, "He fails to discover the one in many, the individual in the aggregate, the simple in the composite." Sir Herbert Risley also observed, "Beneath the manifold diversity of physical and social type, language, custom and religion which strike the observer in India there can still be discerned a certain underlying uniformity of life from the Himalayas to Cape Camorin." Certain scholars have tried to project the image that the ideal of unity is of recent growth in India and it was to a large extent the result of the efforts of the British Government. This view is not fully correct because India has enjoyed unity right from the earliest times and the founders of the Indian civilization were fully aware of this factor. This shall be fully substantiated by the following discussion.

1. Geographical Unity. Geographically, India may not be a united by itself but from times immemorial India has been considered as one country. The single name Bharatvarsha given to this country emphasises this unity. According to the authors of *Advanced History of India*, this name and the sense of unity which it denotes, "was ever present before the minds of the theologians, political philosophers and poets who spoke of the thousand yojans (leagues) of land that stretches from Himalayas to the sea as the proper domain of a single universal emperor". During the medieval times the Muslim rulers also considered it as one country and made efforts to capture all parts. The nature has also bestowed a geographical unity by providing Himalayas in the North and Ocean in the other three sides of the country, and thereby completely separating India from other countries. The rivers of India have also been responsible for giving a sense of unity in the country. Some of the rivers are ascribed divine origin and are considered sacred by every Indian. For example, Ganga is worshipped in all the four directions of the country. Pilgrims from all over the country continue to visit the various holy places situated on its banks. Other rivers like Yamuna and Saraswati are also considered sacred by people all over the country. In short, we can say that in spite of the geographical diversity the country has enjoyed a typical unity.

2. Racial Unity. No doubt, the people of India belong to different races but they are so much absorbed in the Hindu fold that they have virtually lost their separate entity. It is a well-known fact that the people of India, to whichever race or region they might belong, are known as Indian or Hindustani. This is a clear proof of the underlying racial unity of the people.

3. Linguistic Unity. Although India possesses a variety of languages yet she has enjoyed a linguistic unity from the earliest times. In the 3rd century B.C., the Prakrit served as the common language of the people. According to Dr. Ray Chaudhri, "Prakrit was the one single language sufficient to bring the message of a royal missionary to the doors of his humblest subject throughout his vast kingdom." After Prakrit, Sanskrit became the common language of the masses. The other local languages which subsequently gained prominence originated out of Sanskrit. Some of the prominent Indian languages which owe their origin to Sanskrit include Hindi, Gujarati, Telugu and Tamil. In fact, Sanskrit served as the *lingua franca* during the ancient times. During the medieval times also though the Sanskrit language was not extended royal patronage by the Muslim rulers, the rulers in the South continued to patronise it and it continued to flourish. With the coming of British, English became the *lingua franca*. After independence this role has been taken over by Hindi.

The scripts of the various languages used in India also possess a certain amount of uniformity. In fact, almost all the scripts are based on the Brahmi script. The literature produced in different Indian languages also possesses an element of unity. Most of the literature of Indian language drew inspiration from the Sanskrit literature and maintained the unity. No doubt certain local pieces of literature like Vedas, Puranas, Dharma Shastras and Upanishads were written in Sanskrit and are regarded as the common treasure by the people all over the country.

4. Religious and Social Unity. In a religious sphere also despite the manifold diversities a sort of unity prevailed amongst the various religious sects in the country. India was primarily a Hindu country and its culture was based on Varna Ashrama, Dharma Vyavastha, *i.e.* caste Ashrams and Dharma. People in all the four corners of the country followed these principles. The people also worshipped the same Hindu gods all over the country, although they were assigned different names in different regions. The Hindu religious works *Ramayana* and the *Mahabharata* were also popular throughout the country and Indians both in the north and the south as well as east and west attach great importance to these works. Similarly, the Vedas, Puranas and other religious scriptures are given due regard by the people from all parts of the country. Again, every Indian, irrespective of his caste, creed and race believes in the doctrine of transmigration of soul, monotheism, immortality of the soul, re-incarnation Karma, deliverance or Moksha, etc. The people staying in different parts of the country followed the same religious rites and rituals. Even the religious places of the Hindus like Ayodhya, Avantika, Mathura, Gaya, Kashi, Sanchi, and Puri are located in the four directions of the country. Hindu festivals like Holi, Diwali are also celebrated in all the regions of the country. In fact, people from all religions participated in these festivals. Thus, we find that in spite of the religious diversities there has been an undercurrent of cultural unity which to a large extent nullified the peculiar effects of various religions.

Dr. V.A. Smith says, "The essential fundamental Indian unity rests upon the fact that diverse peoples of India have developed a peculiar type of culture and civilization which may be summed up in the term of Hindustani." He further observes, "Her type of civilization has many features which differentiate it from that of all other regions of the world, or rather subcontinent in a degree sufficient to justify its treatment as a unit in the history of the social, religious and intellectual development of mankind."

The religious and cultural unity has also led to unity in the social sphere. The people belonging to various religions have been following common customs both with regard to the dress and eating habits.

5. Political Unity. In the political sphere, the unity of the country has been one of the greatest goals which most of the Indian rulers cherished. No doubt, India was divided into a number of small principalities but the powerful rulers were always keen to bring this area under their control. They were keen to assume the title of Chakravarti. According to Kautilya, Chakravarti kings' domain extended from Himalayas to the seas. In other words, according to Kautilya, the king was considered to be a Chakravarti only when he succeeded in extending his power or supremacy over the whole of the country. Usually such titles were assumed by the king after due performance of rites and sacrifices. In the ancient times, Chandra Gupta Maurya, Ashoka and Samudra Gupta carved out all-India empires. During the medieval times also kings like Ala-ud-din Khilji and Aurangzeb made efforts and succeeded in establishing their control over the entire country. These Muslim rulers have been provided similar system of administration, uniform laws and customs, common coinage, etc. and thus, imparted a type of political unity to the entire country. Thus, we find that despite the variety of religion, cultures, languages, geographical diversity, etc. India has enjoyed some sort of unity.

Economic Life of the Indus People

2

The excavation at Harappa and Mohanjodaro led to the discovery of Indus Valley Civilization at a time when the English people were still living in the jungle age. This unique and important civilisation of the pre-historic times in India was for the first time discovered by Daya Ram Sahni and R.D. Banerjee in 1921 and 1922 respectively. Further excavations were carried out along the Indus between Rupar at the foot of Simla hills and Sutkagendor, 300 miles close to Karachi, where similar remains were discovered. All these discoveries point to the existence of an advanced civilization in pre-historic India which is now popularly known as Indus Valley Civilization or Harappa Culture. Though this civilisation is termed as Indus Civilization, it covered area even beyond the Indus Valley. It extended from the upper Sutluj to the Gulf of Camba to the South and from Makran coast of the Arabian Sea in the west to the Jamuna-Ganges country in the east. Thus, the Indus Civilization was the largest of the early civilisations.

The various objects discovered at the site of Mohanjodaro suggest that it was a prosperous city. The people were fully acquainted with agriculture and different types of agriculture. Implements like sickle have been discovered.

The common agricultural products of the time were wheat, barley, vegetables, cotton, etc. As the land of the Indus Valley was quite productive and had sufficient irrigation facilities, the agriculture seems to have been the mainstay of the people.

In addition to this, people domesticated animals for economic purposes. The main animals which were domesticated by the people of Indus Valley included cow, bull, buffalo, sheep, goat, camel, etc.

Industry. Mohanjodaro was a great industrial centre and a number of industries were practised there. But probably the most important of these industries was weaving. This is proved by the discovery of a number of spindles and spinning wheels in the various houses of Indus Valley. This suggests that spinning of cotton and wool was quite common.

In addition, the people of Indus Valley also knew the practice of dyeing.

People also knew the art of using metals like gold, silver, bronze, copper, tin, led, etc. and they produced various articles with these metals. But probably the most important industry of the Indus Valley people was pottery. The earthen pots of those days which have been discovered now can be broadly classified into two categories—hand made and wheel made. The discovery of a number of pottery kilns shows that the pots were burnt in kilns. People produced a variety of pots, certain pots were meant for daily use and were plain while other pots were meant for the preservation of valuables and were painted.

Trade and Commerce. The city of Mohanjodaro was a great trading centre and both internal and external trade was carried on from there. The international trade was mainly carried on by the land routes in which bullock carts were used.

That the people of Mohanjodaro had trade relations with the people living in South India, Central India and North-Western India, is proved by the common use of precious and semi-precious stones. The trade with foreign countries are mainly carried through water routes. This has been proved by the representation of a boat on a seal. Trade was particularly carried with countries of Western Asia.

The chief articles sent to the foreign countries were the clothes. The presence of certain objects of Indus Valley Civilization in Sumeria suggest that India had trade relations with that country also.

Scholars have expressed the opinion that Mohanjodaro was economically prosperous city only because it was a flourishing centre of trade and commerce.

Weights and Measures. A large number of weights have been discovered from Mohanjodaro and Harappa. These weights differ a great deal in size. While some of the weights are so heavy that they could not be picked up with hands and were used with the help of ropes, the others were so small that it appears that they were used exclusively by the jewellers. But the most common weight which was used by the people of Indus Valley is cubical in shape.

The people of Indus Valley also knew about the footage system. It appears that the State exercised strict control over weights and measures.

The Early Vedic Age

3

From the Vedic literature we know a detailed description of the political, social economic and religious conditions of early Aryans. Particularly the Rig Veda gives a beautiful account about the economic condition of the early Vedic Age.

The people of the Rig Vedic period were essentially rural and lived in villages. The Rig Vedic society was self-sufficient and provided all the necessities of life without any dependence on other countries.

Agriculture. The people of Rig Vedic Age knew about cultivation and agriculture was their mainstay. They usually ploughed the fields with the help of a pair of the oxen bound to the yoke. They knew about tilling of the soil, cutting of furrows, sowing the seeds, and cutting of corn with the help of sickle.

The chief crops cultivated by the people were barley and wheat. Most probably they did not cultivate rice which was discovered at a later date.

The people used manure to increase the fertility of land. They also knew about irrigation and whenever necessary watered their land by artificial canals. Usually they grew two crops a year.

In addition to cultivating the fields the people left certain fields or pastures for the animals to graze.

As the Aryans were mainly pastoral people they naturally attached great importance to keeping of cows and bullocks. The cows were milked thrice a day and were allowed to roam freely in the pastures. The cow-dung was used to make fuel cakes. Sometimes the cow was also given in charity.

The other animals which were domesticated by the people included buffalo, goat and sheep. They also domesticated horse, camel and elephant.

Trade and Industry. The Vedic hymns clearly indicate that trade and commerce was known to the people of the early Vedic period. This trade was not only confined to the country alone but was also carried on with other countries. Barter system of exchange was in vogue. The cow was also regarded as a unit of value during this period. Most probably the people also knew about currency, and the coin used by them was known as Nishka. Some scholars are, however, of the opinion that Nishka was not a coin but an ornament, most probably a necklace. But the Rig Veda contains certain references of gifts being made in horses and Nishkas. This suggests that Nishka must have been a unit of value. However, nothing definite can be said about the coins because no coin has been discovered so far.

The chief items of commerce were cloth and goods made of leather. The goods were carried from one place to another through chariots, horses and bullock carts. Probably the inland rivers were also used for the purpose of trading.

The trade with foreign countries like Babylon and countries of West Asia was carried on by sea.

In addition to agriculture and industry, carpentry, blacksmithy, goldsmithy and weaving were other professions of the people. These professions were not only the monopoly of the men but the ladies also contributed their labour into them.

Generally, women were engaged in weaving, dyeing and embroidery.

The carpenter made chariots, wagons, boats, ploughs, domestic utensils and furniture.

The metal workers made implements and utensils of copper and bronze.

The ornaments were made by the goldsmith.

Amongst the other professions the Rig Veda makes a mention include Medicine, Dancing and Barbers. The physicians were greatly respected in their skill. They treated the patients with the help of herbs and plants and practised some sort of surgery also. Often they also used magic and spells to drive away evil spirits.

Later Vedic Age

4

The period in which Sama Veda, Yajur Veda, Atharva Veda, the Brahmanas, the Aranyakas and the Upanishads were composed is known as Later Vedic Age in the Indian history. During this period, the Aryans had spread over the land as far as the Vindhyas in the South, Bengal in the East and at certain points penetrated into Deccan on the western side by way of Malwa and Gujarat. Thus, we find that the centre of life had shifted to Madhyadesa. Eastern regions like Kosala (modern Oudh), Kashi (Banaras) and Videha (North Bihar) had come into prominence. The Punjab and the western regions had lost their importance and the tribes residing there have received disapprobation in Satapatha and Aitareya Brahmanas. In short, we can say that by this period the Aryans had conquered the whole of northern India as far as northern Bihar and had started penetrating into the south where the kingdom of Vidarbha had been established.

During this period a number of new tribes are mentioned, which did not find any reference in the early Vedic literature. A number of old tribes like Bharatas, and Purus were absorbed by the new tribes like Kurus or Kauravas. Similarly, tribe of Panchala was evolved by the fusion of the old and the new tribes. Some of the other new tribes mentioned in the later Vedic literature are Usinaras, Matsyas, Srinjayas.

On the testimony of Atharva Veda, Aitareya, Taitriya and Satpatha Brahmana we get a glimpse of the economic life prevailing during the later Vedic period. At the outset it may be pointed out that it marked an improvement over the conditions prevailing in the Rig Vedic period.

Agriculture. Agriculture continued to be the mainstay of the people during the later Vedic period. However, the art of agriculture had made much progress since the time of Rig Veda. Very heavy and large ploughs began to be used. Some of the ploughs were so heavy that as many as 24 oxen were harnessed to drive it. The ordinary ploughs also existed, which were driven by two or four oxen. Reference is also made to furrow.

People knew about the art of irrigation and use of manure.

Many types of grains were grown. These included wheat, beans, sesame, etc. We learn from the various texts about the time of sowing and harvesting of the various types of grains. Barley was sown in winter, ripened in summer and that rice was sown in the rainy season and was harvested in autumn. Usually there were two crops a year.

People recited hymns at the time of sowing of the seed and gathering of corn with a view to ward off natural calamities like famine, flood, drought, etc. The prayers for the success in the efforts of the farmer are mentioned in the Atharva Veda.

The cattle breeding also received impetus during this later Vedic period. The people not only left sufficient meadows so that the animals could get their food, but also provided necessary shed and protection to them against extreme cold and heat. The cow was regarded sacred during this period and its slaughtering was punished with heavy penalty.

Trade and Commerce. According to Atharva Veda, trade and commerce continued to flourish during the later Vedic period. The trade was carried on by the businessmen who went from place to place for the transaction of business. The internal trade was carried on both by land and water routes. The business was carried on both by means of barter or exchange and cash transactions. Some type of coins were also in vogue during this period.

According to Dr. B.R. Bhandarker, the Satamana (a piece of gold) was used as a coin. However, this view is not acceptable to other scholars and they contend that the mere fact that the

Satamana was a round shaped gold piece cannot be the conclusive proof that the coins were in existence. These scholars argue that this round shaped piece of gold could be regarded as simple gold also.

However, we have not come across any coins of this period to prove conclusively that the coinage did exist.

The chief article of trade and commerce were garments, coverlets and skins of goat, etc. It cannot be said for certain whether the people of later Vedic period had commercial relations with the foreign countries. However, certain scholars have interpreted the legend of flood in the Satapatha Brahman as an indication of India having relations with Babylon.

During this period, a new class of moneylenders also came into existence. However, we do not know for definite the rate of interest charged by them. The reference to Ganas or corporation and the Sreshthins or eldermen suggests that the merchantmen were probably organized into guilds.

A variety of occupations came into existence. Some of the most prominent occupations of the period included those of potters, carpenters, smiths, smelters, weavers, washermen, barbers, butchers, makers of baskets, ropes, jewels, merchants, magicians and so forth. The women were generally engaged in dyeing, embroidery, and basket making.

Means of Transport. Though the means of transport were quite underdeveloped, they certainly marked an improvement over the Rig Vedic period. We learn from Atharva Veda that some sorts of roads existed. The bullock carts were the chief means of transport. Ships and boats were also popular mode of transport. A special type of vehicle 'Vi-patha' was used for the bad track. The elephants and horses were also used for the purpose of transporting goods. People also used elephants and horses for the purpose of riding.

The Epic Age

5

We have two great epics. They are the *Ramayana* and the *Mahabharata*.

The *Ramayana* and the *Mahabharata* are the two great epics of the Aryans.

According to Lin Yutang, these two epics can be compared with the Greek epics *Iliad* and *Odyssey* composed by Homer.

It is very difficult to say as to when these epics were written, and what particular period of history they cover.

According to the religious tradition, these two epics were composed around 3000 B.C.

But according to Dr. Macdonell, they were composed between 500 to 200 B.C.

According to Pargiter, the drama of the *Mahabharata* was probably staged as early as 1100 B.C.

Prof. Hopkins says that the language of the epics seems to be similar to that of the Sutra Literature and so the stories of the epics belong to the later Vedic period.

Dr. Radha Kumud Mukherjee, a great scholar of ancient Indian history has assigned the period 1500 to 600 B.C. to these epics.

Thus, we find that the scholars have not been able to arrive at an agreed date regarding the age of these epics. However, the most commonly held opinion is that the epics cover the period intervening between the later Vedic age and the Buddhist age.

Agriculture. Agriculture continued to be the main occupation of the people in the epic age and made further progress. On the testimony of the *Mahabharata* we can say that the lands of Kosala, Vatsa, Matsya, etc. were very fertile. People knew about irrigation and used manures to increase the fertility of their lands. The private ownership of the produce was as per its share. In return for this the state not only provided irrigation facilities but also helped the indebted peasants.

During this period sugar cane and indigo, two technical crops, were also cultivated.

Cattle Breeding. Cattle breeding was given special attention and was one of the most important means of income for the people. The cow was the most popular animal which the people domesticated. The other animals domesticated at that time were horses and elephants which were in much demand for the army.

Trade and Commerce. Both internal and external trade flourished during the epic period. Most of the businessmen lived in cities. The merchantmen were organised in guilds which were controlled by the Mahajanas. The growth of a large number of cities or 'nagars' as testified by the epics further shows that the commercial activities were on the increase. Each city had a number of guilds, each guild managing a particular craft. Money had come to be established as a standard of value during the epic period, though exchange by barter was also carried on.

Industry. Cotton manufactures occupied the first place in industry. Silk and woollen clothes were also manufactured. People also knew about the manufacture of mixed cloth and the art of interlacing. The allied arts like dyeing also made considerable progress. Fast colours were produced by the people.

People also knew about the use of minerals. The minerals were excavated and worked upon by the artisans.

During the epic period India produced gold, precious stones and pearls in abundance.

6

Economic Condition between 650-321 B.C.

We get abundant information regarding the economic condition of India between 650 to 321 B.C. from the Buddhist and Jain works.

Therefore, certain scholars have described the period between 650 to 321 B.C. as the period of Buddhism in India.

But scholars like V.A. Smith are not willing to accept this description and have challenged the validity of this title for the period.

According to Dr. V.A. Smith, "Neither Buddhist nor Jain period ever existed in the history. From time to time either Buddhism or Jainism obtained exceptional success but they never became the prevailing religion in India as a whole at any time."

We need not go into this controversy whether this period should be designated as Buddhist period or not, as we are mainly concerned with the study of the conditions prevailing during this period. However, one thing be said for certain that our knowledge about the condition prevailing during this period is mainly drawn from the Buddhist literature, particularly Tripitaka and Jatakas.

Similarly, the Jain literature is of immense value in so far as it provides us with an idea about the conditions prevailing during this period. Though this literature is primarily religious in character, it throws a flood of light on the political, social, economic and religious life in Northern India during the period between 650 to 321 B.C. Let us study the various aspects.

Village continued to be the basis of the economic organisation in India. Most of the people lived in the villages and devoted themselves to agriculture and cattle rearing. Each family had its own fields which are cultivated by the father with the assistance of his sons. The holdings were generally very small, but large holdings were also in existence.

We do not get any reference about the landlords owning large estates and the ultimate ownership of the land belonged to king, who claimed a portion of the produce from the soil. Every village was self-sufficient unit. A spirit of co-operation existed amongst the inhabitants of the villages and they constructed reservoirs, irrigation canals, roads and fencing for the common benefit of the village. Though each householder possessed separate cattle, there were common pastures for these cattle. Cattle were usually entrusted to the care of 'Gapalak' who knew much about the cattle and their diseases. It may be noted that no land could be sold to the outsider without the consent of the village council.

People cultivated rice and several other grains. Sugar cane, fruits, vegetables and flowers were also cultivated. We get frequent references regarding the scarcity due to droughts or floods. Agriculture was mainly the profession of the Vaishyas, even though we come across various references of the Kshatriya clansmen of the republic taking to the cultivation of the soil.

In the matter of administration villages enjoyed complete autonomy. Administration of the village was looked after by the village council headed by the headman selected by the village council. The headman collected the revenue for the king. Usually the land tax varied from 1/6 to 1/12th of the total produce. The headman also performed certain judicial functions and was responsible for the maintenance of law and order within the jurisdiction of the village. The other functions performed by him included works of public utility, construction of roads, building canals, tanks, halls and rest-houses, etc.

Industry and Crafts. A considerable specialisation and localisation of industries had taken place. The Jatakas speak of 18 crafts which existed at that time. However, they name only four of these crafts, *viz.* leather-dressing, smithy, painting and carpentry. But on the testimony of other references we can say crafts like hunters, trappers, fishermen, butchers, tanners, snake charmers, actors, dancers, musicians and rush weavers were also in existence, although they were considered as quite inferior to ivory workers, weavers, confectioners, jewellers, workers in metals, garland makers, hair dressers, potters, and bow and arrow makers.

The sons usually followed the professions of the forefathers but the rules were not very rigid on this issue. People could change their profession without losing their social status and caste. We get a number of references in the Buddhist text when the Brahmanas worked as potters, basket makers, garland makers, tax collectors, traders, etc. Similarly, some Kshatriyas worked in the fields.

The important handicrafts were organised in the guilds (Srenies). At the head of each guild was President or Alderman (Jethaka). Usually the President was an influential person who had an access to the king. The authority of the President has not been clearly defined anywhere but probably he supervised and inspected the goods produced. The guild also worked as endowment trusts and banks. The traders also sometimes formed the unions with a view to control the prices of the articles and to make huge profits. The practice of business partnership was also known to the people. Such partnership could be formed by two or more merchants and sometimes these partnerships were formed by 100 to 500 merchants.

Trade and Commerce. Both internal and external trade flourished. The internal trade was usually carried out in the towns and its markets. The towns were surrounded by walls and admission could be got only through the gates. These towns were usually well connected by network of roads with the various parts of the country. The Jatakas have mentioned several trade routes. One route ran south-east from Savathi to Rajgriha and back. There was trade between Magadha and

Gandhara. The rivers were easy to ford in the route from Savathi to Rajgriha. Caravans also went south-west from Savathi to Patithana. From east to west the traffic was largely through water boats, up to Sahajati on the Ganges and the Kosambi on the Jamuna. Further on overland, the route went to Sindh from where large imports of horses and asses came. Northward lay the great trade route connecting India with Central Asia and Western Asia by way of Taxila and Sangla (modern Sialkot) in the Panjab. Goods were carried both on pack animals and bullock carts. Caravan moved together under the protection of hired escorts.

Trade with foreign countries was carried on both through land and sea routes. The chief articles of export were silk, muslin, cloth, cutlery, armour, broaches, embroideries, rugs, perfumes, drugs, ivory-works, and jewellery of gold and silver. The merchant ship laden with a variety of articles sailed to Burma, Siam and Ceylon. There were trade relations with Babylon also. There is also a mention of traffic with China.

The older system of barter had ended and the new system with its standard and token coins had come into existence. Coins struck in copper and silver known as Karshapanas (Kahapanas) were in general use. They were punch marked on both sides guaranteeing their standard and fineness. Pali texts refer to other coins such as Nikka and Suyanna of gold. The money saved was hoarded in jars and buried under the ground or kept in custody of a friend and a written record was kept of it.

There were no banking facilities but the merchants in different cities issued letters of credit on one another. The system of moneylending was in vogue and the interest was charged on the money lent. The state did not regulate the prices and these were fixed between the producer or consumer or the middleman. Thus, we find that the economic organisation in India as revealed in Buddhist and Jain literature was not primitive but was sufficiently advanced.

Economic Life under Mauryas

7

The historian of the Mauryan period has the advantage of having abundant authentic and varied sources of information. These may be roughly classified as literary and archaeological. The Puranas, the sacred books of the Jains and the Buddhists and the Ceylonese chronicles are the ancient historical traditions. They give valuable things about the Mauryan period. In addition to this, the *Arthasastra* of Kautilya, the *Indica* of Megasthenes and the *Mudrarakshasa* of Visakadatta give a detailed description about the Mauryas and their people. Moreover, foreign references to India are really remarkable evidences to know more about their period. Besides these sources, the remarkable inscriptions of Asoka furnish the most reliable data regarding the extent of Asoka's reign.

Economic Conditions

(i) **Agriculture.** Agriculture was the main occupation during this period. Megasthenes mentions that majority of people were agriculturists, peasants and farmers. The land was fertile. The means of irrigation were simple. There were two seasonal rainfalls in India and the farmers reaped the harvest twice a year. Kautilya has given a description of ploughed, unploughed and rocky lands. The land was tilled with the help of oxen. According to the Junagadh inscription, Pushpagupta, an official of Chandragupta, got Sudarshan lake constructed for irrigation in Saurashtra. In addition to this, *Arthasastra* mentions canals, tanks, wells, ponds and rivers as means of irrigation. Kautilya also mentions about the manure made of the mixture of ghee, honey, fats, cowdung and powdered fish. It was used to increase the fertility of the soil.

Wheat, gram, maize, rice, barley, sugar cane, mustard, peanuts, cotton, tobacco, potatoes, water melons, etc. were the main crops of the Mauryan state. The fruit gardens were of mangoes, grapes, lemons, etc.

(ii) **Occupations.** There were many cloth centres during this period. Among them Kasi, Vatsa, Madura, Vanga, etc. were prominent centres. According to Kautilya and Megasthenes, cotton was produced in great quantity. During those days cloth was prepared out of the leaves and bark of the trees and the fibre of many kinds. Woollen clothes and blankets were produced. Muslin clothes were produced during this period. Silken clothes were imported from China.

(iii) **Metallurgy.** Gold, silver and iron were utilised by the people during this period. Megasthenes and Kautilya have mentioned about these metals in their books. Diving and fishing, pearls and shells and diamonds from the sea was the most difficult task. The utensils were made of metal.

Besides, forests were considered as great wealth.

(iv) **Skins and Hides.** *Arthasastra* mentions different kinds of skins. Skins of different animals were used for manufacturing many things.

(v) **Drinks.** *Arthasastra* mentions the following six types of drinks:

(a) Madaka
(b) Pratyano
(c) Asava
(d) Mairaye
(e) Arishta
(f) Madhes.

(vi) **Trade.** There was brisk external and internal trade. Strabo mentions about this foreign trade. Slave trade was carried on by sea and land routes. The big ships were known as Pravana. There were ports and harbours.

(vii) Coinage. Gold, silver and copper coins were used during this period. The coins were made by the state foundries.

It goes without saying that the economic life under the Mauryas occupies a unique and a prominent place in the entire history of ancient India.

Sangam Age

8

The Sangam economy was very simple. In fact it was mostly self-sufficient. The need and necessity of wealth was insisted in the Sangam literature. It goes without saying that "this world is not for those who have no wealth." During this period there were the rich, the poor and the intermediate class in Tamilaham. The rich people led a luxurious life as that of the royal family. The poor people did not enjoy so much of concessions and benefits in the society. They were greatly experiencing poverty.

The common people were mostly agriculturists (or cowherds, hunters and fishermen) or manufacturers or traders. The king was the owner of the territory over which he ruled.

(a) Agriculture

Agriculture was the chief occupation of the people of Tamilaham. It was an esteemed profession. In whatever occupation others might be engaged, they all must depend finally on the farmer. If the peasants do not till the land even the ascetics will become helpless. Valluvar mentions the fertile land as a necessary feature of an ideal state.

The Palar, the Pennar, the Kaveri, the Vaigai and the Tamraparni, the very important Tamil rivers sustained the fertility of the land. The delta regions were very fertile. It added to the economic development of Tamilaham. The land was fertile and the agriculturist was an active and hard-working person; and so there must easily have been self-sufficiency in the matter of food; rice and millets then, as now, were the staple food. In contemporary literature, the fertility of the Chola

Kingdom is proudly mentioned in many places. The most fertile land (*i.e.* a Veli) yielded a full thousand Kalams of paddy.

During the Sangam Age agriculture was carried on in almost every part of the land. Paddy was the chief product; besides, it has been largely supplemented by millets and other varieties of corn. The land has always been very rich in its yield of coconuts, plantains, sugar cane and cotton.

The agriculturists were the 'ulavar' and their women were 'ulattiyar'; Indira was their god (god of Marudam). He was the very personification of the monsoon rains. They worshipped him with great devotion. They were entirely dependent on him. The cattle were their favourite animals. The chief trees of the Marudam land were Vanji, Kanchi and Marudam. Lotus was their sacred flower.

Valluvar has given a beautiful description in the chapter on 'ulavu' about the fertility and the exploitation of the same for the benefit of all. According to Valluvar, "Agriculturists alone led a truly useful life, the rest being only parasites and sycophants." He warns the farmer against lethargy, he bids him to be active and never dependent. The most important advice the author of the *Kural* has to give to the agriculturist is to guard against absentee-landlordism. Revenue relief was given during the time of natural calamities.

(b) Industry

The Sangam Age witnessed a far-reaching development in the field of industries and crafts. Encouragement was given to indigenous industries. Foreign workmen were invited to settle down in Tamilaham to pursue their specialist occupation. Specialists from Magadha, Avanti, Maharashtra and Rome came and settled in the leading cities of Tamilaham.

Apart from agriculture, spinning and weaving were the most important and widely practised crafts. Spinning was done by patient women in spare time. Uraiyur and Madurai were famous for weaving. *The Periplus* mentions the fineness of Tamil textile fabrics especially those of Uraiyur. Moreover, we have abundant references in contemporary native literature about the beauty and fineness of the textile products. Embroidery cloth was used by them during this period. Dyeing industries existed in the leading towns. Besides silk and cotton goods, woollen goods were sold in Madurai city. There were many tailors. So stitched garments were known to them.

Rope making, manufacture of leather-sheaths, dealing in conches and ivory and especially manufacture of bangles are some industries mentioned in contemporary literatures. Moreover, baskets made of wicker were manufactured by the artisans. There was a smithy in the country. It was an important industrial factory. War weapons were forged and repaired in the factory. Goldsmith engaged in making beautiful ornaments. Carpentry was a very common industry. It was practised as a hereditary profession. The carpenter was engaged in assisting house-building and in building boats, canoes, ships and chariots.

Jaggery cakes were made out of sugar cane in the villages. It was a popular occupation in the villages.

Cutting down the aromatic wood, sandal, and pearl-diving were known Tamil industries.

In coastal areas, fishermen engaged in fishing. In addition to this, salt was manufactured in coastal areas. Building of boats and other industries flourished during the Sangam Age.

(c) Trade

We get a graphic picture about the trading or commercial activities of the Tamils from Tamil literatures. It is amply corroborated by foreign contemporary sources.

Inland Trade

The inland trade was in a flourishing condition during the Sangam Age. Most of the trade was carried on by barter. Paddy was the most commonly accepted medium of exchange, especially in the more rural parts of the land. Well purified white salt was sold for paddy. Honey and roots were exchanged for fish (liver) oil and arrack. Sugar cane and rice flakes were exchanged for venison and toddy. Foodstuffs and vegetables were purchased from street hawkers by paying for them in rice or in paddy. This system continues in urban areas even today.

In the biggest towns, there were established markets or bazaars. They were called 'angadis'.

The salt merchants were called 'usanar'. They were expert in salt trade. It was considered as an important trade during this period. For this we have numerous references in the Sangam literature.

There were two kinds of markets, *i.e.* bazaars in the leading cities like Puhar and Madurai. They were:

(1) Nalangadi — the morning bazaar;

(2) Allangadi — the evening bazaar.

In the above markets such large varieties and such large quantities of goods were sold and purchased. Crowds thronged into the markets for busy transactions. Silappadikaram gives a detailed description of the markets in the city of Puhar.

In Madurai, people of many countries speaking many languages crowded for busy transactions. Particularly foreigners who had come from outside Tamilaham made wholesale purchases of Tamilian goods for sale elsewhere. In the evening bazaar in Madurai, the following persons were busy in selling the buying:

(a) grocers,

(b) the sellers of conch-bangles,

(c) goldsmiths,

(d) appraisers of gold articles,

(e) dealers in foreign cloth,

(f) other textile dealers,

(g) sellers of copper wares,

(h) painters,

(i) dealers in perfumes, flowers and sandal paste.

The following commodities were sold in the bazaar of Puhar:

(a) dyes,

(b) scented powder,

(c) sandal paste,

(d) flowers,

(e) aromatic wood-like ahil.

There were great demand for flowers during festival days. The flower bazaar looked like a forest of flowers.

Normally textile dealers, sellers of perfumes, flowers, sandal paste, scented-powder, sellers of salt, oil mongers, dealers in bronze and copper wares, carpenters, goldsmiths, artists like painters and sculptors, dealer in dolls, lapidaries, those that sold false hair or fashionable wigs, traders in sheep, fish and mutton and sellers of cakes and vegetable edibles thronged the bazaar. The traders lived in separate streets.

There were warehouses near the bazaar. Goods were stored in rooms in those houses.

In the Sangam Age, the merchants functioned often in a body. There were merchant 'guilds' and 'chambers of commerce'. Such merchant bodies were called 'Vanikachchattu'. Such caravans of traders moved from place to place for business. They were escorted by the warriors.

Pearls, gold, diamond and ivory were the chief articles the Tamils exported to the north. The Tamil word 'Muthu' was Sanskritised long ago into 'mukta' and the commodity became so famous in the north as to deserve special mention in Kautilya's *Arthasastra*; and Maurya was the Tamil Mayil (Peacock).

The merchants sold their goods by openly announcing the profit they were aiming at. It was a peculiar feature of the merchants in those days. It was believed that honest trade led to increased trade which meant increased wealth. Generally speaking, integrity in trade was appreciated by all.

Foreign Trade

Extensive trade was carried on with foreign countries from early times in Tamilaham. Normally and usually there was great demand for our goods in foreign markets. This was a great secret of her foreign trade. The following articles were in great demand in the crowded bazaars of foreign lands:

(1) pepper
(2) ginger
(3) rice
(4) sandalwood
(5) almug
(6) cardamum
(7) cinnamon
(8) turmeric
(9) ivory
(10) pearls
(11) aquamarine gems
(12) coriander
(13) cotton fabrics
(14) monkey
(15) deer
(16) peacock
(17) bird
(18) cheetah
(19) tiger
(20) elephant

Hebrews

In ancient time, there was trade contact with the ancient land of the Hebrews. The Hebrew Bible mentions two important objects. They are 'kapim' and 'tukim'. It is very clear that 'kapim' is mentioned as 'kapi' in Tamil, it is 'kavi', *i.e.* monkey, and 'tukim' is the Tamil 'tokai', *i.e.* peacock.

Greece

Tamil trade with Greece is amply borne out by the existence in Greek vocabulary of Tamil names of many objects; the Greeks have 'cossa' for 'rice' from the Tamil 'arisi'. Tamil 'chiruttai' became 'cheetah' in English. 'Corrundum' is clear transliteration of Tamil 'kurundum', sandalwood was derived straight from 'sandana' or 'sandu'.

The Pearl of the Pandyan Kingdom was a great attraction to foreigners in those days.

Megasthenes and Strabo had heard of the Pandyan Kingdom, but they give no account of the ports or trade centres of ancient Tamilaham.

Pliny mentions about Cottanara as a centre of pepper trade. The place Cottanara is identified with Kuttanadu.

From *The Periplus* we know the major ports of India of those days—Naura, Tyndis and Musiris. In addition to this, we know the following market towns and the harbours from *The Periplus*:

(a) Damirica

(b) Camara

(c) Poduca

(d) Sopatma

Rome

We find large hoards of Roman gold coins of the Augustan Age in many parts of South India which are evidence of the brisk trade between Tamilaham and Rome resulting in the inflow of considerable gold into Tamilaham. Such was the magnitude of the trade in the early centuries of the Christian era.

The direct trade route between Tamilaham and Arabia, Egypt and Rome had been well established by the date of *The Periplus*. "One of the most important articles which came from India was cotton and perhaps silk." From Alexandria, glass, metalware and linen were imported.

The eastern trade beyond Tamilaham with Burma, Malaya, Java, Sumatra and China was mostly in the hands of the Tamils.

The Pandyan Kings sent two 'embassies' to Augustus in 20 B.C. to win his favour. Thereafter the trade became very active and more extensive. The trade had further increased very much during the first half of the second century A.D.

The direct and brisk trade between Rome and Tamilaham declined during the third century because of the growing anarchy in the Roman empire. But the trade did not die out.

It is mentioned by Gibbon in his *Decline and Fall of the Roman Empire*.

The Greeks, the Romans and the Egyptians came and colonised certain parts of Tamilaham. From literature we know the Yavanas' (the Romans) settlement in Puhar. The Yavanas who permanently settled in Tamilaham entered royal service and served as bodyguards, palace guards and guards in the military camps.

The Tamils were great seafarers. The Chola Kings maintained a great navy; ship-building was a native industry in Tamilaham. The ship was called 'Marakkalam' as it was made of wood. All kinds of boats were in use in Tamil ports—*i.e.* ambi, pahri, odam, padagu, timil, etc. Paratavar community dominated the coastal areas.

The Pattinappalar gives a graphic picture about the harbour of Puhar. Warehouses were built near the beach. 'Limitless quantities of goods' were collected in these warehouses and they lay there waiting to be shipped abroad.

The chief ports had lighthouses. They were called 'Kalam Kavai Ilanguchudar'.

During the Sangam Age excellent Yavana wine was imported to Tamilaham. They exported to Tamilaham 'Sugar Candy' also. Many novel wares were introduced by them. Horses with a noble gait came to Puhar by the sea. The merchants of Puhar imported the following articles:

(1) Gems and gold from the north;
(2) Sandalwood and akil from the western mountains;
(3) The pearl of the southern sea;
(4) The coral of the western sea;
(5) The yield of the Kaviri;
(6) Foodstuffs from Ceylon; and
(7) Other consumer goods from Kalingam.

The Periplus gives the following items of imports to Muziri:

(1) Coins
(2) Topaz

(3) Thin clothing
(4) Linen
(5) Antimony
(6) Coral
(7) Crude glass
(8) Copper, tin, lead
(9) Wine, and
(10) Wheat.

The exports from there were:

(1) The pepper
(2) Pearls
(3) Ivory and
(4) Silk cloth.

Pliny says that the Roman ladies exposed their charms much too immodestly by clothing themselves in the "web of woven wind", as he called the muslins imported from India. From this we know that the wise Tamil weavers made the nice clothes in those days.

From the above account it is very obvious that the foreign trade of Sangam Tamilaham was very brisk and extensive.

(I) ECONOMIC CONDITION UNDER PALLAVAS

The Pallava period witnessed excellent economic progress. The revenue of the government increased day by day. Dry lands were brought under cultivation. Lakes and canals were utilised for irrigational purposes. In short, there was many sided progress in the economic field.

(a) Lands

We come to know that there were many kinds of lands from the copper plates of Kuram, Kasakudi, Patatal Mangalam and Bahur.

Lands donated to Brahmins are called Brahmadeya lands.

Lands donated to an individual (Brahmin) is called Ekaboga Brahmadeya lands.

These above lands were exempted from tax. Moreover, these lands were not to be sold out.

The Brahmins who mastered four Vedas lived in Chaturvedimangalam. Besides, the Brahmins lived in Agraharas like Dayamuga Mangalam, Pattatal Mangalam, Udayachandra Mangalam, etc. These places developed later on.

Lands donated to temples were called Devadanas.

The revenue from the lands were spent for temples. The temples extended loans to the people during the time of famine or drought.

Lands given to Jain monasteries are called Pallichandam.

The above lands were exempted from tax.

Lands given to renovation of tanks are called Eripatti.

(b) Revenue

The Kasakkudi and Velurpalayam plates mention eighteen kinds of taxes, 'ashtadasaparihara'. Land revenue was the chief item of royal income. The following professional taxes were levied and collected during the Pallava period:

(1) Slamputchi (Tax levied on toddy-tappers)

(2) Tattukkanam (Tax levied on goldsmith)

(3) Kusakkanam (Tax levied on potters)

(4) Visakkanam (Paid by the people to the village chief)

(5) Thirumukkanam (It was levied to transmit information from one place to another)

(6) Kattikanam (Tax levied on blacksmith)

(7) Pattigaikanam (Tax levied on spinners)

(8) Pavaikanam (Tax levied on washermen)

(9) Kalyanakanam (Tax given during marriage)

(10) Idaiputchi (Tax levied on shepherds)

(11) Tharagu (Tax levied on mediation)

(12) Naivilai and Charmvari (Tax levied on Palmyra and coconut trees)

(13) Sengodikanam and Kannithukanam (Tax levied on herbal plants)
(14) Tharikkurai (Tax levied on weavers)
(15) Nedumparai (Tax paid by those who beat drums)
(16) Sungavari (Excise duty)
(17) Mannupadu (Tax levied in counts)
(18) Puttagai Vilai (Tax levied on cloth sellers).

Lakes, tanks, wells, rivers and even trees were counted and registered for purposes of tax assessment. Some varieties of flowers were also taxed.

(c) Treasury

Treasury was in vogue during the Pallava period. It was managed by efficient officers. Central exchequers were appointed to supervise the divisions of the country. There was an official called Manikkappandarakappon besides the head of the treasury.

(d) Measurements

The Uruvapalli grant presents a detailed account of land survey according to arable and waste lands. The entire lands of the kingdom were measured. In addition to this, every village was measured and a sketch was drawn. There were two kinds of lands, *viz.* Puyal and Adai. The income of the former was shared by landowners and cultivators, the latter lands were crown lands. These lands were cultivated by farmers on lease. For measurement of lands kalappai or ploughs were used. Satas-Sahasra meaning 1,00,000 ox ploughs was used as a land measurement, according to the Hiragadahalli plates.

Navaratna, pattika, padakku, kuli, veli, etc. were important longitudinal measurements. Navaratna was the extent of the land that one can draw from a specific place by walk in a given time. Padagam stood for 240 kudis of arable land.

Sealed weights and measures were in use during this period. To measure ghee and oil, 'pidi' was used as measurement. Paddy was measured by sadu, nali, marakal, padakka, kuruni, kadi and kalam. For the measurement of gold, kalanju and munchadi were used by the people.

(e) Irrigation

Dry lands and waste lands were brought under cultivation. For this purpose, lakes, canals and wells were used by the people. The government, village boards and some private people looked after the water tanks. The important lakes were:

(1) Thenneri
(2) Rajathadagam
(3) Vali Eri
(4) Velleri
(5) Marudanadu Eri
(6) Mahendra Thadagam
(7) Parameswara Thadagam
(8) Chitramega Thadagam
(9) Vairamega Thadagam
(10) Kanaga Valli Thadagam.

The above lakes depended mainly on rains and river waters.

A large number of wells were constructed for drinking and irrigational purposes.

The following canals were used for irrigation:

(1) Vairamega canal (Trichy)
(2) Perumbidugu canal (Chingleput)
(3) Ganapathy Vaikkal
(4) Sridara canal.

Moreover rivers like Vegavathi and Palar greatly helped in irrigation of surrounding villages.

Marutadu inscription mentions that Kongavaiyar Naina Perumal built a sluice to protect the lake. Many sluices (Kalingal) were built during that time.

Tank committee was created to look after tanks, wells and canals. This committee was managed by the village Sabha. For the purpose of maintenance rich people gave gold and lands, common people gave paddy and labour. Apart from this, government extended its help in very many ways.

(f) Crops

Sennel, Narnel, Coconut trees, Palm trees, Senkodi, Karusaranganni, Marikolundu and Nilerpalam were cultivated during this period. There is a reference about Thulasi plant. Particularly these herbal plants were taxed by the government so as to increase its revenue. From the Velurpalayam plates we come to know the cultivation of Ulli (Vettiver) and Iruveli.

(g) Drought

Droughts occurred in the Pallava kingdom due to scarcity of rain. One such drought occurred during the time of Parameswaravarman. Periyapuranam also mentions about a drought.

Another cause for drought was the wars that occurred during the Pallava period. It is clearly indicated by Dandin, a great poet of Rajasimha. Moreover, a serious damage to the country was caused by the war that took place between Nandivarman and Cholas.

Relief measures were undertaken by the government. A separate Board was created for this purpose. This Board (Panchavariya Committee) collected and stored paddy from the villagers. This Board distributed the same to the people during drought. During the time of Dandivarman and Nripatunga many tanks were dug to avoid drought. To wipeout drought condition, monasteries and schools took all possible steps in the land. We get informations about this from Periyapuranam and the accounts of Hiuen Tsang.

(h) Trade and Commerce

The Pallava period witnessed a considerable development in the field of trade and commerce.

Regarding inland trade, every village had shops in those days. Inscriptions speak of the commercial activities of those shops. The following commodities were sold in the shops:

(1) Oil

(2) Ghee

(3) Arecanut

(4) Vegetables

(5) Flowers

(6) Coconut

(7) Sugar

(8) Cloth

(9) Sandals.

From the Ulagalantha Perumal temple inscription at Kancheepuram it is inferred that licences were given to these shops.

Mahabalipuram was an important port during the Pallava period. It is often mentioned by Thirumangai Alwar and Hiuen Tsang in this masterpieces.

In addition to Mahabalipuram, Nagapattinam was also a remarkable port. There was trade relationship between Kancheepuram and China and South-West Asia. Nandi Kalambagam gives a beautiful account of the trade that was going on between Kanchi and China.

(i) Coins

Many coins of Pallava rulers are available to us. Wheel, Swastik, Umbrella, Sangu, Arrow, Fish, Crab, Tortoise, Lion, Horse, etc. were found on the obverse of the coins. Coins bearing the emblem of Nandhi and two ships are also available to us.

Generally, coins were made of gold, silver and copper. Many inscriptions speak about the various coins available to us.

(II) ECONOMIC LIFE UNDER CHOLAS

(a) Agriculture

Agriculture was the backbone of economy. The heart of the Chola country lay in the Kaveri delta. Kaveri delta was highly responsible for the progress of the people. The lands of the Chola period can be broadly divided into three divisions on the basis of the property rights. They were:

(i) Vellan Vagai

(ii) Eleemosynary Tenure

(iii) Service Tenure.

(i) Some professional agriculturists had hereditary right over the lands. They paid tax to the state. Such lands were called Vellan Vagai. Those who enjoyed such lands were called Irai Kudigal. Those who owned large lands were called Perumkudigal. Later on they paid tax to the Siva temples.

(ii) Under Eleemosynary Tenure the following items of lands were brought for cultivation:

(1) Brahmadeyam (Lands given to the Brahmins)

(2) Devadanam (Lands donated to Siva)

(3) Salabhogam (Lands given to Brahmin Sivayogins)

(4) Pallichantam (Lands donated to Jain and Buddhist shrines)

(5) Tiruvidaiyattam (Lands given to Vishnu temples)

(6) Madapuram (Lands given to the Mathas).

During the time of Rajaraja I Brahmadeya lands were given liberally. There were 240 Brahmadeyas in the Chola country during his reign.

In some places the entire village was given to the Brahmins. It was called Ekabhoga-Brahmadeya.

The above categorical of lands were mostly tax-free lands.

(iii) Land given for meritorious service of public servants is called Service Tenure. They were Jivitam, Puram, Patti, Parru, Bhogam, Vritti and Kani.

Jivitam is a kind of land which was given to the officers instead of monthly salary. After the death of a particular officer it was redistributed to his wife and children.

Lands like Puram, Patti and Parru were given mostly to the menials of the temples for their service.

Bhogam is another kind of land which was given to the Brahmins who performed Archanas or Pujas in the Siva temples.

The lands given to the Brahmins for their teaching are called Bharata Vritti, Purana Vritti and Veda Vritti (Vritti lands).

The lands given to dancing damsels, dance masters, drummers and music masters are called Kani lands.

Efforts were taken to reclaim forest and wastelands as in the days of Kaduvettis (the Pallavas).

(b) Irrigation

The Chola Kings took series of successful steps for the improvement of irrigation. They constructed many water reservoirs like the Viranarayanameri, Cholavaridi, Gandavadityaponeri, Cholagangam, Sembiyam Mahadevi Eri, etc. The Cholagangam near Gangaikondacholapuram had a channel running to 60 miles. Rivers and tanks were christened after the name of the kings. Virasala Vadavam and Madurantaka Vadavam were named after the titles of Parantaka I. He also renovated Kunjaram Mallan Perani. During the time of Rajaraja I, Uyyakkondam and Kirtiman were dug for irrigation. Mudikondan river and Virasalan river were dug during the time of Rajendra I and Vira Rajendra respectively.

(c) Land Measurement

Periodical land surveys were conducted for assessment of taxes. Rajaraja I and Kulottunga I undertook large scale measurement of lands. During the time of Kulottunga III also, lands were measured. The units of measurements were 'kuli', and 'veli'. The title of 'Ulakalanthan' was given for those who helped to measure the land during the Chola period. They used a stick to measure the lands. It was called 'Ulagalanthakol'. It was the veritable unit of measurement during this period.

(d) Industry

Cottage industries flourished as it is in modern times. The metal workers had expert knowledge on metallurgy and produced images and utensils in gold, silver, bronze, copper, brass, etc. It is said that the "jewellers' art reached its high water-mark under the Cholas". The following ornaments were popular during this period:

(1) Kiridam (head)

(2) Kuntalam (ear)

(3) Kandikai (neck)

(4) Aram (chest)
(5) Skandamala (shoulder)
(6) Udarakandam (3″ above navel)
(7) Oddiyanam (hip)
(8) Rings
(9) Bangles
(10) Padasaram (anklets).

Kanchi was an important centre of textile industry. Silk, cotton and dhairs of the animals were used for wearing in many industrial centres. In addition to Kanchi, Uraiyur and Trichy occupied a prominent position in this industry.

Fine and strong ships were built by the carpenters of the Chola period. The following centres were very famous for ship-building:

(1) Kanyakumari
(2) Aduthurai
(3) Marakkanam
(4) Ariyur.

Beautiful images of various gods and goddesses were made by the coppersmiths and goldsmiths. War materials were produced by the blacksmiths of this period.

(e) Taxation

Taxation was known as 'vari' or 'irai'. Dandam and 'mampadu' were possibly fines or levy. Tax free lands were known as 'iraiyili'. Taram-perranilam were assessed lands and those non-assessed lands were Tavamili. The primary items of state revenue were:

(1) Land revenue
(2) Customs taxes
(3) Professional taxes
(4) Taxes on mineral wealth
(5) Taxes on forest
(6) Spoils of war

(7) Tributes from feudatories

(8) Other sources.

Land revenue was one-sixth or one-third according to the fertility of the soil. The following were some of the important taxes levied on various categories of people:

(1) Kusakkanam (potter)

(2) Kannalakkanam (marriage)

(3) Ilaikkanam (betelnut)

(4) Tarigurai (weavers)

(5) Sekkirai (oilmongers)

(6) Vannarapparai (dhobi)

(7) Porvari (war tax)

(8) Ilamputchi (toddy droppers)

(9) Odakkudi (boatman)

(10) Sangam (export and import taxes)

(11) Idaippattam (shepherds)

(12) Nilanirpattam (using water from tank)

(13) Ankadipattam (shopkeepers).

During the time of Uttama Chola 'Iravuvari' (night tax) was collected from the people.

Severe punishments were given to tax evaders. It cannot be denied that there was malpractice and corruption during this period among the administrative officers.

Towards the end of the Chola rule there was heavy taxation. People suffered a lot due to the tax burden. Some people experienced untold sorrows and sufferings.

(f) Expenditure

The chief items of state expenditure were the king, his household, secretariat, armed forces, allowances to members of royal family, benevolences, etc. Besides, the kings spent the State revenue on wards and famine relief measures. Moreover, they directed a portion of the revenue for constructing temples. Renovation work was also carried out by them in an excellent manner.

(g) Weights and Measures

Various kinds of weights and measures were in use during the Chola period. A decimal fraction of a veli of lands for assessment of revenue was known. The various kinds of measurements are:

(1) Liquid and grain measures

2 sevidu	=	1 pidi
5 sevidu	=	1 alakku
2 alakku	=	1 ulakku
2 ulakku	=	1 uri
2 uri	=	1 nali
8 nali	=	1 kuruni or marakkal
2 kuruni	=	1 padakku
2 padakku	=	1 tuni or kadi
3 tuni	=	1 kalam

(2) Cubic measures

4 kani	=	1 ma
5 ma	=	1 kuruni
2 kuruni	=	1 manjadi
10 manjadi	=	1 kalanju (68 to 72 grains)

(3) Linear measures

8 torai (rice corn)	=	1 viral
12 viral	=	1 jan
2 jan	=	1 mulam

(4) The day and year calculation

7½ nalikai	=	1 samam
8 samam	=	1 day
7 days	=	1 week
15 days	=	1 pakkam
2 pakkam	=	1 month
6 months	=	1 ayanam
2 ayanams	=	1 year

(h) Trade and Commerce

The Cholamandalam, *i.e.* Coromandel was a busy coast frequented by ships from China and Arabia. Mamallapuram, Saliyur, Korkai, Quilon, etc. were important ports. Brisk trade was going on between the Chola Kingdom and the neighbouring countries. Chan Ju-Kwa refers to the trade in pearls, elephants, cardamom, cotton textiles, etc. Pepper, perfumes, textiles, drugs, ivory, coral, pearl, etc. were chief among the exports. Horses were imported from the Arabian peninsula.

According to Benjamin of Tudela, the ships entering the Chola ports were required to pay tolls. All sorts of protections were given by the State to those ships and their cargo. Kulottunga I was known as Sungamtavirtta Chola (who abolished tolls) in the history of Tamil Nadu.

During this time local bodies, levied fines on rotten drugs. It is mentioned in an inscription found in Thanjavur.

Barter system was followed during the Chola period.

Manikiramattar and Nagarattar were well-known traders.

Robbery was prevented by a special army kept by the merchants.

The Cholas had trade relations with the following countries:

(1) Persia

(2) Burma

(3) Java

(4) Sumatra

(5) Ceylon

(6) Maldive Islands.

Thus, brisk trade existed in the Chola country.

(i) Coins

During the Chola period gold, silver and copper coins were in use abundantly. Gold coins were made by pon. After Kulottunga III Kasu was in use. It was a copper coin. Its value was very small. The coins of Rajaraja I bear the figures of the other countries. It indicates the Chola domination over other countries.

(j) Hospitals

Hospitals (Adula Salai) were maintained by the Chola Kings. It is mentioned in many inscriptions. For the maintenance of hospitals lands were given by the government. From Tirumukkudal inscription we know that a hospital was named after Vira Chola. Many diseases were cured by the doctors of the Hospital. It was under the control of a chief physician. He was paid annually 80 Kalams of paddy, 8 Kasus and a grant of certain land. Apart from the doctors, the other staff members of the hospital like the nurse, barber (performed minor operations) and waterman were also given remuneration. Treatment was given to the following diseases in the hospital:

(1) tuberculosis

(2) jaundice

(3) fistula

(4) dropsy

(5) anaemic diseases

(6) enlargement of the spleen

(7) general disability.

(k) Role of Temple in Employment

Many towns came into existence during the Chola period. It goes without saying that they grew around the temples. Liberal donations were given to those temples. So the temple provided the means of livelihood for a large number of artists and servants. From the inscription of Brihadeeswar Temple at Thanjavur, we know that a large number of servants performed their duties and received considerable remuneration for their work during this period. Among the servants of the temple, the dancing girls topped the list. There were nearly 400 dancing girls. The dancing girls were transferred from one temple to another temple.

(III) ECONOMIC LIFE UNDER PANDYAS

The fertile lands of the country were immensely important for the growth of economy. People utilised the fertile lands for their progress and prosperity. They settled on the fertile plains of Vaigai and Tamiraparani. They made use of the rivers for their agriculture.

(a) Agriculture

During this period lands were measured properly. After proper measurement boundary stone was laid and regular fencing work was undertaken by the government. It is mentioned in many copper plates. Moreover, the periodic land surveys are indicated by reference to scales like Sundara Pandyankol and Via-Pandyankol. Kuli, ma and veli were four kinds of lands, *viz.*

(1) Vellan Vagai

(2) Brahmadeyam

(3) Devadanam and

(4) Service Tenures

(1) *Vellan Vagai*

In this kind the landowners were called Vallan Vagai. They were brought under the control of the State. They paid the taxes regularly. It is stated that they had to pay an annual tax of 642 Kalams of paddy and 40 Kalanju to the government.

(2) *Brahmadeyam*

Brahmadeyam lands were given to the learned Brahmins as an honour by the Kings and Queens. Rich people also gave this kind of lands to the Brahmins. Parantaka Viranarayanan gave a village called Dinachutar Mangalam as Brahmadeyam. It is mentioned in the Chinnamanur copper plate.

(3) *Devadanam*

Devadanam lands were given to the learned Brahmins as an honour by the kings, queens and the rich people.

(4) *Service Tenures*

This kind of lands were given to the villagers for their meritorious service. Besides the villagers, soldiers were also given such lands for their heroic deeds in battles.

Tax remission was given to the people during the time of drought and famine.

(b) Irrigation

The main sources of irrigation were Vaigai and Tambaraparani rivers. The secondary sources were Vellaru and other canals. River irrigation was in vogue to a greater extent. Several canals were dug in Vaigai river for the purpose of irrigation. Many tanks and canals were constructed by Parantaka Viranarayanan. Among the canals the following were very important:

(1) Parakrama Pandyan grand canal

(2) Vasudeva grand canal

(3) Veerapandyan canal

(4) Sri Vallabha grand canal

A dam was constructed during this period. It was called Parakrama Pandya Kallanai. Apart from these irrigation works, a canal was dug in River Pennai for the irrigation of the farmers at Tiruvannamalai.

The kings maintained Eri Variyam to look after the lakes. Tanks and lakes were properly maintained by the Variyam.

(c) Reclamation of Wastelands

Barren lands and uncultivable lands were brought under cultivation in those days. Series of successful steps were undertaken by the government to remove the sands from the fields affected by heavy floods. No wonder the government authorities paid great attention to increase the yield of these lands.

(d) Industry

A significant development took place in the field of industry. The following occupations were prominent in those days:

(1) Pearl fishing

(2) Fishing

(3) Salt manufacturing

(4) Conch shells cutting

(5) Weaving

(6) Spinning

(7) Making of ornaments

(8) Pot making

(9) Sculptural work.

Paradanars mostly engaged in fishing.

During the Pandya period, pearl fishing was a famous trade.

Both men and women were engaged in weaving. 'Tari irai' was collected for this occupation.

(e) Coins

Enough references to trade guilds are found in the inscriptions. A good many number of Pandyan coins have been discovered and are found mentioned in inscriptions. A double carp on the obverse with an inscription is the common type of Pandyan coins. The coins of Srimara Srivallabha, Maravarman Sundara Pandya I, Jatavarman Sundara Pandya I and Jatavarman Vira Pandya were known as avanibhasekhara kolakai, Sonadu Kondan, eliam talaiyan and valal vali tirandan kulikai respectively. Achchu, anai-achchu, kasu or sempon kasu, panam, palankasudrahmam, kanum, pudu kulagai panam, anrada narpadu kasu, palan soliakkasu, palasurdai anai achchu, etc. are some of the varieties of coins listed by historians.

Korkai was the minting place of Pandyas. It was called Akkasalai, *i.e.* several coins.

(f) Inland Trade

Inland trade was in a flourishing condition in the Pandya Kingdom. Trade guilds existed in Pandianadu. Such guilds were:

(1) Nagarattar

(2) Nanadesikan

(3) Ainuruvar

(4) Anjuvanathar

(5) Tisaivairathar.

The above guilds promoted exports of the country. They had cordial trade relationship with Sri Lanka, Sumatra, Java and Malaya.

Kayal was a famous port in those days.

The trading communities did wonderful service to the temples also.

(g) Foreign Trade

The overseas commerce which flourished under the Cholas was continued by the Pandyas. The foreign accounts of a galaxy of travellers given an excellent peep into the commercial activities of the age. According to Wassaf, "The curiosities of Chin and Machin and the beautiful products of Hind and Sind, laden on large ships (which they call junks) sail like mountains with the wings of the winds on the surface of the water are always arriving there.... The wealth of the Isles of the Persian Gulf in particular, and in part the beauty and adornment of other countries from Iraq and Khurasan as far as Rome and Europe are denied from Malabar which is so situated as to be the key of Hind."

According to Marco Polo, "It is at this city that all ships touch that come from the west, as from Hormes and from Kis and from Aden, and all-Arabia, laden with horses and with other things or sale...there is great business done in the city of Cail." The Tamil kingdoms invested huge sums for purchase of horses from the Arabia.

According to Wassaf, "10,000 horses at the value of 2,200,000 Dinars were imported annually. But the horses were ill-fed and with no trained cavaliers to take care of them, they died. Kayal was the famous centre of horse and pearl trade. The earlier enthusiasm of the Tamils in trade was waning."

The Arabs brought in large quantities of spices in addition to horses during their trade.

The Ceylonese exchanged their goods in Pandianad.

The Pandya King Kulasekaran had political relations with the Chinese emperor Kublai Khan during the 13th century.

(h) Taxation

There was a department of revenue called puravu-vari-ti—naikalam, Irai, pattan, kadani, antarayam, uludukkudi, padidkkavai, tattapattam, inavari, idai vari, etc. were the various synonyms for taxes.

The taxes due to the state were collected by local officials and deposited in the royal treasury.

All kinds of professions and commercial groups were taxed.

Land revenue was the principal source of income in addition to royalty from pearl fishing and port taxes.

The levy and collection of taxes were done on consultation with local officials.

The taxes mentioned in inscriptions are:

(1) Vaykkalpattam
(2) Archchuvari
(3) Kaviyavarachi
(4) Vellipattam
(5) Panjupili
(6) Sandiviggirahappam
(7) Vasalpen
(8) Ilani naipperu
(9) Tari-irai
(10) Sekkirai
(11) Pasipattam
(12) Taxes levied on courtesans.

Remission of taxes on festive occasions like the King's coronation were ordered.

The lands offered free of tax were davadana (to Siva temples), tiruvidaiyattam (to Vishnu temples), pallichandam (to Jains and Buddhist temples), Brahmadeya (to Brahmanas) and Madappuram (to Maths).

(IV) ECONOMIC CONDITION UNDER VIJAYANAGAR RULERS

(a) Agriculture

Agriculture was the backbone of economy. There were three types of villages during the Vijayanagar period. They were:

(1) Villages granted as donations—Devadanam, Brahmadeyam, Madappuram, Thirunamathukkavi and Tiruvidaiyattam.

(2) Privileged villages of the government—Pandaramadai and Amaram.

(3) Privately owned villages—certain private people had their own villages.

Villages were not properly planned and constructed. There was poor sanitary condition in those villages. Many choultries and Mandapas were constructed for common purpose of the villagers. Travellers also utilised these choultries and Mandapas for their sojourn. Thannir Pandals (Drinking Water) were established on the roads for the use of travellers. An ideal village consisted of many houses, streets, cultivable lands, pasture lands, wastelands, public places, etc. Rich people lived in big houses whereas poor people lived in huts. Social groups lived in separate streets. The Europeans lived in palatial buildings.

The village lands were divided into three categories, *viz.* wet lands, dry lands and gardens. The people cultivated paddy, ragi, varagu, thinai, green grams, black grams, horse gram, maize, turmeric, surgar cane, gingelly, cotton and indigo. We get information about the cultivation of spices from the accounts of the foreigners. Mango, coconut, orange, lemon, jackfruit, arecanut and plantain trees are mentioned in their accounts.

Wooden ploughs were used by the farmers to plough the lands.

Irrigational system was very excellent in those days. Irrigation was carried on through rivers, tanks and wells. Canals were constructed for the purpose of irrigation. Irrigational conflicts were solved by the government smoothly. There was no hindrance for the distribution of water.

The condition of the farmers was not satisfactory. They lived on debts. The debtors were treated as slaves. Most of the agriculturists were very poor. During the off season they were engaged in fishing. They had to pay heavy taxes to the government.

(b) Industry

Weaving was the major industry during this period. Many small industries were encouraged by the government. Jaggery making and oil pressing were other flourishing industries. Pot making industry was given great impetus during the Vijayanagar rule. Potters provided their pots and other things to temples. Fishing was also encouraged by the government.

Weaving was in prosperous condition. Cotton and silk products were in great demand. Silk was imported from Karnataka. Kaikolas and Saliyars engaged in weaving. Generally their condition was very pathetic and pitiable. The income of the weaver was very meagre. The government gave tax exemption to those weavers on certain occasions. Dyeing factory also existed during this period. Particularly there were many expert dyers in Kanchi and Madurai.

Carpenters, blacksmiths, dhobies, barbers, chettys and cattle rearers were engaged in their respective professions.

Pearl fishing occupied a significant place during this period. Kayal was the centre of pearl fishing in Tamil Nadu. Portuguese showed keen interest in purchasing the pearls.

The Telugu and Kannada speaking people migrated to Tamil Nadu during Vijayanagar rule.

(c) Trade and Commerce

Trade and commerce—both inland and foreign—were carried by Chettis or Komatis. Brisk trade was going on between Tamilaham and neighbouring countries. Cows, oxen and horses were sold in fairs. Fairs were organised weekly in those days. For example, the Friday shandy (Fair) of Senji was a popular one. Rice, kandalas' sugar, etc. were exported to Aden, Ormuz and Ceylon. Besides these items, the following things were also exported to those countries:

(1) Coconut

(2) Spices

(3) Dyes

(4) Indigo

(5) Sandal

(6) Iron

(7) Precious stones

(8) Pearls
(9) Cotton, silk and calico clothes.

The following things were imported from Aden and China:

(1) Gold
(2) Silver
(3) Tin
(4) Lead
(5) Copper
(6) Opium.

Some precious stones were imported from Ceylon. Akil, camphor, spices, etc. were imported from Sumatra, Java and Malacca Islands.

Trunk roads were constructed for the purpose of trade and commerce. Bullock carts were utilised for transporting goods from one place to another. Moreover, boats, catamarans, ships and small boats were utilised for transporting goods through water.

The following ports were very prominent during this period:

(1) Nagapattinam
(2) Thirumalairayanpattinam
(3) Tharangambadi (Tranqubar)
(4) Parangippettai (Porto Novo)
(5) Thevanampattinam
(6) Sadurangapattinam (Sadras)
(7) Pazhaverkkadu (Pulicat)
(8) Mylapore.

The capital of Vijayanagar was connected with Mylapore through a great trunk road. Chandragiri, Tirupati and Pazhaverkkadu were important towns in the above route. Another great road connected the towns of Kalahasti, Tirupati and Kanchi. Still another route connected the towns of Tiruvannamalai, Chidambaram, Madurai and Rameswaram.

Merchant guilds were organised during the Vijayanagar rule. The merchant guilds, the Nanadesis and Ainnurruvar, etc.

continued to function. There were 18 such guilds in the Tamil country. Kammala had their own guild in Kancheepuram. There was a guild for weavers in Virinjipuram, Chittrameliperianattar guild for Vellalas also existed during this period.

The Portuguese, the Dutch, and the Dane were vigorously engaged in business along with Muslims during the Vijayanagar period. After the fall of Vijayanagar in the Battle of Talikota in 1565 the Portuguese trade began to fall rapidly.

(d) Revenue

Since no government can be run without finance and governmental finance is got mostly through taxation. Tamil governments from very early times knew and levied many kinds of taxes. The Vijayanagar rule in Tamil Nadu was not an exception to this. Many kinds of taxes were imposed and collected during this period. The government earned the income through the following services:

(1) Land tax

(2) Profession taxes

(3) Wealth tax

(4) Excise duty

(5) Irai or Thirai or tribute

(6) Fines

(7) Commercial taxes.

(1) During the reign of Krishnadevaraya lands were properly surveyed. Taxes were levied according to the fertility and nature of the lands Remission of tax was given during the time of famine and drought.

(2) Professional taxes were collected from carpenters, blacksmiths, dhobies, barbers, fishermen, weavers, cattle rearers and chettis.

(3) Taxes were levied upon huts and tiled houses. It was called wealth tax.

(4) Excise duty was imposed upon goods imported to our country.

(5) The Nayaks paid tribute to the Emperor to recognise their states.

(6) Fines were collected to add to the resources of the country.

(7) The government secured huge revenue through the commercial taxes.

Besides, the government received income through courts and confiscation of properties. In addition to this, the officials collected tax from Shandys (markets).

Thus, the revenue administration of Vijayanagar period clearly indicates the various sources of income to the government.

(e) Expenditure

The government spent the revenue on the following items:

(1) Wars

(2) Construction and maintenance of roads

(3) Construction of temples

(4) Renovation of old temples

(5) Construction of choultries and rest houses.

(f) Coins

The medium of exchange in all commercial transactions was gold. A good many number of coins of Vijayanagar period are available to us. Gold coins called 'Ramadunga' are available in plenty. The people used 'Pagoda' as medium of exchange (one pagoda is equal to three rupees). 'Panam' and 'kasu' were in use during this period. Frier has mentioned that one pagoda was equal to eight shilling; one panam was equal to three shilling and one kasu was equal to one panam. Figures were inscribed on both sides of the coin. Figures like Uma Maheswarar, Hanuman, Lakshmi and Narayanan were inscribed on one side of the coins. Figures of ox, pig and elephant were inscribed on the other side of the coins. There were three minting centres during the Vijayanagar rule. They were established at Tanjore, Trichy and Vellore. In the Ramadunga kasu figures of Rama and Sita were inscribed on one side and the figures of Hanuman on the other side. Generally the coins were round (circular) in shape.

(g) Weights and Measures

Various kinds of weights and measures were in use. The following units of measurement were used for measuring liquid and grains:

(1) Manu
(2) Param
(3) Veesam
(4) Palam
(5) Ser
(6) Tola
(7) Kanam
(8) Ulakku
(9) Kalam
(10) Marakkal.

Besides these units, lands were measured by the following units:

(1) Veli
(2) Ma
(3) Kuli.

Moreover, lands were measured by a measuring rod or stick (Kol).

(h) Famines

Famine and drought greatly affected the economy of the people. Virtually they crippled the economic condition of the society. Added to this, flood and epidemic diseases also wrought havoc in the society. Famines visited the country in 1381, 1402 and 1450. In 1402, there was a great famine in Tanjore. In 1450, another famine visited Ramanathapuram, Pudukkottai and Trichy. It was really a terrible famine. The government took famine relief measures. From Kuthalam inscription we know some more details about famine which occurred during this period.

Guptan Age (Gupta Period)

9

We get a clear picture about the economic condition of the Gupta period from the literary and archaeological sources. The foreign accounts also give valuable information about the Gupta period. The Puranas, *Kaumudi Mahotsava*, *Devi Chandraguptam*, *Harsha Charita* and the coins of the period give a detailed description about the economic condition of the Gupta period. Moreover, the accounts of Fa-hien and It-sing (Chinese travellers) are really remarkable evidences to know more about the period. Besides these sources, the remarkable inscriptions, cave paintings and sculptures furnish the most reliable data regarding the extent of the reign of the Gupta rulers.

Agriculture. During this period the Gupta rulers did wonderful service. The people were prosperous and happy. There was peace and tranquillity in the land. People witnessed many sided developments. So the period is regarded as the "Golden Age" in the history of India.

Agriculture was the main occupation during this period. There was no government interference. Hence, there was marked development in this field. Production increased by leaps and bounds. The people were happy and contented.

From the literary sources we know that the majority people were agriculturists and farmers. The Chinese travellers Fa-hien and It-sing also mention the same thing in their accounts. The land was fertile. The means of irrigation were simple. There were two seasonal rainfalls in India and the farmers reaped the harvest twice a year.

The peasants and farmers used manure to increase the fertility of the soil.

The main crops of the people were wheat, gram, maize, rice, barley, sugar cane, mustard, peanuts, cotton, tobacco, potatoes and watermelons.

There were fruit gardens in those days. There were gardens of mangoes, grapes and lemons.

Occupations. There were many cloth centres during this period. Besides the cloth centres, other industries flourished in those days. They were very prosperous. Particularly silk industry witnessed a significant development during the Gupta period. During the time of Kumaragupta many families engaged in this occupation. From the Mandasor inscription we know that those people helped to a great extent for the growth of silk industry.

Metallurgy. Gold, silver and copper were utilised for coins during this period. They were also utilised by the people for making ornaments and jewels. Added to these metals, pearls and diamonds were added attractions of the people during this period.

Leather industry also flourished during the Gupta period.

During this period people were engaged in mining and other allied industries.

Trade. There was brisk internal and external trade during the Gupta period. Fa-hien mentions about this foreign trade. There were ports and harbours.

Coinage. During this period coins were issued in silver and copper. Chandragupta's gold coins show the pomp, power and prosperity of the empire. The gold coins bear the effigy of the emperor handling a bow, and on the reverse a figure of goddess seated on a lion. In others he is slaying a lion instead of a tiger. Generally the gold and silver coins issued by the Gupta emperors bear simple testimony to the prosperity of the country. On the obverse side of the coins the figure of the king and on the reverse side the figure of Lakshmi or Durga or Saraswati were depicted.

The figure of the king is depicted in different poses like shooting a tiger or riding a horse. Coins of Samudragupta and Kumaragupta issued after their Ashwamedha sacrifices bear the figure of a horse tied to the Yupasthamba. Chandragupta coins bear the picture of Garuda eating a snake. The coins issued by the Gupta emperors infer the originality and skilfulness of the craftsmen.

Economic Life in Ancient India

10

Agriculture

Agricultural technique has been changing through the ages; in the ancient times as even today land was ploughed with the plough yoked to a pair of oxen. There is mention in the later Vedic age of heavy ploughs drawn by as many as twenty-four oxen but their use must have been rare. Iron plough shares were known. The yield and fertility of the Indian soil and ability of her cultivators, who raised two crops a year, impressed the Greek travellers and diarists who accompanied Alexander. The yield then must have been better than now as the soil was less exhausted. The main food crops raised were wheat, barley, rice and millets. Sugar cane, oil seeds and cotton were grown over most parts. Sugar was exported to western countries. Malabar was well-known for its spices, particularly pepper, ginger, cardamom and cinnamon, which were widely in demand in Europe. Vegetables, leaf, gourds and roots of different kinds were grown everywhere. Trees yielding fruits and nuts were specially grown in orchards. The most valued fruit was the mango, which grew during summer. The banana was grown in all wetlands. The tamarind was grown all over south India. In the ancient period the palmyra was known but not the coconut, which was imported in the Middle Ages from Indonesia. The arecanut which was first grown in the south was introduced into north India in the early centuries of the Christian era. The sandal, much loved for its fragrance, grew in the south. The date, the walnut, the grape and the almond were importations from the Middle East, particularly Persia, and are little mentioned in ancient literature.

Stock Breeding

In the early rural and in the still earlier pastoral communities cattle were the chief movable property. It was absolutely essential for cultivation and transport. The cow, the bull, the buffalo and the goat were the first animals to be domesticated and great attention was paid to their breeding and feeding. Each village had its own professional breeder, who maintained breeding bulls. Stall-feeding was not known. There was more pasture and wasteland than now and the cattle of each village were led out for grazing in the morning by the communal cowherd, who drove them back home only in the evening. The Krishna legend suggests that there must have been communities of professional herdsmen, who probably led a semi-nomadic life in the wilder parts of the country. The Yadavas and the Abhiras, who established their own kingdoms in the historical period in Malwa and Western Deccan traced their descent from such communities. Milk, ghee and butter were important articles of diet and the Krishna legend speaks of their plentiful stock in every household. Though beef was eaten the cow was held sacred and inviolable. The ox was the usual beast of burden. The buffalo was sacrificed to the goddess Durga and the cult became popular in the Middle Ages. The goat's and the sheep's wool was used in the manufacturing of blankets.

The horse was a luxury animal, maintained by the warrior class. In India horse breeding was confined to Sind and the north-west. Horses were imported from Arabia and Persia and supplied throughout the country. It is known that the elephant was domesticated as early as sixth century B.C. Kings maintained special forest tracts as elephant preserves and employed trackers, hunters and tamers to catch wild elephants and tame them. The elephants were used in war and as vehicles for kings. They were also maintained by temples to adorn festive processions. The camel was known and used as a beast of burden in the dry regions of north India. The dog was as common in ancient India as it is today. Though used in hunting it was never treated as a domestic pet. Indian dogs of a large breed from cold hills of north India were in great demand in Persia and Egypt for use in war and hunting.

Among birds the fowl, the peacock and the parrot were well-known. Though the fowl were reared eggs did not form an important item of diet. Peacocks were kept both for food and ornament and there were whole villages of peacock rearers. In the Middle Ages they ceased to be used as food. The parrot was reared and kept in cages in the houses of nobles; it was a bird of beauty believed to possess powers of talking. Literature refers to it as a pet of ladies, who devoted much time in teaching it to talk. Though silkworms were bred and reared in India, especially in Assam and Bengal silk weaving was not mastered before the Christian era. The earliest silks were imported from China and the *Arthasastra's* reference to Cheenapatta is significant.

Industry: Crafts and Craft-guilds

Industrial crafts developed and grew in complexity along with the growth of town life and the needs of royal courts. Stone cutting and polishing, metallurgy, carpentry, spinning and weaving were the major industries. Ancient Indian craftsmen worked with simple tools but attained a high degree of technical skill and perfection as attested by the Asokan pillars, the Iron Pillar of Delhi, and the great demand in the Roman empire for the fine cotton cloth of India. The Asokan pillars, made of sandstone from Chunar, some 30′ to 40′ in height and weighing about 50 tonnes, were so well polished that several foreign visitors had mistaken them for metallic pillars. The Iron pillar of Chandra (probably Chandra Gupta II) at Mehrauli, near Delhi, about 24′ in height, is a single piece of iron, "of a size and weight which could not have been produced by the best European iron founders until about a hundred years ago". The fabrication, conveyance over long distances and erection of the monolithic Asokan pillars and the rust free iron pillar, which has withstood the rains of 1,500 years, are eloquent testimonies of the skill of the ancient Indian engineers and metallurgists. Her spinners and weavers produced silks and muslins, which were

, to make them almost transparent; ancient sculpture so ne limbs through folds of such textiles.

ancient India there were individual craftsmen, state actories and craft guilds. The individual craftsman had orkshop in his home worked with the help of the members s family and usually sold his wares at his doors. Occasionally individual craftsman became wealthy and owned more than one workshop. From an early Jain source we learn that there was a wealthy potter, by name Saddalaputta, who owned 500 pottery workshops and a fleet of boats, which supplied his wares throughout the Ganges valley. The state owned textile and artillery workshops had employed salaried craftsmen. It also owned and worked the mines.

Our chief sources for an understanding of the ancient Indian craft guilds are the Buddhist scriptures in Pali. The craft guild was an industrial and mercantile organization, which included all craftsmen of a particular trade. Every town had its own guild in each trade; sometimes a guild was so important that it embraced several towns; in any case each trade had its own guild, even thieves organizing themselves in guilds. As guilds were organized on the basis of trades and professions and as caste and sub-castes too developed on similar lines it is difficult sometimes to distinguish between the development of a craft guild and that of a trade caste. Each trade has its own guild, even thieves organized themselves in guilds.

The craft guild (Sreni) was headed by a chief called the Elder (Jyeshtaka Sanskrit, Jethaka Pali), who was assisted by a council of senior craftsmen and merchants. The Jethaka was often the richest craftsman in the trade and his office was hereditary. He was influential and his advice was sometimes sought by the king. Each guild was a corporate body and enjoyed considerable autonomy. It had its own court with full jurisdiction over all members and distinguishing insignia like banners and chamaras, which were carried in festive processions. Major guilds had their own militias, which fought along with the king's army if required. The guild council framed rules of work and fixed standards, wages and prices. If any member violated a rule he was tried by the guild court, whose judgement was upheld by the state. The court heard and decided ca dispute. It could expel a member from the guild which m mean ruin as he could not practise his trade any more. provided for the maintenance of widows and orphans and sic members. The expenses were met out of a reserve fund built from subscriptions paid by members. It received deposits and gave loans, and acted as trustees of religious endowments made by benefactors; on their behalf it regularly carried out certain services in a temple or during a festival. Numerous inscriptions on walls of temples record such services rendered by guilds; often the guild itself made endowments. In short, the craft guild was the hub of the economic and social life of the craftsmen belonging to a particular trade.

The guild system did not always work well. Sometimes there were rival guilds belonging to the same trade and inscriptions refer to their better quarrels.

Currency and Credit

A money economy is essential for trade and it came into existence in India not earlier than the sixth century B.C. The earliest Indian coins were uninscribed punch-marked silver and bronze pieces of irregular shape but fairly accurate weight. The punch-marks like those on the Indus seals were probably emblems of kings or chieftains or merchants, who issued them. The Graeco-Bactrians introduced inscribed coins of a better shape and finish of gold, silver, bronze and nickel. The Satavahanas of the Deccan issued coins of lead and various alloys. The Kushana coins were of gold and copper. The gold dinar was based on the Roman denarious. The Guptas issued gold, silver and copper coins, which are the best examples of early Indian coins. By this time a large range of silver and copper coins of different weight and character issued by kings and chieftains had come into circulation. The coins were accepted for their bullion value and the ideas of legal tender and token money were unknown. Coins issued by defunct dynasties and foreign coins, *i.e.* Greek, Roman and Persian, were in circulation. Some dynasties like the Palas of Bengal did not issue their own coins but managed with those of other states. Naturally some types of coins became localised. For small payments cowry shells were regularly used for a long time.

Moneylending was recognised by the Dharmasastras, which laid down rates of interest often calculated monthly. For secured loans the rate of interest was 1¼ per cent per month or 15 per cent per year. For unsecured loans Brahmans, according to Manu, were charged 24 per cent, Kshatriyas 36 per cent, Vaisyas 48 per cent and Sudras 60 per cent per annum. The *Arthasastra* gives a schedule of rates for traders: merchants trading within the town 5 per cent per month or 60 per cent per annum, merchants carrying their wares through forest 10 per cent per month or 120 per cent per annum, those doing overseas trade 20 per cent per month or 240 per cent per annum. These rates "are measures of both the profit and the risk of ancient commerce". Defaulting debtors were imprisoned or as bondsmen of the creditors they repaid their debt by means of their labour. The *Arthasastra* lays down the rules that interest payments should cease when the total interest paid equals the principal and that loans on securities which are used by the creditors for his own profit should be free of interest. Credit was provided by guilds, sometimes by temples and often by individual bankers, professional moneylenders and merchants.

Inland Trade: Merchant Guilds

The local merchant (Sreshtin, Chetti, Sait) combined trading with moneylending. He was often wealthy and honoured by the king. He bought the products of craftsmen and those of the peasants and sold them for profit. He specialised in distribution. Just as producers formed themselves into craft guilds, the distributors or merchants formed merchant guilds or mercantile companies, some of which are mentioned in the inscriptions and literature of south India. A famous mercantile corporation called Manigrama carried on business not only in south India but also in Ceylon through its agents. The merchant guild, like the craft guild, was a corporate body. It employed mercenaries to guard caravans, owned warehouses in different towns, in which the members might strict their goods, helped members or their families during periods of trouble or loss, maintained quality by preventing adulteration and avoided competition.

Thus, co-operation both of producers (industrial and not agricultural) and distributors was known but we do not hear of consumers' co-operation.

Retail trade was often in the hands of craftsmen themselves, who displayed their wares at their doors. Each trade was concentrated in a street, *e.g.* the potters street, the metal smith's street, the weaver's street, etc. We have noted above that the market officials of the Mauryas regulated market prices and enforced quality. From the days of the Buddha there were hawkers and pedlars too, who carried their wares from house to house.

Trade Routes: Transport

In the days of the Mauryas the entire country was served by trade routes. The main trade route of north India linked Tamralipti (near Calcutta) with Takshasila *via* Pataliputra, Banaras, Kausambi, Mathura and Sakala (Sialkot). From Takshasila the trunk road went to Central Asia along Kabul valley. A branch took off from Mathura and went to Patala (Hyderabad in Sind) *via* Rajasthan. Another branch linked Kausambi with Bhrigukaccha (Broach) on the mouth of the Narmada *via* Ujjain. Numerous feeder roads linked these main roads with the interior. The main southern route ran through western Deccan. It linked Ujjain and Broach with Pratishthana (Paithan), the ancient Satavahana capital, near Bombay. From Pratishthana the road crossed the Godavari and the Krishna and ran to Kanchi and Madurai. Feeders and branches linked the main road with the other southern cities. The eastern route from Bengal did not proceed beyond Orissa at least up to the Gupta period.

Transport was dangerous. From the Asokan inscriptions, the *Arthasastra* and the *Sukraniti* we learn that roads were wide, and frequently provided with drains but the numerous rivers were not bridged and could be crossed by ferries only and even the best roads were dusty during summer and impassable during the season of heavy rains. When the rivers were in spate all travel ceased. The roads often passed through dense jungle inhabited by tigers, elephants and snakes. Bands of professional robbers were a perennial menace. Under such conditions merchants travelled in a huge caravan which sometimes consisted of 500 men, moving with their merchandise in bullock carts and on pack animals, *viz.* oxen, mules, asses and camels. Pali literature mentions the caravan leader or Sarthavaha the land-pilot or Thalaniyyamaka and bands of professional caravan-guards who undertook to provide safe conduct over a particular route.

Merchandise

Long and short distance trade was carried on in a variety of commodities. The southern country supplied gold, gems, spices and sandalwood; from the east, *i.e.* Bengal and Banaras, came silks and muslins; the hills supplied musk and saffron. Iron was mined in south Bihar and copper in Rajasthan and parts of the Deccan. These metals were carried through the length and breadth of the country as well as sugar and salt, both sea salt and rock salt. Salt was manufactured at several places along the coast and there were rock-salt deposits in the Punjab (Salt Rangers).

Overseas Trade

Classical Tamil literature as well as the accounts of the Greek travellers like Strabo, Pliny and Ptolemy and the anonymous *Periplus of the Erythraean Sea* (Geography of the Indian Ocean) testify to an active trade between India and the West, particularly the Roman empire in the first few centuries of the Christian era and probably earlier. In the days of the Buddha Indian sailors sailed along the coasts of south India and probably visited Burma, Malaya and Indonesia. With the fall of the Roman empire the western trade declined but it revived with the growing demand of medieval Europe for the eastern products; but in the later Middle Ages the trade was carried not by the Hindus but by the Arabs. In the east the trade with Malaya, Indonesia and China, particularly from south India, never flagged until the Muslim conquest.

Trade with the Roman Empire

Spices, perfumes, precious stones, jewels, muslins, ivory, both raw and carved, pearls, sugar, Indian iron which was liked for its purity and hardness, rice, dyestuffs like lac and indigo, wild animals, birds and monkeys were regularly exported from India to the parts of the Roman empire. Indian elephants, lions and tigers were required for the wild gladiatorial shows and games of the circus arranged by the Roman emperors and noblemen. Parrots, peacocks and even monkeys from India were kept by wealthy Roman ladies as their pets. The wild animals were transported by the land route and the rest were sent by sea, up the Persian Gulf to Persia and Babylonia and up the Red Sea to Egypt. The elephants were accompanied by their mahouts. Indian fortune-tellers and prostitutes travelled along with merchants and settled in Rome. The Greek writers like Strabo and Pliny refer to several embassies sent by Indian kings to the Roman emperors. The earliest mission sent by a Pandya king met Augustus, the first Roman emperor, at Athens about 20 B.C. One of the members of this mission was an ascetic called Zarmanochegas (Sramanacharya) who is said to have burnt himself to death at Athens having grown tired of worldly life. Justinian (527-565 A.D.), the emperor of Constantinople, had an Indian cook. It is interesting to note that the Graeco-Latin terminology to indicate the Indian articles of trade were adaptations of Sanskrit or Tamil names, *e.g.* emerald from *marakata*, ginger from *sringavera*, pepper from *pippali*, sugar from *sarkara*, cotton from *karpasa*, rice from *arisi*, etc.

Extent of Indian Sea-faring

Though most of the western trade was carried in Greek and Roman ships which were bigger and heavier than Indian ships, the latter, it is known sailed as far as Alexandria, Babylon, and Madagascar. Socotra (Sukhataradvipa), a small island south of Arabia, had a large Indian colony. In the east the Indian vessels sailed to China, Burma, Malaya and the islands of Indonesia. The eastern trade was practically in the hands of south Indian seamen.

Chief Ports

The chief ports of ancient India were Tamralipti, Kavirippattinam (Puhar) and Korkai on the east coast and Patala, Bhrigukaccha, Supara (near Bombay) and Muziris (near

Cranganore) on the Cholas, Korkai that of the Pandyas and Muziris that of the Cheras. These were dynasties of Tamil kings who ruled over the extreme south in and around the beginning of the Christian era (the Sangam Age). They maintained their harbours in good condition and provided them with lighthouses, wharves and warehouses.

IMPORTS FROM THE ROMAN EMPIRE

Yavana Settlements

In return for her exports to the west India imported chiefly glassware, pottery, tin, lead, wine and slave girls, but these were quite inadequate to pay her exports, the bulk of which had to be paid in gold. The balance of trade, in other words, was very favourable to India. Pliny attributed the great drain (net loss) to the cost fo 100,000,000 sesterces year after year (1 sesterce = half a rupee) to the degenerate and luxurious life of Rome, particularly of the women. Roman coins of all types have been found in large quantities in many parts of south India. Greeks and other subjects of the Roman empire came to India in the wake of trade and settled at various places. Inscriptions mention one such western trading station at Arikamedu near Pondicherry. Excavations at this site have revealed the remains of several depots of foreign merchants containing chiefly glassware and sherds of Roman pottery. A temple was erected at Muziris to emperor Augustus. Indian literature refers to the western traders and settlers as Yavanas, though the term was originally used to denote the Greeks only. Tamil literature contains numerous references to the Yavanas, who were employed by kings and chieftains as bodyguards and military engineers, and to the Yavana merchants, whose ships were big and beautiful and whose prosperity never waned. Kavirippattinam was a busy port, where were to be seen many foreigners and where the foreign ships were busy loading and unloading.

The Eastern Trade

We have already referred to Indian exports, particularly from the southern ports, to Burma, Malaya, Java (Yavadvipa), Sumatra (Suvarnadvipa), Borneo, Bali and other islands of Indonesia, and China. From China south India and Ceylon bought silk and porcelain ware. This trade continued for centuries. In the wake of peaceful commercial enterprise the Buddhist and Hindu faiths and cultures migrated to these regions and Buddhist and Hindu kingdoms and colonies were established in Sumatra, Java, Malaya, Cambodia (Kamboja) and Annam (Champa). These settlements were in a flourishing condition throughout the Middle Ages.

Decline of Foreign Trade

India's foreign trade gradually passed into the hands of the Arabs in the west and the Chinese in east, who outstripped her craftsmen in the art of ship-building. Indian merchants preferred to sell their wares towards the close of the Middle Ages at their own depots to foreign lands. The idea gradually developed in this age that foreign travel, particularly across the sea, brought impurity to one's caste. Sailing came to be looked upon as dangerous and unsuitable. "The Muslim invasions encouraged xenophobia, and the people who had planted their colonies from Socotra to Borneo became, with religious sanction, a nation of landlubbers."

Sultanate Period

11

The Delhi Sultanate was basically a theocracy in which the Sultans were endowed with both the powers, *i.e.* religious and temporal. Their avowed object was to rule the country as per the tenets of the Quran and to propagate Islam.

Most of the Sultans considered themselves to be the deputies of the Khalifa of Baghdad and received investitures from them.

The Sultan was assisted by a council of six ministers in the day-to-day administration of the country. Besides, there were other departmental heads. Barid-i-Mamalik was the head of the Agriculture department.

In those days agriculture was the main occupation of the people.

India was traditionally popular for its economic prosperity and this can be testified by the innumerable list of war spoils and booties seized by Muslim invaders like Ghazni, Ghori and Timur. Agriculture was the main occupation of the people. Firoz Tughlaq had undertaken many agrarian projects. In the towns guild system of trade flourished. There were separate guilds for each handicraft. It was able to thrive because it was based on the caste system. The Sultan founded Karkhanas or factories in Delhi for the manufacture of silk, cotton, cloth, silver and gold articles and so on. India exported grains, cotton and silk clothes, opium and indigo. Horses occupied an important place in the items of import. During the period of Sultans, India had a favourable balance of trade. This fact is testified by the evidences of the accounts of Marco Polo and Ibn Batuta.

In spite of its riches, there was no equitable distribution of wealth among the people. While the Muslim nobles rolled in luxury, the common people led a miserable life even without the basic necessities. These common people had to bear the burden of heavy taxation. Besides, the vicissitudes of monsoon combined with famine also affected the people very much. Price level was not maintained uniformly because of inadequate transport facilities.

REVENUE POLICY

The Sultan had five main sources of revenue. They were as follows:

(1) Zakat

It was a tax collected only from the Muslims. One-forty of their property was collected as Zakat from them. Such property should be possessed by them at least for a period of one year. The amount collected under this was used for the benefit of the Muslim community and for religious purposes like reconstruction and renovation of mosques and tombs.

(2) Jizya

It was a poll tax imposed on non-Muslims. Non-Muslims were considered to be Zimmis or people living at the mercy of the Sultan. Non-Muslims were given the option of either conversion to Islam or paying Jizya for exemption from conversion. Three grades of Jizya taxes were levied upon Hindus, namely 48, 24 and 12 Dirhams. However, women, children, monks, beggars, the blind and the crippled were exempted from this tax.

(3) Kharaj

It was another tax collected from non-Muslims. It varied from 1/10 to 1/12th of the total produce of the lands.

(4) Ushr

This was also a land tax but collected from the Muslims. It was one-tenth of the produce of the lands irrigated by natural means.

(5) Khams

It was one-fifth of the spoils of war confiscated from the infidels. The remaining four-fifths of the booty went to the soldiers.

Besides these taxes sanctioned by the Quran, there were also other taxes such as customs duties, excise duties, tax on income from mines, tax on heirless properties, house tax, grazing tax and water tax.

LAND REVENUE

Agricultural lands were classified for the purpose of collecting land revenue and the revenue collection was entrusted to tax farmers and Jagirdars. There were four kinds of lands divided for the purpose of collection of land tax. They were:

(1) Khalisa lands which were directly administered by the Sultan.

(2) Lands divided into Iqtas which were held by Muqtis either for a certain number of years or for lifetime.

(3) The Hindu principalities who have acknowledged the suzerainty of the Sultan.

(4) Inam lands awarded to Muslim scholars and saints.

Collection of Land Revenue

Officers like Chaudharis were appointed to collect land revenue from farmers cultivating Khalisa lands. The officers in the upper ranks were Amil who used to collect revenue from the Chaudharis and remit it to the Government.

In the case of Iqtas, the collection of revenue was made by Muqtis who used to remit to the Government after deducting the required share for themselves. An officer called Khawaja was appointed to supervise the revenue collection made by Muqtis.

The Hindu chiefs paid their annual tributes to the Sultan, whereas the Inam land holders were exempted from taxation.

Mughal Period

12

The economic life of the people during Mughal reign was satisfactory. Though there was much difference in income between the privileged people and the lower class of people. Much information was not available about the period of Babur and Humayun. Sher Shah did a lot to improve the economic condition of the people. Like Sher Shah, Akbar introduced many economic reforms and measures such as the Revenue System of Raja Todar Mal and the Mansabdari System. From the economic point of view, the period of Jahangir and Shah Jahan was most glorious and it began to dwindle in the time of Aurangzeb. Manucci said, "All things are in great plenty here, fruits, pulses, grains, muslin cloth, gold and silver."

Nature of Agriculture

Agriculture was the main occupation of the people. Sher Shah and Akbar did a lot for the improvement of agriculture. Further the peasants were willing to devote all their time and energy to produce more. The farmers were given all the facilities and all sort of things that are found in the modern India were present during the days of Mughals. Rice, barley, wheat and pulses were the significant crops. Cotton was cultivated in Deccan. Bengal was famous for high quality sugar cane. Lower quality of indigo was also cultivated in north India. The chief items of non-agricultural production were fisheries, minerals, salt, opium, liquor and indigo.

Industries

Cotton industry flourished in Mughal India. The famous textile centres were Banaras, Jaunpur, Khandesh and Lahore. The dyeing industry was also on the road of progress. Leather products were produced in plenty. Lahore, Agra, Fatehpur Sikri were the important places of silk weaving centres and Akbar encouraged this industry by giving all the facilities to the weavers. The shawl and carpet weaving were also patronised by Akbar. Moreland said, "So much of cotton cloth was produced in the country that after clothing the people of India, the same was exported to Africa, Arabia, Egypt, Burma and Mecca." Precious and costly stone industry also flourished and by means of these stones Mughal Emperors built many monuments including the Taj Mahal, one of the wonders of the world. Metal industry was also developed in Mughal period and the metal swords, daggers and other tools were popular. As people used gold ornaments, gold and silver industries were prevalent during the Mughal period.

Export and Import

Akbar took keen interest in the foreign trade. The important harbours were Cambay, Surat, Bengal, Malabar coast, etc. India used to export all kinds of cloth and spices to other countries. Gold, silver, copper and other valuables were imported. The emperor took certain effective steps for the advancement of the trade. The nature of trade changed after the death of Akbar. During the reigns of Jahangir and Shah Jahan, the Dutch and English set up direct trade link between India and the West. Surat was the famous centre of European markets and they permanently set up their trade establishments in 1650 and before the end of the Mughal rule, the English controlled the whole trade of Surat. The Indian merchants had to face a stiff competition with the English merchants and finally they established their monopoly over trade in the Mughal Empire.

Growth of Industrial Cities

As many industries were developed in the Mughal period, there was a growth of industrial cities such as Lahore, Agra and Fatehpur Sikri. Fitch writes, "Agra and Fatehpur are two very great cities, either of them much greater than London and very populous. Between Agra and Fatehpur are twelve miles, and all the way is a market of vehicles and other things." In eastern India, Banaras, Patna, Burdwan and Dacca were the prosperous cities. Kabul was the centre of trade between Central Asia and India.

Revenue Administration under Sultans

13

The financial resources and economic stability are very essential for the stability of a state in all times.

During the Sultanate period the revenue administration was not well organised. Even the fiscal resources of the state were very limited because the state's authority extended over the limited territory in North and East of India, and the major parts of Central and Southern India remained beyond their influence. But the early Sultans were quite intolerant and tried to squeeze maximum of money from the Hindus. Ala-ud-din Khilji intentionally and deliberately followed the policy of reducing the Hindus to poverty.

Land Revenue. As agriculture was the main occupation of the people the land revenue was the chief source of state income. But there was no fixed share which the cultivator had to pay to the state. This was determined differently by the different Sultans and ranged from one-tenth to one-twelfth of the total produce. For example, Ala-ud-din Khilji charged 50 per cent of the agricultural produce as state share.

According to the Islamic Law there were two types of land taxes—Ushr and Kharaj.

Ushr was the land tax charged on the lands held by the Muslims. It was usually one-tenth of the total produce.

Kharaj was the tax charged on the lands owned by the Hindus and it varied from one-tenth to one-half.

The Jagirdari System was in existence and the Jagirdars acted as middlemen between cultivators and the state. They collected the revenue on behalf of the state. In addition, they also claimed a share for themselves. After payment of these taxes nothing substantial was left with the cultivator.

Ala-ud-din Khilji paid some attention to improve the revenue administration and introduced a number of vital changes. His primary objective in introducing the changes was to collect the maximum revenue for the state so that he could maintain a strong army, which was needed to combat both the Mongol danger and to effect fresh conquests. In the first instance he ordered the resumption of all landed grants which the nobles held as Inam (reward) or Waqf (gifts) and turned them into crown lands. All the lands were measured and after ascertaining their produce the government's share was fixed at 50 per cent. The share of the state was rather high and was unprecedented. The agriculturists had, in addition, to pay certain other taxes and they were virtually reduced to sore straits.

Barani tells us how the Hindus, who had the monopoly of agriculture, were greatly impoverished so much so that there was no sign of gold or silver left in their houses and the wives of Muqaddams used to seek jobs in the houses of Mussalmans, work there and receive wages.

Apart from increasing state's share in land revenue Ala-ud-din Khilji took drastic steps to eradicate corruption prevailing in the revenue department. He increased the salaries of the Patwaris, but inflicted heavy punishment on them if they resorted to corrupt practices. He also ensured that the Patwaris properly assessed land revenue and did not show favour to any one.

According to Dr. R.P. Tripathi, "Ala-ud-din was apparently the first Muslim ruler whose hands reached as far as Patwaris who were the best source of information in all matters pertaining to the land and its revenue."

The Revenue Administration set by Ala-ud-din Khilji continued to work under his successors, but it lost much of efficiency. It was Ghiyas-ud-din Tughlaq who softened the rigours of Ala-ud-din's revenue policy and administration. He found the state share of 50 per cent of the land revenue rather harsh and inconvenient. He fixed the state share at one-tenth of the total produce. During his time many barren and ruined lands were brought under cultivation and he paid much attention to the welfare of the peasants. He disallowed the system of farming. According to Prof. S.R. Sharma, "We do not come across such tender consideration for the country until the days of Sher Shah Suri two centuries later."

Mohammed Bin Tughlaq, the successor of Ghiyas-ud-din, also introduced important reforms in the revenue administration. He got prepared a comprehensive register of the income and expenditure of the Sultanate in order to introduce a uniform standard of land revenue and to bring every village under assessment.

Another great experiment of Mohammad Tughlaq, which brought much odium upon him, was the increase of taxation in the Doab. Mohammed Tughlaq required lots of money for his conquests and administration and decided to raise the same by increasing the land revenue in the Doab, an area known for its fertile lands.

There is no unanimity amongst the scholars regarding the exact increase. According to Ferishta, the tax was increased three or four times. However, Barani holds that it was raised ten or twenty times. The view of Barani certainly seems to be rather exaggerated. The people could not have afforded such heavy taxes.

Barani has severely criticised the tax increase in Doab and observed, "It operated to the ruin of the country and decay of the people...the backs of the ryot were broken. Those who were rich became rebels...the lands were ruined and cultivation was arrested. Grains became dear, the rains were deficient, so famine became general and widespread. It lasted for years and thousands upon thousands of people perished."

But it appears that Barani, who himself belonged to Doab, has greatly exaggerated the sufferings of the people. The Sultan had cogent and convincing reasons to justify the increase in taxation.

Earlier, Ala-ud-din Khilji had also been charging 50 per cent of the gross produce. Furthermore, Doab was a rich and fertile land and the king could expect better income with least labour and inconvenience to the people of the land. The only misfortune was that he carried out this measure at a time when a severe famine was stalking the Doab and the distress of the people was greatly aggravated by its disastrous effect.

One of the commendable things done by Mohammed Tughlaq was the establishment of the department of agriculture Diwan-i-Kohi. This department made efforts to bring more and more lands under cultivation.

Firoz Tughlaq, who succeeded Mohammed Tughlaq, found the revenue system in complete chaos, people suffering due to extortion and famine. He paid attention to the improvement of the revenue administration. An inquiry was held into the titles and tenures. Those who were illegally deprived of their lands, were asked to file their claims in the courts of law. He reduced state's share of land revenue. He provided 'taqavi' loans to the cultivators and provided greater facilities for irrigation. He is credited with having got dug four canals which were source of perennial irrigation. He increased the salaries of the revenue officers so that they may not exploit the poor peasants.

Firoz Shah did away with the variety of taxes which were charged from the people. Instead he levied only four taxes which are sanctioned by Quaran, *viz.* the Khiraj, the Zakat, the Jizya and the Khams. Khiraj was the land tax. Khams meant one-fifth of the booty captured during wars. Jizya was a tax levied on the Hindus and Zakat was the tax realised from Muslims for religious purposes. In addition to these four types of taxes, later on Firoz Tughlaq added irrigation tax on those agriculturists who made use of the water from the canals. It was charged at the rate of one-tenth of the produce of the irrigated area. It may be noted that for the imposition of this tax Firoz sought the approval of the Ulemas. The Revenue System adopted by Firoz Tughlaq continued to operate under the later Sultans.

Revenue Administration under Mughals

14

Ishwari Prasad in his masterpiece *A Short History of Muslim Rule in India*, J.N. Sarkar in his *Mughal Administration*, S.R. Sharma in his popular work *Mughal Administration* and R.P. Tripathi in his *Rise and Fall of the Mughal Empire* have given a beautiful picture about the revenue administration of the Mughals.

The revenue administration under the first two Mughal rulers—Babur and Humayun—continued to operate as it was under the Sultans of Delhi. Babur was so much engrossed in the various wars during his four years of rule that he could hardly get any time to devote to the revenue affairs. Humayun, his successor, also found himself in trouble soon after his accession to the throne and had to spend most of his life in exile. Accordingly, he also did not get any chance to improve the revenue administration.

It was Sher Shah Suri, who intervened between Humayun and Akbar, who provided an excellent land revenue system. He has acquired good knowledge of the working of the revenue system as Jagirdar of Sasaram, Khawspur and Tanda. When he became the emperor of India he tried to introduce this system on a large scale.

First of all he ordered the measurement of the lands according to a uniform standard. The cultivable land was divided into three categories—good, middling and bad. The average of these three was taken to determine the produce of the land per bigha. State's share was fixed at one-third of the gross produce. This could be paid both in cash and kind, although the former was preferred.

In addition to this each cultivator was to pay in kind 2½ per cent of the revenue he paid to the state. In lieu of this he got grain at very cheap rates during the times of famine and other calamities. The revenue could be paid either through the Maqaddams or directly to the Pargana treasury.

Sher Shah paid great attention to the welfare of the peasants and therefore, reduced or remitted the revenue in times of calamities. He had issued specific instructions to the revenue officers to be lenient at the time of the assessment but once the assessment had been made the tax was to be collected with severity. The Sultan kept an eye on their conduct so that they may not exploit or tyrannise the peasants. Sher Shah gave severe punishments to the soldiers if they destroyed the crops. Thus, the revenue system established by Sher Shah was efficient and elastic.

For some time following the death of Sher Shah there was complete disorder in the country and much of the valuable work done by him in the field of revenue administration was destroyed. Akbar, who succeeded Humayun was only a child at the time of his accession. He first paid attention to the security and consolidation of the empire. After he had entrenched himself on the throne he paid attention to the revenue administration and made efforts to improve on the revenue system set up by Sher Shah. In this he got the assistance from experts like Muzaffar Khan, Itimad Khan and Raja Todar Mal.

First of all Akbar collected complete information about land and reorganised the whole land revenue system. He introduced Zabti System in eight provinces of his empire. Under this System, the cultivable lands were measured with the standard gaz known as Jarib which was an improvement over the measurement methods adopted by Sher Shah. The officers were given strict instructions to do the measuring work honestly and not to accept any bribe from the cultivators.

After getting the lands measured he tried to ascertain the produce of the land for the purpose of determining state's share of land revenue.

For this purpose the land was classified into four categories.

Polaj was the first category of land which was always in cultivation. Throughout the season it had some crop ready according to the season.

The second category of land was Parauti, which had to be left fallow for one or two years to recoup the fertility.

Chachar was the third category of land which had to be left out of cultivation for three or four years to gain the fertility.

The fourth category of land was known as Banjar or barren land. It had to be left fallow for five years or more.

The first two categories of lands were further subdivided into three types according to their fertility—good, middling and bad. The produce of three grades of land was calculated and their average was considered to be the actual produce of the land. The state's share was fixed on the basis of this actual produce.

This share of the state was determined for the various categories of lands on the basis of the fertility of the soil and the produce of the last ten years. The state share in respect of Polaj and Parauti was fixed at one-third of the average produce of the three grades. On the Chachar land the state's share was one-fifteenth of the produce in the first year, two-fifteenth in the second year, one-fifth in the third year, four-fifteenth in the fourth year and one-third in the fifth year.

Similarly, on the Banjar land the government charged one-twenty-sixth of the produce in the first year, one-thirteenth in the second year, two-thirteenth in the third year, three-thirteenth in the fourth year and one-third in the fifth year. Though the states share was fixed in kind, it was commuted into cash according to the current prices. This practice was not proper and caused much inconvenience to the cultivators. Therefore, later on Todar Mal fixed the cash rate on the basis of the average of the last ten years.

In certain other parts of the empire certain other systems of land revenue also existed, *viz.* Ghalla Baksha, Nasaq, etc. Ghalla Baksha was the old system of assessment by crop division and it worked in Thatta and certain parts of Kabul and Kashmir. According to this system the government took one-third of the total produce after the harvest as its share. Under the Nasaq system a general estimate of the expected yield on the standing crops was made and the state claimed one-third of the expected yield.

This land revenue system adopted by Akbar has been greatly admired by scholars.

According to V.A. Smith land revenue system of Akbar was based upon sound principles and state issued instructions to the officers from time to time to keep the system up-to-date. But one "cannot help feeling considerable scepticism concerning the conformity of practice with precept." He further opines that Todar Mal's system was devised to prevent the State from being defrauded rather than to protect the interests of the ryot. In fact there is no specific instance cited by V.A. Smith to prove that the system operated to the detriment of the ryot.

On the other hand, on the testimony of Abul-Fazl in *Ain-i-Akbari* it can be said that "the land revenue system of Akbar was highly efficient and the peasants were quite happy". The state demand being fixed, there was very little scope for extracting more from the peasants than was due. The officers were usually honest. Exactions and extortions, if brought to notice, were severely punished. In case of drought or excessive rains the land revenue was often remitted. The needy peasants were given loans by the government.

The land revenue system introduced by Akbar continued throughout the Mughal period with more or less no change. The system appears to have worked very satisfactorily. It is evident from the fact that the land revenue under Babur stood at Rs. 2.60 crore, in Akbar's time it stood at Rs. 17.50 crore. In Jahangir's time at 17.60 crore and under Shah Jahan it was 21.15 crore. Under Aurangzeb it rose to 29.77 crore.

Though the land revenue was the chief source of state revenue it resorted to certain other taxes to supplement its income. These included toll tax, customs, mints, presents which the king received from the Governors and Ministers as well as Jagirdars on important occasions; fines which the state levied on the criminals. Another source of income was indemnity from vanquished or defeated ruler. This indemnity was paid either once or regularly as a token of subordination to the emperor.

It will thus be observed that the revenue administration during the medieval times underwent many improvements and the revenue of the state continued to grow. It may be noted that the fiscal resources of that state at that time were very limited. But as the state did not undertake any welfare activities its expenditure was also very limited. Most of the revenue collected by the state was spent on the wars and personal luxuries of the rulers. For example, Aurangzeb, who inherited an overflowing treasury from his father, squandered huge amounts in his Deccan wars and ultimately left an almost depleted treasury for his successors. He even resorted to the much hated Jizya on the Hindus to find additional funds for meeting the expenses of these wars.

Economic Life in Medieval India

15

Agriculture

As at present, even during the medieval times India was predominantly an agricultural country. The people produced sufficient to meet their requirements and were self-sufficient except during famines, or other natural calamities. Usually in normal times the peasants produced much more than what was actually needed by the people, leaving sufficient scope for export of food-grains. Though there are no contemporary references regarding the system of cultivation, it must have resembled the present one. In addition to the food crops, the people cultivated medicinal herbs, spices and fragrant wood, which had a good foreign market. The chief crops at that time were oilseeds, pulses, wheat, barley, millet, peas, rice, sugar cane and cotton, etc. The practice of storing or stocking the surplus grains was in vogue. The grain was usually stored in grainpits or khattees, where it could be preserved for sufficiently long time.

Fruits of numerous varieties were produced in different parts of the country. The Sultans of Delhi and other rulers took special pains to improve the quality of the Indian fruits. They paid special attention to gardening, which indirectly led to improvement of the quality of fruits. Firoz Tughlaq is particularly credited with having 1200 gardens in the neighbourhood of Delhi, eighty on the Salora embankment and forty-four in Chittor. The most popular fruit of that time was mango, although melons were also quite popular. Amongst other fruits grapes, dates, pomegranates, plantains, peaches, oranges, apples, grapefruits, figs, lemons, etc. were found in abundance. The coconuts were found in the coastal areas.

Village was the basic unit of economic organisation. The chief feature of the Indian village community was a "harmonious co-ordination of the specialized functions of its various component groups of workers". Each member of the village community performed a function which was determined by his birth and upbringing. The villages were not only economically self-sufficient but also fed a number of rural industries, *viz.* making of ropes and baskets and manufacturing of sugar, scents, oils, etc. Certain craftsmen like weavers, leather-workers, dyers, wood-workers, etc. were also found in each village. Usually every village possessed a small market where necessities of life were sold by petty shopkeepers. Every village also had its own blacksmiths who were conversant with the process of smelting iron-ore and manufactured various agricultural implements, arms and other items of common use in the Indian homes.

Industries on large scale existed only in certain selected areas which were either located at places where the raw materials were found or were situated at the mouth of certain navigable rivers through which the raw materials could be supplied. There were very few industrial centres at other places. In view of the special navigation facilities available in Bengal and Gujarat, most of the industrial centres were located there. They also served as the collection centres of the surplus of finished products from inland centres, and exported them abroad. The entire trade and commerce at these centres were monopolised by a handful of rich people, who made huge fortunes by their trade with the foreign countries. This naturally led to the emergence of certain cities and big towns, which served as centres of distribution for the agricultural and industrial products.

The state took a large share of the produce from land in the shape of land-tax and various other duties. Out of the remainder the peasant distributed fixed share to the various classes of domestic and other labours. A certain share was also earmarked for the priest and the domestic animals. As a result the peasant was left with sufficient stock to meet his day needs. The peasant usually worked hard and unceasingly. His wife and other members of the family also shared the burden with him. In return for all this he could merely get a square meal every day. Prof. K.M. Ashraf says, "There are very few and very vague references to the life of the peasants but it can be asserted with confidence that their lot was very miserable and they lived constantly in a state of semi-starvation."

The famines were quite frequent and the state made no provision for relief to the affected peasants. Even the remission in revenue was negligible. The condition was no better under the Mughals. The sufferings of peasants and people knew no bounds "...because the Mughal State then made no systematic and prolonged efforts to provide relief and affected no substantial remission in revenue collection. The little that they did was insufficient to alleviate the acute miseries of the myriads of the people who died of starvation and the pestilence that closely followed it."

Industries

Apart from the various cottage and home industries existing in the villages, number of other industries also made considerable progress during the medieval period. The most important of these industries were textiles, metal work, stone work, sugar and paper. But these industries differed substantially from the modern factories or big enterprises. The Sultans of Delhi set up the best equipped and most efficiently organised factories at Delhi. They were popularly known as karkhanas or workshops. These workshops or karkhanas mainly produced for the royal consumption. The items produced by these karkhanas for royal consumption included caps, shoes, curtains, tapestry, waist-bands, embroideries, saddles, etc. Even the gifts to be presented to other monarchs by the Sultans were manufactured by these stores.

In addition, the private industries also continued to flourish despite the shocks of foreign invasions and internal disturbances. The most important private industries were textile industry, which manufactured cotton, woolen and silk cloth, dyeing industry, printing industry, sugar industry, metalwork, paper industry and numerous others. Let us examine about these industries in some details.

Textile Industry. The textile industry was the biggest industry of India during the medieval age. It manufactured cotton and woollen cloth as well as silk. The raw material for the manufactures of the various clothes were either provided indigenously or imported. The textile industry also provided incentive to other allied industries like embroidery, good thread work and dyeing. The textiles were produced in sufficient quantity to meet the internal demand, and a surplus was left to be exported to other countries. Quality-wise these products could favourably compete with the products of other countries.

Because of their location Bengal and Gujarat were the chief centres for the manufacture and export of textile goods. Deogir and Mahadeva Nagari in Deccan, Delhi in the North, Cambay in Gujarat and places like Sonargaon, Dacca and Banjala in Bengal were the most famous centres of cloth manufacture. Talking about Cambay in Gujarat, Barbosa says, "Cambay was the centre of manufacture for all kinds of fine and coarse and printed cotton cloth, besides other cheap varieties of satins, valvets, taffetas and thick carpets. Varieties of printed cloth and silk muslins were also manufactured in other parts of Gujarat." The manufacture of carpets, cushions, coverlets, bedding (durries) and bed-stings were also manufactured in abundance. The dyeing industry also prospered because of the taste of the people for bright colours. The calico painting was also popular. Coarse cotton cloths were either dyed or printed with a "variety of well-shaped and well-coloured flowers or figures which were so fixed in the cloth that no water could wash them out."

The textile industry continued to flourish under the Mughals and the Indian cloth was exported to countries east of the Cape of Good Hope, Middle East, Burma, Malaya, Java, etc. During the times of Akbar the silk industry was given special patronage.

Metalwork. Next in importance to the textiles was the metal industry, which continued to make progress both under the

Sultans and the Mughals. The Indian metalworkers handled the various metals like iron, brass, silver, zinc with great skill. They not only manufactured various types of armery but also manufactured things of daily use like basins, cups, knives and scissors. They made great advancement in the manufacture of inlaid ornaments, embroidered and damascened work. Greater refinement was attained in the metalwork under the Mughal Emperors and it reached its zenith under Akbar. Abul Fazal has paid warm tributes to the excellence to the skill of these goldsmiths.

Stone and Brick Work. The Indian artisans and masons displayed great skill in stone and brick work. They not only constructed some of the outstanding buildings of Hindustan, but also displayed their skill by constructing a number of buildings in Kabul, Ghazni and Samarkand. The state accorded special patronage to the masons and craftsmen. Ala-ud-din Khilji is said to have employed 70,000 workers for the construction of the state buildings. Babur also speaks highly of the skill of the Indian workmen and takes pride in claiming that he engaged 680 stone cutters in the construction of his buildings at Agra. The Dilwara temples at Mount Abu and the buildings of Chittorgarh in Rajasthan are also a testimony of the brilliant skill of Indian craftsmen in stone and brick work. The period also witnessed the introduction of the use of enamelled tiles and bricks, which continued to grow in the subsequent centuries.

Leather Work. The leather industry also considerably developed during the medieval age. Leather was used increasingly for purposes like manufacture of saddles and bridles for horses, scabbards of swards, shoes and other items of common use by the upper classes. Even the ordinary peasants made water buckets of leather. But probably the most excellent item made out of leather was the leather mats made of red and blue leather and exquisitely inlaid with figures of birds and beasts. Gujarat also exported the dressed skins in large quantities to Arabia and other countries.

Sugar Industry. The Sugar industry also made tremendous progress during the medieval age. Sugar was generally made from the sugar cane. Bengal led in the field of sugar production.

It produced so much sugar which was sufficient not only to meet the internal demands but also left sufficient surplus for exports. The sugar was exported to other country in parcels of untanned and sewn leather.

Paper Industry. During the medieval times the people of India knew the use of paper. Nicolo Conti refers to the use of papers in Gujarat. Similarly, Khusru mentions the use of paper called shami in Delhi. The various manuscripts and other documents which have come down to us from medieval times further confirm the existence of paper industry in India. Khusru makes a clear mention of the regular market of booksellers in Delhi, which suggests that the paper was quite commonly used. Under the Mughals the paper industry made further progress and paper began to be manufactured in Sialkot, Kashmir and Gaya as well. In Shahjoodpur, special quality of paper was manufactured.

Shipping Industry. It is commonly believed that the maritime activities of India greatly declined during the medieval times and the shipbuilding industry almost went into abeyance. However, this view is not supported either by the contemporary literary references or the observations of Nicolo Conti. For example, Nicolo Conti says, "...that the Indian ships are much bigger than our ship." The Mughals established a centre in the Bay of Bengal for the construction of ships. The Indian shipbuilding industry earned such a high reputation that even the Portuguese had some of their best ships built in India. The shipbuilding activities were mainly carried on the western coasts of India.

Other Minor Industries. Certain other minor industries also flourished in various parts of the country. For example, coral work was done in Gujarat and Bengal. Ivory work and manufacturing of imitation jewellery were carried out in various parts of the country. Scented oil was manufactured in Delhi. Usually the artisans working in these industries followed the family trade and there was a great demand for their manufacturers.

Trade and Commerce. Trade and commerce flourished during the medieval times. The trade was mainly the monopoly of the Vaisyas. Though the main business was done through regular shops in the market or Mandis, petty shopkeepers and dealers also carried on their business in movable stalls and pack horses. The Mandis served as a convenient media of exchange for the surplus of corn or goods produced in vicinity. These Mandis were located in cities like Multan, Lahore, Delhi, etc. The purchase and sale of all kinds of cattle (horses, oxen, camels, cows, etc.) usually took place in cattle fairs, which were occasionally organised.

In addition to the regular business community which carried on the entire trade, certain other categories of people were also dependent on trade. For example, the Banjaras carried the agricultural and other products of one part of the country to the other part on large scale through huge caravans. The brokers and the carriers of goods also depended for their livelihood on trade. The brokers charged commission from both the parties—the seller and the purchaser—and usually tried to raise the prices of commodities. Certain Sultans tried to suppress this class of traders. For example, Ala-ud-din Khilji is said to have put all sorts of curbs on the activities of the brokers. Despite all this it cannot be denied that the brokers played an important role in trade. According to Manrique there were as many as six hundred brokers and middlemen in Patna and most of them were wealthy. At Agra he found merchants of great wealth and speaks of vast sums of money piled up like heaps of grain in their houses. Similarly, in Dacca he saw money heaped up in such large quantities that, counting being difficult, it used to be weighed.

The successful prosecution of internal trade and commerce depends on a reasonable security of life and property. During the medieval times, particularly under the Mughals "roads were fairly secure in the interior of the country, although in less settled parts the traders were protected by guards as is testified by Terry's account as well as by innumerable documents called 'Dastaks' in the Central Records Office, Hyderabad (Deccan). These 'Dastaks' served the purpose of travellers' passports for providing facilities to persons proceeding on a journey from one subah to another." The highway from Agra to Lahore was shaded by great trees on both sides. This, according to Terry, was looked upon by the travellers, who found the comfort of that cool shade, as one of the rarest and most beneficial works in the whole world. Generally in inter-provincial highways sarais and wells were provided for the comfort of the traders and other travellers.

A class of native bankers existed which discharged some of the commonly accepted functions of the present banking. They advanced loans against hundis as well as lent money on interests. The rate of interest charged was rather very high and the Sahus and Mahajans, as the moneylenders were known, made huge profits. The loans were mainly taken by the people of the upper classes, who could not provide sufficient funds to meet their extravagant habits. The poor people also sometimes borrowed money from the Mahajans, but due to their incapacity to repay they usually fell in heavy indebtedness.

The prices of the goods were not uniform in all parts of the country due to the primitive means of communications. The things were cheap in normal times but during the times of famine and scarcity the prices went abnormally high. The price of wheat during the normal times of Ala-ud-din Khilji was seven and a half jitals per maund. But during the times of Mohammed Bin Tughlaq when a famine occurred the prices soared high and the wheat was sold at sixteen to seventeen jitals a seer. During the times of war also the prices shot up by eight to ten times.

During the Mughal period by and large the prices of things of daily use like grain, fruit, milk, ghee, meat, fish, clothes, etc. were low. According to the contemporary records the normal rates of various articles during the reign of Akbar were—wheat 12 maunds a rupee; barley 18 maunds a rupee; best rice 16 maunds a rupee; moong 18 maunds a rupee; meat 17 seers a rupee; and so on. No doubt the prices of the goods of daily use were very low, but the wages of the workers were also low. An unskilled labourer usually got 2 dams or one twentieth of a rupee a day. The skilled workers like carpenters got much higher wages, *viz.* 7 dams a day. As a result of the cheap prices of the goods of daily use the common man was greatly benefited and he led a life of contentment. According to Prof. A.L. Srivastava,

"Though the income of the common man during the Mughal period was not high, he did not suffer from starvation. Nor did he feel the pinch for want of corn and other necessities of life, which were plentiful and cheap. Moreover, the common man had fewer needs and more contentment than his successor of our times. He was more honest and led a more contented and purer life than his representative of the twentieth century."

Terry, a foreign traveller, has also observed in his *Voyage to East India*, that the fish could be purchased 'at such easy rates as if they were not worth the valuings' and that generally speaking 'the plenty of all provisions was very great throughout the whole monarchy and everyone there may eat bread without scarceness'. The government was greatly concerned with the welfare of the general people and there are numerous references in the official documents laying emphasis on the duty of the state to promote general welfare. For example, one of the kins of Akbar says, "Every man of sense and understanding knows that the best way of worshipping God consists in allaying the distress of the times, and in improving the condition of man. This depends, however, on the advancement of agriculture, on the order kept in the King's household, on the readiness of the champions of the empire, and the discipline of the army. All this is again connected with the exercise of proper care on the part of the monarch, his love for the people and with an intelligent management of the revenues and the public expenditure. It is only when cared for that the inhabitants of the towns and those of the towns and those of the rural districts, are able to satisfy their wants, and to enjoy prosperity."

Foreign Trade. India had always maintained substantial commercial relations with the other countries, particularly with the Mediterranean countries. During the medieval times this commercial intercourse continued and showed some progress. Indian goods were carried by the Arabs to the Red Sea and from there found their way to Damascus and Alexandria. The Moorish merchants carried the Indian goods to East Africa, the Malay Island and China in the Far East. India carried on trade with Central Asia, Afghanistan and Persia through land route of Multan, Quetta, Khyber Pass and Kashmir.

India exported numerous items like textile goods, spices, indigo, saltpetre, ginger, opium and sugar. Some of the countries round the Persian Gulf depended for their food supply entirely on India. But the Indian cloth was the chief item of export to European and Near-Eastern countries. Abul Fazal has mentioned thirty-three types of silk and thirty types of cotton as being exported to various countries. In return India imported gold, silver, horses, copper, tin, zinc, lead, mercury, coral, amber, precious stones, velvets, perfumes, China goods, wines and African slaves from abroad. During the earlier medieval period the chief articles of import mainly consisted of certain articles of luxury meant for the upper classes, but subsequently guns, gun-powder and other mechanical weapons also began to be imported. Horses were imported in large number both to meet the military demands as well as to meet the needs of the people who used them for pleasure riding and racing.

It is not possible to give an accurate idea of the volume of foreign trade in the absence of reliable statistics regarding imports and exports. However, one thing can certainly be said that as compared to the huge and growing volume of foreign trade at present, the volume of foreign trade was rather limited. It is also difficult to say for certain whether India enjoyed a favourable balance of trade or not. Prof. A.L. Srivastava holds that the value of Indian exports was much greater than that of the imports, and the balance of trade was always in favour of India. He corroborates his version by pointing out that it was generally believed that "Merchants of all countries never ceased to carry pure gold into India, and to bring back in exchange commodities of herbs and gums."

Though the quantity of foreign trade was small during the Sultanate period, it showed an increase as the years passed by. It is recorded that during the reign of Jahangir no less than fourteen thousand loads of merchandise passed between India and Qandhar through the Bolan Pass every year. Under Shah Jahan this quantum further increased. The sea trade carried through the coast of Surat also considerably increased. India imported silver and jewellery from Turkey and Iraq and exported cotton yarn to Ormuz and Basra. Khafi Khan has recorded that the imperial ship 'Ganje Sawai' which was bringing gold and silver worth fifty-two lakhs of rupees from the sale of goods at Mocha and Jeddah, was attacked by the English pirates in the Indian Ocean. This incident throws much light on the volume of trade between India and Arabia alone.

During the Mughal period efforts were made to encourage trade with European countries. A number of European powers were permitted to establish their factories on the coasts of India. The main European powers who were given this concessions included the Portuguese and the English. It may be noted that as the Mughal rulers possessed no efficient navy, they were forced to make these concessions.

It may be noted that the foreign trade was mainly in the hands of the foreigners although a small community of Indian traders mainly consisting of Gujaratis, Banias and Chettis of South were also engaged in it. But as the time passed and the Indians became aware of the profitability of this enterprise, they devoted more attention to foreign trade. The sea trade was mainly in the hands of the Moors domiciled in India. Prof. Ashraf has pointed out that Indians could not take to foreign trade on a national scale because they were discouraged by their manners, customs and outlook.

Economic Structure of Society. Any account of the economic conditions in the medieval items would be incomplete without acquiring an insight into the existing economic structure of the society.

Broadly speaking the medieval society consisted of three classes. At the top was a small group of enormously wealthy nobles and high officials who enjoyed certain privileges and rights which were beyond the reach of an ordinary citizen. These officials and nobles mainly hailed from high caste. These officials had enormous wealth at their command and spent it lavishly on items of luxury. They used costly dresses and lived in big mansions. They also had a large array of servants at their command.

The middle class, mainly consisted of professionals (teachers, maids, etc.), merchants and important clerks. Though the

middle classes were not that rich, their condition was quite comfortable. The businessmen, particularly those engaged in coastal trade, were much better off than other members of the middle classes. Though the members of the middle classes were quite well off, they never made a demonstration of their correct position due to the fear of being harassed by the rulers. Probably this explains for the observation of Bernier that there was no middle class in Delhi.

The lower class consisted of labourers (carpenters, smiths, weavers, artisans, etc.), small businessmen, soldiers, peasant workers, etc. Their condition was quite miserable and did not have sufficient to satisfy their needs. The government demand on the people's productive capacity was quite exorbitant and the tiller was left only with roughly one-third of his produce. But as the demands of the lower classes were very few and things of everyday use were quite cheap, they managed to escape starvation. However, during the times of famine or other natural calamity the common people died in large numbers and the state took no measures to save them.

The living standard of the common people was rather miserable, as is testified by a number of foreign visitors. For example, Pelsaert writing about the habitations of the people during the times of Jahangir records: "Their houses are built of mud with thatched roofs. Furniture there is little or none except some earthenware pots to hold water and for cooking and two beds; their bed clothes are scanty, merely as sheet or perhaps two serving as under and over-sheets. This is sufficient in the hot weather, but the bitter cold nights are miserable indeed."

Talking of the houses of the upper and middle classes Pelsaert says: "They are noble and pleasant, with many apartments, but there is not much in the way of an upper stores except a flat roof on which to enjoy the evening air. There are usually garden and tanks inside the house; and in the hot weather the tanks are filled daily with fresh water, drawn by oxen from wells. The water is drawn, or sometimes raised by a wheel, in such quantity that it flows through a leaden pipe and rises like a fountain; in this climate, water and plants are a refreshment and recreation unknown in our cold country.

These houses last for a few years only, because the walls are built with mud instead of mortar, but the white plaster of the walls is very noteworthy, and is far superior to anything in our country.... They have no furniture of the kind we delight in such as tables, stocks, benches, cupboards, bedsteads, etc. but their cots, or sleeping places, and other furniture of the kinds unknown in our country, are lavishly ornamented with gold or silver, and they use more gold and silver in serving food than we do, though nearly all of it is used in the mahal, and is seen by scarcely anybody except women. Outside the mahal, there is only the diwan-khana or sitting-place, which is spread with handsome carpets and kept very neat and clean."

No doubt the condition of the peasantry, unskilled workers and menial servants showed some improvement under the Mughals but from the times of Akbar onwards, it started deteriorating and became really miserable under the later Mughals.

Sir Jadunath Sarkar says that during the reign of Aurangzeb itself agriculture, industry and trade were badly affected by his incessant wars and inefficient administration and resulted in "the great economic impoverishment of India, not only a decrease of the 'national stock' but also a rapid lowering of mechanical skill and a standard of civilization, a disappearance of art and culture over wide tracts of country".

Prof. A.L. Srivastava also holds the view that the economic condition of the people became miserable in the later Mughal period. He says that "...after the death of Aurangzeb, the economic system broke down almost completely consequent on the break-up of the empire and the establishment of the provincial dynasties in several parts of the country. The weakness of the central government, the Maratha ravages, the foreign invasions of Nadir Shah and Ahmed Shah Abdali, the piracy of the Portuguese and abuse of the trade privileges by the European traders and their agents caused economic distress to a vast majority of the people. Thus at the time when the country passed under the alien sway of the English East India Company it presented a low economic state of affairs with more than half the population leading a miserable life."

Economic Condition under Marathas

16

The rise of Marathas in the South is considered as the most significant development of the Mughal period.

Shivaji was not only a great soldier and conqueror, but also an excellent statesman and efficient administrator. Since he was an enlightened despot, he took series of successful steps to improve the economic condition of the people during his period.

Shivaji reorganised the land revenue system. His system was based upon the principles laid down by Todar Mal and Malik Amber. More details have been given in this respect in the next chapter.

Shivaji and his successors took keen interest to improve the economy of the country. Hence, they considered agriculture as the main occupation for the same. To increase production, irrigational facilities were provided to the people. Now and then the officers of Agriculture Department toured the country so as to redress their grievances.

At the same time it cannot be denied that there were many shortcomings in the revenue administration.

(a) Agriculture

Agriculture was the main occupation during this period. There were five kinds of lands, *viz.* wasteland, dryland, garden, poramboke and barren lands. The villages of this period may be divided into the following three kinds on the basis of the yield:

(1) Ekabhogam

(2) Palabhogam

(3) Samudayam

(1) The entire lands of the village was owned by a single individual. Such lands were called Ekabhogam.

(2) Under this type, the lands of village were distributed to many people. Those lands were called Palabhogam.

(3) The entire lands of the village was owned by Samudayam or society. Such lands were called Samudayam.

There were many Agraharams during this period. Brahmins lived in these Agraharams.

Two-thirds of the land was under *ryotwari* tenure during the Maratha period.

Land revenue was the important source of revenue in Tanjore. The other sources of revenue were:

(1) Tax on toddy and arrack;

(2) Tax on bricks;

(3) Tax on pearl-fishing;

(4) Customs duties.

The agriculturists had the right of selling their produce in the country. The estimate was done by the government. Price list was registered in the register. Besides, there were Palayagar System, Veesabhuti System, Alamani System and Mirasi System.

The estimate of land tax and the payment of land tax were differed from year to year. During the time of Ekoji the Brahmins paid 37% of tax and others paid 20% of tax; but during the time of Pratap Singh the Brahmins paid 47% of tax and others paid 30% of tax. Most of the villages were self-sufficient and independent.

There was a village headman (leader) for each village. He was assisted by a host of officers in the village administration. Added to this, there was a village council to advice the leader. The leader was the link between the village and the government. Among the village officers the Kanakkar, Kavalkarar, Talaiyari and Vettiyan were very important.

According to Fullerton, there were 5783 villages during the Maratha rule. The total number of Ekabhogam villages were 1807; the total number of Palabhogam villages were 2202; and the total number of Samudayam villages were 1774. The ideal village consisted of residential houses, public places, cultivable lands and temples. Some lands were cultivated once in a year; some twice in a year and some thrice in a year, *i.e.* One Bhogam, Irubbhogam and Munru Bhogam. Tanjore was a fertile area. It was (is) due to Kaviri. The following items were cultivated in Tanjore during the Maratha rule:

(a) Kar, Sambha paddy

(b) Millets

(c) Ragi

(d) Maize

(e) Green gram

(f) Horse gram

(g) Gingelly

(h) Groundnut

The main source of irrigation was Kaviri river. In addition to this, tanks and wells were utilised for irrigation. Many canals were dug to improve the irrigational facilities.

Famines and droughts brought loss to the people. There was a severe famine in 1730. It brought untold sorrows and sufferings to the people. The people witnessed another famine in 1781. They suffered a lot during this time. Moreover, the invasion of Haider Ali caused serious sufferings to the people.

The Pattak System introduced by Bava Pandit, the able minister of Tuljiji became an utter failure. According to this system, the resources of the villages were united while the Pattakdar became the sole Manager of the operation of the lands and receiver of the government share. Bava's successor Shiva Rao made this system a paramount one. Consequently, the Pattakdar became oppressive and suppressive and even repressive in their dealings with agriculturists. Finally, this system was abolished by the British Government.

(b) Industry

Weaving industry flourished during this period. The Kaikolas and the Sowrashtras showed great interest and enthusiasm in this industry. Cotton and silk clothes were produced enormously. Fine clothes and Calico materials were exported to foreign countries. Towns like Arni and Kumbakonam were famous for silk *sarees*. Government patronised the silk industry of those two towns. Members of royal family and rich people were fond of silk clothes.

During the Maratha period blacksmiths occupied a prominent place in making weapons and other materials. Goldsmiths carpenters and craftsmen contributed their mite for the industrial field.

(c) Trade and Commerce

Brisk trade was going on during the Maratha rule. The commodities were sold in the markets at reasonable prices. At that time Chettiars engaged in trade and commerce. It is mentioned that the Brahmins also engaged in trade during this period. There were two kinds of markets (Fairs) in those days, *viz.* daily market and weekly market. The markets were called Pettais during their regime in Tamilaham. There existed betel-leaf Pettai, Paddy Pettai, Sarayappettai, etc.

In Tanjore region, the Muslims showed keen interest in horse trade. Precious stones were sold in the markets. Many European traders are mentioned in the sources. The important trading centres were:

(1) Nagapattinam

(2) Porto Novo

(3) Tranquebar

The Dutch, the Portuguese, the Danish and the English were engaged in trade and commerce in these centres. Ekoji made a commercial treaty with the Dutch East India Company. Accordingly, industrial centres were established in Nagapattinam, Tirumalairayampattinam and Karaikal. He got 4200 gold coins from them. For the same, consequently many European settlements came into existence in the country. It paved the way for their exploitation in India.

Charities

Regarding charities they did a lot in the Tamil country. They made large gifts of lands. They constructed many temples; repaired the old temples; built many choultries; they constructed many tanks. The foreigners were given shelter and they were not permitted to interfere in the local affairs. All castes of people were fed in the choultries freely and they were utilised for the travellers for their sojourn. Many choultries were built in memory of their queen. The following were mentioned in the account of the foreigners:

(1) Serfoji's choultry at Orathanadu.

(2) Pratab's chatrams at Tanjore, Needamangalam and Manamelkudi.

(3) Tuljiji's chatrams at Darasuram, Rajamadam and Ammachatram.

Choultries did a wonderful service to the people in very many fields. They functioned as schools and hospitals. For example, Serfoji's choultry at Orathanadu.

Revenue Administration under Marathas

17

S. Abid Hussain (*Indian Culture*), H.M. Elliot and John Dowson (*History of India as Told by Its Own Historians*), K.M. Munshi (*History and Culture of Indian People*), Jawarharlal Nehru (*Discovery of India*) and Venkateswara (*Indian Culture Through the Ages*) have given a detailed description about the economic conditions of the people under Marathas and the revenue administration of the Marathas in their respective works.

The Marathas under Shivaji also paid attention to an efficient system of revenue administration and reorganised the same.

For the purposes the entire kingdom was divided into prants each under a Subedar.

The prant or suba was further divided into a number of tarafs, each under a Havaldar.

The village was the lowest unit of revenue administration and was under the charge of an official known as Patel.

Shivaji got all the lands measured with the help of measuring rod known as Kathi.

Further, these lands were classified into various categories according to their fertility to ascertain their produce correctly.

The state's share of revenue was fixed at 30 per cent of the gross produce. This share was later on raised to 40 per cent and all other taxes were abolished.

According to Fryer, Shivaji's land revenue system was very oppressive. The officers were dishonest and selfish; the peasants were oppressed and cruelly tortured and in fact "the great fish prayed on the little and even Bijapur rule was milder than that of Shivaji". However, these observations of Fryer do not quite match with the various stories of Shivaji's benevolence and generosity towards the peasants. He said to have undertaken a number of projects for the welfare of the peasants. The account of Fryer is one-sided and prejudiced.

In addition to land revenue, Shivaji tried to raise funds for the state through imposition of two other taxes, *viz.* Chauth and Sardeshmukhi. Chauth, according to Ranade, was not merely a military contribution without any moral or legal obligation, but a payment in lieu of protection against the invasion of a third power. He compares it with Wellesley's Subsidiary Alliance System. However, Sardesai holds that it was a tribute exacted from hostile or conquered territories.

Prof. J.N. Sarkar is of the opinion that Chauth was only a means of buying off one robber and not a subsidiary system for the maintenance of peace and order against all enemies. Thus, Chauth was a military contribution paid to ward off any attack of the Marathas. It was roughly equivalent to one-fourth of the revenue of the district invaded, although in actual practice it used to be much more.

Sardeshmukhi, was another tax which Shivaji claimed as the hereditary Sardeshmukh of his country. It was charged at the rate of ten per cent.

Impact of British Rule on Indian Economy

18

The British came to India primarily as traders but ultimately succeeded in carving out a strong empire in India. During their rule of over two centuries, they brought about far-reaching changes in the economic system of India. They completely destroyed the isolationist and self-sufficing character of the village; they brought money to the villages and substituted it for barter; they contributed to the growth of new urban centres by opening up opportunities for trade and evolving credit instruments; they also contributed to the establishment of large-scale industries, destruction of handicrafts, concentration of workers in certain areas and thus, contributing to the growth of slums, etc. In this chapter, we shall deal with the impact of the British economic policies with special reference to commercialisation of agricultural indebtedness, growth of agricultural labour, destruction of handicrafts industries, drain of wealth and growth of modern industry and rise of capitalist class in India.

Commercialisation of Agriculture

The term commercialisation of agriculture is generally used for the process of production of crops for market to be sold for cash rather than for family use or subsistence. This process of commercialisation of Indian agriculture started in the beginning of the nineteenth century and gained momentum in the later half of the nineteenth century. As a result of this process, the agriculture was no more devoted to the production of food, etc. for internal consumption. It was made to subserve the new commercial policy. More and more land was brought under cultivation for the purpose of exportation.

It may be noted that even in ancient times India exported agricultural products and handicrafts to foreign lands and built up large reserves of gold. But at that time only the surplus product of the village society was traded. However, during the British rule not only the surplus products of the village were traded, the peasant also produced at least partly for the market for the sake of money. Further, now the Indian exports exclusively consisted of primary agricultural products because the British systematically destroyed the Indian handicrafts and replaced them by British manufactured goods.

The British came to realise the export potentials of Indian agricultural products like indigo, cotton, jute and oilseeds, etc. towards the close of the eighteenth century. It took an initial step in this regard in 1833 when jute cultivation was introduced in Bengal with a view to export the same to foreign markets. Soon after it undertook cultivation of cotton in the Deccan and also introduced certain foreign varieties of cotton. However, during these earlier stages the volume of Indian exports was very limited. It was only in the later part of the nineteenth century that rapid progress was achieved in the direction of commercialisation of agriculture.

Factors Responsible for Commercialisation of Agriculture. The main factors which contributed to the transition of the Indian agriculture from production for self-consumption to production for sale for cash were as follows:

(1) In the first place, the introduction of the system of payment of land revenue in cash by the British in place of the existing system of payment in kind, obliged the peasants to sell a part of their produce for the payment of revenue. This presented the problem of finding markets for the peasants' product. This problem was overcome through export of foodgrains to Britain.

(2) Secondly, the commercial middlemen, who made huge profits by collecting the produce from villages and selling them with a premium, also induced the farmers to grow commercial crops. Often they advanced money to the farmers and induced them to grow particular commercial crops. In course of time some of the farmers also realised that it was more advantageous to grow commercial crops than foodgrains, because with the money obtained through sale of cash crops they could procure food from the market.

(3) Thirdly, the agricultural policy adopted by the British East India Company also greatly contributed to the commercialisation of agriculture. The Company encouraged the diversion of domestic production towards those articles which could bring higher profits. Thus, they encouraged the cultivation of tea, indigo and poppy. The government encouraged commercialisation of agriculture through its new irrigation policy as well. Vast tracts of land in Punjab and U.P. were brought under cultivation and bumper crops of wheat were procured. In some areas certain crops were encouraged chiefly for the purpose of export.

(4) Fourthly, the policy of ruthless suppression of Indian manufacturers followed by the British resulted in millions of artisans being thrown out of their jobs and they were forced to fall back upon agriculture. Mostly these artisans were encouraged to take to commercial crops.

(5) Fifthly, the process of commercialisation of agriculture received great fillip on account of the development of roads and railways. As a result, it became possible to transport huge quantities of crops from one part to another part and even to foreign markets. This encouraged the peasants to produce for the world market where Indian foodgrains, rice, wheat, etc. commanded ready market. It may be noted that towards the close of the nineteenth century huge

quantities of Indian wheat was shipped to Europe. Indian rice also commanded worldwide market and was shipped not only to Europe but also Straits, Ceylon, East Africa and other parts of Asia, West Indies and America. All this became possible on account of the extensive network of roads and other means of communication which made transportation of bulky and even perishable agricultural commodities to far off distances without loss of much time.

(6) Sixthly, the American Civil War of 1861-65 also greatly contributed to the acceleration of the pace of commercialisation of agriculture in India. The British manufacturers of cotton goods who were getting bulk of their raw material supplies (cotton) from United States grew apprehensive about regular supplies from U.S.A. and started looking for alternative sources of supply. They procured the supply of cotton from Indian ports like Bombay. As the English offered quite high price for the cotton the Indian cultivators tried to considerably increase the cotton production. The British Government also adopted a deliberate policy to encourage the Indian agriculturists to grow commercial crops like cotton, jute, oilseeds, etc. for export to Britain. Thus, we can say that American Civil War provided encouragement to the policy of commercialisation of agriculture by increasing demand of Indian cotton and pushing up its prices. It is estimated that during a short span of four years from 1859 to 1864 the export of the Indian cotton rose from five lakh bales to 134.5 lakh bales. There was also a four-fold increase in the prices of cotton. This naturally gave incentive to greater cotton cultivation.

(7) Finally, the opening of the Suez Canal in 1869 also greatly contributed to the commercialisation of Indian agriculture. As a result of the opening of the Suez Canal the distance between India and Europe was greatly reduced. This not only cut short the time and cost of Indian exports to Europe but also made it

possible to export those goods which earlier ran the risk of getting spoilt due to long journey through the Cape of Good Hope. The opening of the Suez Canal also encouraged competition among the shipping companies and resulted in considerable reduction in freight charges. This naturally provided a fillip to the Indian exports and large quantities of raw materials were exported to England and other European countries.

Impact of Policy of Commercialisation of Agriculture. As the commercialisation of agriculture in India was encouraged by the English primarily with a view to feed the British industries, it naturally benefited only British planters, traders and manufacturers. No doubt it also led to the establishment of some industries in India as well but it was a poor consolation because these industries were managed and controlled by the British capitalists. On the whole the common Indian people greatly suffered on account of the policy of commercialisation of agriculture. It resulted in considerable decline in the area under food crops cultivation. Even the Department of Agriculture set up by the British Government tried to encourage the cultivation of commercial crops. As a result of this policy while the area under cultivation of commercial crops continued to grow steadily the area under cultivation of food crops declined. As a result the Indians could not get sufficient supplies of foodgrains to support their own needs. The things assumed serious dimensions on account of tremendous increase in the Indian population, and fragmentation of land due to increasing pressure on land. Even the Prices Enquiry Committee in its report submitted in 1914 observed that "The requirements of foodgrains for internal consumption have increased in a larger proportion than the total production of foodgrains."

The commercialisation of agriculture also led to the break-up of the self-sufficiency of villages. As the village markets were linked with the outside markets as well as the foreign markets they ceased to be more local markets for agricultural commodities. In other words, the agricultural prices in India came to be linked with the world prices. No doubt for some time this helped the farmers to increase their incomes by assuring them more remunerative prices for their products, it also linked their fate with the world events. The American Civil War and the Great Depression (1929) left a deep impact on the Indian farmers.

Yet another impact of commercialisation of agriculture in India was the growth and increasing dominance of the moneylenders over the village economy. Majority of the peasants lived in debt to the moneylenders who charged exorbitant interests and exploited the poor peasants. The growth of this class of moneylenders was also encouraged because the government considered them as the mainstay for the payment of revenue. Thus, the moneylenders became, though indirectly, the instruments of colonial exploitation of India.

The commercialisation of agriculture in India also had some good effects. More and more land was brought under cultivation to increase the production of cash crops. For this purpose certain areas, best suited to the cultivation of particular crops, were selected. For example, sugar cane was cultivated in UP and in irrigated areas in the South; tea in Assam; wheat in Punjab; jute in Bengal and cotton in Berar and Khandesh. As a result, different areas specialised in cultivation of different crops.

Commercialisation of agriculture greatly added to the income of the agriculturists. As they produced the various crops keeping in view the demand and prices prevailing in the market, they were able to considerably add to their income. As a consequence there was an overall improvement in their income.

Again, commercialisation of agriculture led to introduction of a number of new crops like tea, coffee, potato, groundnut and different varieties of fruits, oilseeds, etc. As most of these crops were meant for export this resulted in widening of the markets for Indian agricultural crops. It may be observed that the construction of roads and railways greatly contributed to the expansion of markets for Indian agricultural products.

In short, it can be said that commercialisation of agriculture was a mixed blessing.

Rural Indebtedness

Rural indebtedness has been a traditional feature of Indian rural economy. As the traditional rural economy worked on the basis of self-sufficient village and principle of hereditary division of labour, it was not possible for the individual to come out of the system. But it was under the British rule that the problem of rural indebtedness assumed more serious dimensions. Edward Maclagan has acknowledged this fact and observed, "It has long been recognised that indebtedness is no new thing in India. The writings of Munro, Elphinstone and others make it clear that there was much debt even at the beginning of our rule. But it is also acknowledged that the indebtedness has risen considerably during our rule, and more specially during the last half century." As a result of commercialisation of agriculture and the policy of monetization which accompanied it, a class of moneylenders made its appearance which worked as tools of colonial exploitation. These moneylenders lent money to the peasants on the basis of the legal contract and could realise these loans through legal machinery. Thus, moneylending became an easy method of earning an income and subsequently of acquiring valuable titles to land.

It may be noted that under the traditional moneylending system the farmers could acquire loans from the village sahukar (trader-cum-moneylender) on the basis of his personal creditworthiness. The practice of mortgaging the land was not in vogue. Further, the amount of interest on the borrowed money was never permitted to exceed the principal money. It was only with the establishment of the British rule that full personal rights in land were recognised and it began to be treated as a marketable commodity. Often the ryot lost ownership rights in land to the moneylenders on account of default in payment of debts. The loss of property by the cultivating classes often culminated in riots against the moneylenders. Serious agricultural riots broke out in Poona and Ahmednagar in 1875 which forced the government to appoint a Commission of Inquiry and look into the problem more seriously. Before we deal with the remedial measures taken by the government it shall be desirable to have an idea about the causes of rural indebtedness.

Causes of Rural Indebtedness. Scholars have expressed divergent opinions regarding the causes of rural indebtedness among the rural Indians. Darling attributes the indebtedness to the habit of "extravagance and improvidence" of the Indian agriculturists. He asserts that the habit of rural people to spend large sums on occasions like marriage, funeral and other conventional ceremonies was responsible for their indebtedness. In other words, he holds that the habit of the rural people to spend beyond their means was the chief cause of their indebtedness. However, this view was rejected by the Deccan Riots Commission, set up in 1875, which observed that "undue importance has been given to the expenditure on marriage and other festivals—the expenditure forms an item of some importance in the debt-side of the ryots' account but it rarely appears as the nucleus of his indebtedness."

Prof. S. Bose attributes the rural indebtedness to the general poverty of the cultivating classes. He asserts that "the small and fragmented holdings, the low productivity of the land, made uncertain by the vagaries of the monsoon, hardly gave enough to a peasant to make both ends meet." During bad season his position became still worse and forced him to take debts.

According to yet another view the system of rigid and regular collection of land revenue by the British was the chief cause of rural indebtedness. The British not only levied a very high rate of land revenue but also collected the same before the crop was harvested. As the cultivators did not have sufficient money to pay the instalments of revenues they were obliged to borrow and fell under debt. The Famine Commission of 1880 also confirmed this view and observed, "Had the recovery of instalments being more coincident with the marketing of the crop, instead of falling too early and sometimes too late, much temporary borrowing could have been avoided."

Some scholars hold the British colonial system responsible for the rural indebtedness. While admitting that even before the advent of the British the Indian peasants were under debt, they contend that the colonial rule made their condition still worse. But bestowing the ownership of land on the peasants they raised the limits of his creditworthiness. So far the moneylenders lent money to the peasants to the tune of surplus of an occasional good crop. Now they were willing to extend credit to the tune of the proprietary rights of the peasants. In other words, now the moneylenders were willing to lend more money to the peasants. This encouraged the peasants to contact more loans and they sunk heavily under debt. The British also contributed to the indebtedness of the peasants by encouraging the moneylenders and the new methods. Again the British colonialism contributed to the indebtedness of the agriculturists by adopting a deliberate policy of discouraging cottage industries and thereby depriving the peasants of some extra income which they could raise through cottage industries. Above all, the practice of the British Government to collect revenues through intermediaries considerably increased the tax burden of the peasants. Often there were a score of intermediaries involved in rent collection each claiming some share of profit, thus, enormously increasing the tax burden of the peasants. As the peasants were not always able to bear the burden of high taxation they often sold their produce at cheaper rates to the local bania, and even borrowed money to discharge their revenue liabilities.

The legal system provided by the British also greatly contributed to the rural indebtedness. So far the peasants used to get loans from moneylenders without any formal contract and the terms were settled between the creditor and the debtor by mutual consent. Under this arrangement the village community was always able to protect the interests of the peasants, and prevent their undue exploitation by the moneylenders. The British introduced the system of civil courts and the cultivators were obliged to conclude formal contracts with the moneylenders for the necessary loans. If the cultivators were not able to discharge their liabilities, under the contract the law courts assisted the creditors to realise their credits. This change clearly went in favour of the moneylending classes, which was left free to charge exorbitant interest rate and in case of the inability of the debtor to discharge his liability realise the same by attaching the cattle, implements, etc. of the debtor.

The high rate of interest charged by the moneylenders and the various types of malpractices adopted by the moneylenders to squeeze interest from the debtors also greatly contributed to the rural indebtedness. The exorbitant rates of interest charged by the moneylenders made it difficult for the peasant to clear off the principal. As a result, while they continued to pay huge sums of money as interest the principal amount always stayed, rendering the peasants under debt perpetually. The contribution of this factor towards the indebtedness of the peasants was acknowledged by the Bombay Committee which observed, "It is not that the agriculturist pays too little; he often pays too much. It is the high rate of interest and the malpractices followed by the moneylenders that tend to perpetuate his indebtedness."

Thus, we can say that the problem of rural indebtedness arose on account of numerous causes but most significant contribution in this regard was made by the British Government. As the Royal Commission on Indian Agriculture observed, "The general expansion of the credit of the landholder, his illiteracy and the temptation he has to relieve present necessities by mortgaging his future income and even his capital, have on the one hand, led to the increased indebtedness, while on the other the position of the moneylender has been strengthened by the rapid development of commerce and trade, the introduction of established law and permanent civil courts, and the enactment of such measures as the Contract Act."

Impact of the Rural Indebtedness. The growing rural indebtedness left a deep impact on the Indian economy. In the first place it greatly added to the miseries of the cultivators. As the cultivators were not able to the high rates of interest on the money borrowed by them they were obliged to mortgage their land to the moneylenders. Generally, they were not able to get the land redeemed and it remained with the moneylender. As a result, large number of cultivators were reduced to the position of tenants. This change in status of the cultivators greatly dampened their incentive and adversely effected the produce. In India the transference of lands into the hands of moneylenders did not result in consolidation of holdings and large-scale production (as other countries of world). On the other hand, it led to subdivision and fragmentation of land which resulted in lower production.

Still more serious impact of the rural indebtedness was that the peasants were reduced to the position of serfs. The peasants not only lost their lands to the moneylenders, but also often mortgaged their personal liberty in return for loan. As they were never able to repay the loans they continued to work as labourers on the land of the moneylender and virtually reduced to the status of a livelong slave of the creditor.

The exploitation of the peasants by the moneylenders generated lots of social tension and gave a rude stock to the traditional peace and harmony of village life. This growing tension often found outlet in the shape of incidents of looting and murder of moneylenders. In certain areas this anger of the peasants against the exploitation of moneylenders erupted in the form of rebellions. For example, the Santhal Rebellion of 1855 in which hundreds of peasants proceeded to take possession of the country and set up a government of their own and the Deccan Riots of 1875 in which the peasants spontaneously rose in many places and robbed and wrecked the houses of the moneylenders, were expression of the peasants' anger against the moneylenders.

Measures to Check Indebtedness

In view of the far-reaching consequences of the growing rural indebtedness the British Government took a number of measures to check the same. For the sake of convenience these measures may be studied under the following head:

1. Restrictions on Borrowing. Realising that the best way of relieving rural indebtedness was to check the habit of the people to borrow. This was sought to be achieved through enactment of a number of laws imposing restrictions on borrowing. The government was convinced that the unrestricted power of transferring the land by sale or mortgage was the chief factor which encouraged the peasants to borrow liberally. Therefore, in 1900 Punjab Land Alienation Act was passed which prohibited the non-agricultural classes from buying land from an agriculturist or to keep it in mortgage for more than twenty years. In other words, it prohibited the taking over of the agricultural land by the non-agriculturists in lieu of debt repayment. Similar restrictions were imposed in other parts by different acts, *viz.* Land Revenue Act of 1901 in Bombay, and extension of the Punjab Land Alienation Act to NWFP in 1904 and enactment of identical acts in Bundelkhand and United Provinces. However, no restrictions were imposed on the transfer of land to the agricultural classes. This gave rise to the evil of benami transfers, under which though the agricultural land was nominally transferred to an agriculturist in reality the land belonged to the non-agriculturist. These defects were rectified by certain amendments carried out in 1938-39 which imposed restrictions on benami transfers and acquisition of land by the agricultural moneylenders.

2. Improvement in Civil Law. To protect the peasants against usury and fraudulent practices, resorted to by the moneylenders, the government effected certain improvements in the civil law. Through an amendment to the Indian Contract Act in 1899 if the state found that the debtor had entered into a senseless bargain under pressure of moneylender, it could provide him necessary relief. Similarly, the Usurious Loans Act, 1918 authorised the courts to reopen any transaction if it found the rate of interest excessively high, or the transaction unfair. In such cases the court could give relief to the debtor against excessive interest. Changes were also made in the civil law relating to execution of decrees against the farmers. Cattle and materials of agriculturists household were exempted from attachment or sale. Similarly, the farmers were exempted from arrest from a decree of the court and also allowed certain concessions regarding repayment of his debts.

3. Regulation of Moneylending Business. The government also tried to regulate the moneylending business and passed a number of laws for this purpose. Under the Deccan Agriculturists Relief Act of 1879, the moneylenders were required to show accounts and give receipts. However, this did not resolve the problem and led to lot of litigation. The moneylenders became more cautious and there was a considerable decline in rural credit. To protect the peasants from extortion of moneylenders the maximum rate of interest was fixed through an amendment of 1926 in Usurious Loans Act of 1918. It also granted to the mortgager the right of redemption. System of licensing and control of moneylenders was introduced under the Punjab Regulation of Accounts Act, 1930. Under the Act all persons, whether moneylenders or shopkeepers who lent money on interest, were required to keep an account of each debtor and to supply him every six months a signed statement of the account of principal and interest. If a separate account was not kept for a debtor, the creditor was liable to lose his interest in case of a suit. Similarly, the Bihar Moneylenders Act required the moneylenders to register themselves. Despite all these measures the moneylenders devised ingenuous methods and successfully bypassed these regulations. For example, they resorted to the practice of obtaining promissory notes for higher amounts than actually lent. Similarly, they charged the interest on higher rates than prescribed by law, but charged the excess interest in advance at the time of lending the money. The fact of the evasion of these rules and regulations was also acknowledged by the Rural Credit Survey Committee which observed in its report, "Legislation to curb usury had become a complete failure. The moneylenders evaded the law by obtaining a promissory note for larger amount of principal than actually lent or by computing interest at illegal rates and deducting the advance from the amount lent."

4. Debt Relief. Efforts were also made to provide some relief to the debtors through voluntary reduction of debts. For this purpose laws were passed in Central Provinces in 1933; Punjab in 1934; Bengal and Assam in 1935; Madras in 1936 and Sindh in 1939 whereby Debt Conciliation Boards were set up to work for the reduction of debts of debtors with the consent of the creditors. These Boards tried to persuade the creditors to provide some relief to the debtors and accept repayment in easy instalments. The agreement thus arrived through the Debt Conciliation Boards was to be binding on both the parties. No doubt, the Debt Conciliation Boards succeeded in procuring considerable relief for the debtors through scaling down of the debts, still the relief was quite inadequate and beyond the repaying capacity of debtors. Further, this debt conciliation was purely voluntary in character and benefited only big-borrowers.

No doubt subsequently in certain areas debts were scaled down on compulsory basis and certain rules were laid down in this regard. For example, under the Madras Agriculturists Relief Act of 1938, the creditors were not to recover in aggregate more than twice the original loan. Similarly, the laws enacted by other states also advocated principles like: (a) the total interest paid or payable should not exceed the principal; (b) repaying capacity of the debtors; (c) regulation of mortgages; (d) protection of agriculturists against certain legal proceedings; (e) exemption of specified items of property from attachment, etc.

The debt relief measures take by the government gave a great set back to the confidence of the moneylenders and resulted in shrinkage of credit. To ward off the danger of scaling down of debts they started insisting on the mortgage of land or on a conditional sale deed.

5. Provision of Alternate Sources of Credit. Realising that the problem of rural indebtedness could not be solved unless people were freed from the exploitation of moneylenders by making available alternative sources of credit. Therefore, the government took a number of measures in this regard. In 1883, under the Land Improvement Act the government made available Takavi Loans for permanent improvement on land such as wells and embankments, etc. In 1884, it passed the Agriculturists Loans Act which provided short-term loans for current agricultural needs such as purchase of seeds, cattle, manure, implements, etc. In 1904, the government provided agricultural credit facilities to co-operative societies. However, these measures proved quite inadequate. The procedure for grant of various kinds of loans was quite cumbersome and the interested parties had to wait for long before these loans were actually made available to them. Further, the recoveries of these loans were effected in a mechanical manner without taking into account the actual condition and capacities of the debtors. As far as the agricultural credit facilities through co-operative societies were concerned, very limited funds were made available and only a small fraction of the agriculturists could benefit from it. In short, it can be said that the various credit facilities made available by the government were not in keeping with the seriousness of the problem and no wonder failed to resolve the problem.

Growth of Agricultural Labour

The growth of the agricultural labour in India was largely the result of the British rule. Before the advent of the British in India the Indian economy was largely based on the principle of self-subsistence in which cultivation was carried on by the farmers with the help of other family members. There did not exist an independent class of landless labourers. It was only after the British destroyed the self-sufficient village economy that the old production relations underwent a change and a large number of peasants who were deprived of their lands emerged as agricultural labourers. The number of agricultural labourers in India which stood at 12.5 million in 1881 has shown constant rise since then.

Causes for the Growth of Agricultural Labour. Scholars have attributed the rise and growth of agricultural labour to different causes. According to Nanavati and Anjaria, it was on account of increase of population. However, this view is difficult to accept because contrary to the growth of population in almost all the parts of the country the agricultural labour grew only in certain regions. For example, in Madras, Bombay and Central Provinces the number of agricultural labour was the largest. On the other hand, in Punjab, North-Western Frontier Province, and United Provinces it was the lowest. It clearly shows that there is no co-relationship between the growth of agricultural labour and rise of population. On the other hand, the number of agricultural labour grew maximum in those areas which suffered a decline of village handicrafts and faced increasing indebtedness of the peasantry and land mortgages.

According to D.R. Gadgil, the rise of agricultural labour was due to import of manufactured goods from Britain which resulted in decline of Indian handicrafts and forced the persons working in cottage industries to take to cultivation. As they did not possess lands of their own they were obliged to take up jobs as agricultural labourers.

The British also contributed to the growth of the agricultural labour through its policy of commercialisation of agriculture, demanding revenue in cash, and making land transferable, etc. As a result of all this the peasants sunk deeper and deeper into debts, till ultimately their land was consumed by the moneylenders and they were rendered landless labourers.

Dr. R.K. Mukherjee attributes the growth of landless labourer to the revenue policy of the British. He argues that the British conferred proprietary rights only on a limited number of persons, which were exploited by the traders and moneylenders and these persons were reduced to the status of landless labourers. Dr. Mukherjee substantiates his point with reference to the tribes and states of tribal areas and quotes instances of Gonds and Bhils of Central Provinces, the Karwas in United Provinces and Mundas in Chhotanagpur.

Categories of Agricultural Labour. The agricultural labour was not of the same type and can be classified into following four categories on the basis of their relationship with the landowners.

(1) In the first place there were labourers who virtually lived as slaves. This category of labourers came into existence because they undertook to serve the man from whom they borrowed money till it was repaid. As they could not repay the loans they got converted into bond slaves of the creditors. These labourers depended for food on the creditors and for all other purposes virtually lived like medieval serfs. They were sold, purchased and even mortgaged like ordinary commodities. This type of bonded labour even passed from one generation to another generation. This category of labour was found chiefly in Madras, Bombay, Madhya Pradesh, Chhotanagpur and Bihar where there were a large number of landless labourers and there were very limited opportunities for securing a livelihood. According to one scholar, there were about 2.3 million bonded labourers in India in 1931.

(2) In the second place there were agricultural workers who did not entirely depend on the farm work. They pursued some other occupation and took to farm work with a view to

supplement their income from the main occupation as the same was not adequate. Most of these labourers worked on their tiny holdings and were unemployed in the sense that they did not get adequate earnings from their cultivation. Generally, women and children of the families swelled the ranks to this category of labour and the head of the family continued to pursue the main family occupation. This category of labourers were mostly found in Bengal, Bihar, U.P. and Punjab. Their number was around 32 million.

(3) The third category of labourers consisted of under-employed landless labourers. This category of labourers chiefly consisted of those labourers of the first two categories who lacked alternative means of employment and had cut off their ties with the landowners or the land. This category of labourers kept on moving from place to place in search of work. They travelled in family groups and received wages in cash. Generally, these labourers were employed during the harvesting season and for the rest of the year they were either unemployed or under-employed. This category of labourers were predominantly found in Maharashtra, Gujarat, Tamil Nadu and Central Provinces.

(4) Finally, there were full-time landless labourers who were employed by the capitalists and well-to-do farmers in their plantations. These labourers were recruited by the capitalists and employed in thinly populated areas where the plantations were located. As they were completely cut off from the rest of country and also lacked necessary trade unions they were no better than the bonded labourers. Rajni Palme Dutt describes them as 'plantation slaves'. Another kind of agricultural labourers were employed by the capitalist farmers in areas which supplied dairy products, fruits, vegetables and such other product to cities. These labourers were also employed on more or less long-term basis.

In addition to the above, there existed 'forced labour' of *begar*. According to this practice, the landholders in order to retain the labourers in service for long time, advanced loans or allotted plots to the labourers and extracted their labour either at nominal wages or even without payment of any wages.

Condition of the Agricultural Labourers. The condition of the agricultural labourers was indeed very miserable. As they lived on the margin of subsistence they easily fell victims to disease, pestilence and famine. As most of them remained unemployed for a substantial part of the year, this further aggravated their sufferings. The extremely low wages paid to them also added to their miseries specially when the prices of foodgrains rose. In view of the low wages often all the members of the family took to work to make their both ends meet. This resulted in substantial increase in the labour force and brought about a further decline in the wages of labour, specially male workers.

According to certain scholars, there was an improvement in the condition of the agricultural labourer on account of the rise in their wages between 1891 and 1911, however, this view is not universally accepted. Again it has been contended that the condition of agricultural labourer improved during the inter-war period as well as during the Second World War. However, this increase was to a large extent nullified by the increase in the cost of living. Even the Agrarian Reforms Committee set up by the Congress arrived at the conclusion that during 1939-47 the rise in agricultural wages was more than offset by the greater increase in the cost of living in different parts of the country, resulting in further deteriorating in the condition of the agricultural workers.

Even in the post-independence period the condition of the agricultural workers has not shown any appreciable improvement. Their condition continues to be much worse than the industrial workers as well as other sections of rural population. The only solace is that the Central and State Governments are now keeping a close watch on the progress of various development programmes, specially those which are concerned with the welfare and development of agricultural workers.

Destruction of Handicraft Industries

It has been often argued that India has never been an industrial country and nature has destined her to be an agricultural country. This impression is ill-founded and is contrary to the facts of history. In fact India had emerged as industrial workshop of the world before the advent of the Europeans. Despite her predominantly agricultural economy, a variety of other industries also flourished in India. Even the Industrial Commission (1918) appointed by the British Government observed, "At a time when the west of Europe, the birth place of modern industrial system, was inhabited by uncivilized tribes. India was famous for the wealth of her rulers and the high artistic skill of her craftsmen. And even at a much later period, when the merchant adventurers from the West made their first appearance in India, the industrial development of this country was, at any rate, not inferior to that of the more advanced European nations."

There are ample other proofs to establish the highly advanced nature of the Indian handicrafts and industries. For example, the Egyptian mummies dated back to 2500 B.C. have been found wrapped in Indian muslin. Again the gossamer muslin of Dacca, the beautiful shawls of Kashmir and the brocaded silks of Delhi adorned the proudest beauties at the court of Caesar, when the barbarians of Britain were painted as savages. Even in the face of various foreign invasions and conquests these handicrafts continued to flourish and exported to foreign countries. In fact the rivalry between the various European powers in the seventeenth and the eighteenth centuries was also chiefly due to their desire to acquire Indian manufactures and crafts.

Even after the British acquired a foothold in the country and ultimately succeeded in establishing their political control, these handicrafts continued to flourish. It is a different matter that the various handicrafts continued to thrive in different parts of India and their demand as localised. Thus, Dacca, Krishnagar, Chunderee, etc. continued to be the centres for the manufacture of fine muslins; cotton fabrics were manufactured at Lucknow, Ahmedabad, Nagpur, Madura, etc. Silk manufacturer was confined to Murshidabad, Malda, Benaras, Ahmedabad, Poona, etc. Brass, copper and bell-metal wares were made in Benaras, Nasik, Poona, Hyderabad, Vizagapatam, Tanjore, etc.

Destruction of Handicrafts

The Indian handicraft industries suffered a decline during the middle of the nineteenth century. This decline was caused by the deliberate policy of the Britishers in India, even though the other factors also made a considerable contribution in this regard. Let us examine this point in some details:

1. Hostile Policy of the British East India Company and the British Parliament. The hostile policy of the British East India Company and the British Parliament towards the Indian handicrafts was one of the major causes for their decline. No doubt, during the initial stages the East India Company encouraged Indian handicrafts because it could make huge profits out of their exports to the European markets. But soon the East India Company was forced by the English manufacturers to change its policy and concentrate mainly on the export of raw-materials which were needed by them. The favourable balance of trade enjoyed by India which resulted in flow of gold from England to India also obliged the British to think of restricting Indian imports and increase export of English factory manufactured goods to India. To ensure that the Indian textiles did not offer competition to the British goods heavy customs duties were imposed on the Indian goods. These duties were removed only after the mid-nineteenth century when the Indian handicraft industries had already been crippled. R.C. Dutt, the author of famous *Economic History of India* has brought out the impact of the hostile policy of the British East India Company and the British Parliament on the Indian handicraft industries thus, "The East India Company and the British Parliament following the selfish commercial policy of a hundred years ago, discouraged Indian manufacturers in the early years of British rule in order to encourage the rising manufacturers of England. This policy pursued during the last decade of the eighteenth century and the first decade of the nineteenth century, was to make India subservient to the industries of Great Britain and to make the Indian people grow raw produce only, in order to supply material for the looms and manufactories of Great Britain. This policy was pursued with unwavering resolution and fatal success; orders were sent out to force Indian artisans to work in the company's factories; commercial residents were legally vested with extensive powers over villages and communities of Indian weavers; prohibitive tariff excluded Indian silks and cotton goods from England; English goods were admitted into India free of duty or on payment of nominal duty."

2. Impact of Foreign Rule. The very existence of the foreign rule also contributed to the destruction of the handicraft industries. With the assumption of power by the British in India a new class of professional officers made its appearance. These officials looked upon the products of indigenous industries with disdain and preferred use of cheap European cotton goods, printed calicos, etc. Even the newly educated class of Indians, a product of British rule, accepted the European fashions and standards and turned their back on indigenous handicraft products. They did not want to incur the displeasure of the higher European officials by using Indian goods, which were immensely disliked by European officials. Therefore, they took to European goods. The British also developed certain conventions which encouraged the use of European goods rather than the Indian handicrafts. For example, there was a convention which permitted an oriental to retain a pair of patent leather boots in the presence of British superiors, but on the other hand if they wore embroidered shoes they were expected to put off the same in the presence of the superior officers. This naturally encouraged the use of patent leather shoes as against embroidered shoes and contributed to the decline of embroidered shoe industry. Similarly, the English imposed restrictions on carrying of arms by the Indians. This gave a setback to the production of inlaid arms, weapons and shields. Again, the emergence of the British also gave a serious setback to the guilds which regulated the trade and sought to maintain high standards of workmanship. As a result, the Indian handicrafts suffered a decline in workmanship and excellence.

3. Competition with Machine-made Goods. The competition posed by the machine-made European goods also greatly contributed to the destruction of Indian handicrafts, specially the textiles. As a result of the industrial revolution in England large scale production of goods was undertaken which could be made available to the consumers in India and other markets at a much cheaper price than the Indian handicraft products. It is true that in matter of quality the Indian craftsmen could favourably compete with the British machine-made products but in terms of price they could offer no competition. The construction of railways and improvement of other means of communication made it possible for the British machine-made goods to penetrate in all the corners of the country and push out the products of Indian cottage industries and handicrafts. The opening of the Suez Canal, which considerably cut short the distance between India and Britain and brought about considerable saving in the shipping cost, also greatly contributed to the decline of the Indian handicrafts by flooding the Indian markets as a result most of the artisans were forced to give up their traditional jobs and take to cultivation. This converted India into supplier of foodstuffs and raw materials to the advanced countries of the West. As Ranade observed, "The great Indian dependency of England as during this (nineteenth) century come to be...regarded as a plantation, growing raw produce to be shipped by the British agents in British ships, to be worked into manufactured articles by British skill and capital and to be re-exported to this dependency by British merchants to their corresponding British firms in India and elsewhere."

4. Change in the Tastes of the People. The change in the tastes of the richer classes which had been the chief patrons of the Indian handicrafts also considerably contributed to the decline of Indian handicrafts. As Dr. Vera Anstey writes, "Richer classes in India began to adopt European fashion and either purchased imported goods or were content with the cheaper indigenous products sold to Europeans that previously they would have scorned.... There came a craze for everything Western and a hatred for everything Indian. One of the harmful effects of a foreign rule is the imposition of the conquered people's ideals of the conquerors and the newly created Indian bourgeoisie showed itself during the later half of the last century extremely ready to accept European standards and to pour scorn on everything Indian."

5. Policy of *Laissez Faire*. The policy of *laissez faire* deliberately and consistently followed by the English East India Company as well as the British Indian Government and their refusal to afford any protection to the Indian handicrafts also greatly contributed to the destruction of the handicraft industries. It was not till 1923 that the British Government offered some sort of half-hearted protection to the Indian handicrafts but it was too late by then. On the other hand, the British Government continued to give every possible encouragement to the English manufacturers in exploiting the Indian markets. No wonder with this protection they succeeded in completely eliminating the Indian handicraft industries out of competition.

6. Disappearance of Native Courts. The emergence of the English as supreme power also gave a serious setback to the Indian handicraft industries. So far these industries had thrived on account of the patronage extended by the native rulers, princes and nobles. For example, the muslin, cotton and silk industries of Bengal flourished chiefly because of the patronage extended to it by the Mughal Emperors and their countries. Similarly, in Lucknow the dyeing industry flourished because of the patronage extended to the coloured clothes by the Nawabs of Oudh. When these native rulers were eliminated by the English the patrons of Indian handicrafts also disappeared, thereby bringing about decline in the handicraft industries. With the loss of patrons the Indian craftsmen lost all incentive to produce outstanding pieces of handicrafts. No doubt the agents of the Company often requisitioned the services of these artisans to continue the production but they offered very unremunerative wages to them. This compelled the artisans to abandon their tradition profession.

Thus, we find that the decline of the handicraft industries in India was largely due to the British rule and the policies of the British Government.

Impact of Destruction of Indian Handicraft Industries

The Indian handicraft industries which occupied place of pride in the Indian economic system suffered a complete decline towards the close of the nineteenth century. In fact by 1895 the handicraft industries had suffered such a decline that they merely remained memories of the past. This decline of Indian handicraft industries left a deep impact on the Indian economy.

In the first place of liquidation of the artisans gave rise to the problem of unemployment on an unprecedented scale and considerably added to the miseries of the craftsmen. A large number of them died of starvation. Lord William Bentinck recorded in 1834, "The misery hardly finds a parallel in the history of commerce. The bones of the cotton weavers are bleaching the plains of India."

It was not the textile industry alone which suffered decline even other industries like iron smelting, salt-petre industry, bangle-making, glass manufacture, paper-making, etc. also faced a complete decay.

The decline of the handicrafts caused a pressure on land. The craftsmen and artisans who were thrown out of jobs on account of the decline of handicraft industries could not find suitable employment in urban industries took to agriculture and increased the pressure on land, which became one of the major factors for the poverty of the Indian masses.

Drain of Wealth

The term 'drain of wealth' is generally used for the transfer of resources from India to England either without getting anything in return or getting only a disproportionately small part of such transfer of resources. The theory of 'drain of wealth' was advocated by Indian nationalist leaders like Dadabhai Naoroji, R.C. Dutt, etc. towards the close of the nineteenth century in the process of analysing the causes of poverty of the Indians. When they compared the prosperity of India before the arrival of the English with the abject poverty of the masses during their times they arrived at the conclusion that consistent exploitation by the British was responsible for the miserable plight of the people.

The first systematic attempt to demonstrate the drain of wealth from India was made by Dadabhai Naoroji in 1871 in his book *Poverty and the Un-British Rule in India*. In this book, he not only tried to quantify the magnitude of the drain but also sought to demonstrate that the poverty of Indians was the direct consequence of draining of wealth from India by the Britishers.

In fact the British from the very beginning followed a systematic policy of transferring the economic resources of India to Britain and carried away more of Indian wealth to their country than the loot and plunder made by the Mahmud of Ghazni and Nadir Shah. As a result of this systematic exploitation they left in India "poverty amidst plenty" and turned the people into hewers of wood and drawers of water. According to Dadabhai Naoroji, the following items contributed to the drain of wealth from India:

(a) Remittances to England by European employees for support of families and education of children—a feature of colonial system of government.

(b) Remittances of savings by employees of the Company, since most employees preferred to invest at home.

(c) Remittances for the purchase of British goods for the consumption of British employees as well as purchases by them of British goods in India.

(d) Government purchase of stores manufactured in Britain.

(e) Interest charges on public debt held in Britain (excluding interest payments on railway loans and debts incurred for productive works).

Though the various scholars have come to the common conclusion that there was draining of wealth from India to Britain they have not been able to agree on the quantum of the drain on account of lack of necessary data. No wonder they offer quite fluctuating estimates of drain. Even though they are not able to agree on the amount of drain there seems to be a fair amount of agreement about the medias of this drain. The chief sources of economic drain before 1833 consisted of tributes paid by the Indian rulers to the English, investment of surplus revenue of Bengal in exports from India by the Company, payment of dividends to the shareholders of the Company, savings out of salaries received by the Company's servants, and profits made out of private trade by the servants of the Company. However, after 1833 some of these methods like tributes from Indian rulers, and transfer of surplus revenue from India to England were abandoned. Instead the British took to new methods like home charges, interests and profits on private foreign capital insurance and shipping charges, etc. For a proper understanding of the process of draining of wealth it shall be desirable to know about these methods in some details:

1. Home Charges. In the first instance the home charges constituted a substantial drain on the wealth of India. The Government of India was required to pay huge amounts to the people of England on account of political, administrative and commercial connections between England and India. This included interest on public debt raised in England, annuities on account of railway and irrigation works, payments in connection with civil departments where Englishmen were employed, expenses including pensions to officials working in India or who had worked for India in England and retired there, pensions to army and naval personnel. Even the expenses on employment of missions in foreign countries (such as Persia and China) which worked for the protection and promotion of the imperial interests were charged from India. Likewise India was required to meet the expenses of campaigns in Abyssinia, Malta, Afghanistan (Second War), Egypt, Sudan, Burma, etc. Even the expenses incurred on the recruitment, training and maintenance of forces were paid by India. The English army officers were generally paid salaries at a much higher rate than the Indian soldiers. The responsibility for the transportation of British troops from England to India and back also rested with the Indian Government. Prof. Vakil highlights the impact of this arrangement on the drain of Indian wealth thus, "The British soldier was recruited at India's expense, was brought to India at India's expenses, was given valuable field experience at India's expense, was sent back home at India's expense to join the Reserve Forces of England. To the extent the pension, furlough and other charges could have been reduced by the employment of Indians in the higher military services, there was drain from India."

R.C. Dutt, who considered the British rule over India as a gift of providence, is also highly critical of the system of home charges. He records, "It is not fair that all the expenses incurred in England down to the maintenance of the Indian office and the wages of the charwomen employed to clean the rooms at Whitehall, should be charged to India.... If Great Britain and India are both gainers by the building up of British Indian Empire, it is not fair or equitable that India alone should pay all the cost of the maintenance of that superb edifice."

2. Dividend to Proprietors. Huge amounts were paid to the proprietors of the East India Company as dividends, which constituted a serious strain on the Indian wealth. No doubt after 1833 when the Company was stripped of its commercial functions, bid was made to regulate the dividends payable to proprietors and the annual dividend was fixed at £6.30 lakh. This continuous flow of dividends greatly stained the Indian economy.

3. Interest on Public Debts and Profit on Private Foreign Capital. Huge amounts were paid to England as interest on public debts incurred by the Government of India for financing battles against the Indian rulers. At the time of Mutiny this debt stood at £49.2 million to which the mutiny added another £44 million. This increase in public debt resulted in corresponding increase in interest. It was indeed ironical that the Indians were made to bear the expenses of the adversary. We do not find any such parallel in history where the victor raised loans to finance the war against and to be paid by the vanquished. Vera Anstey, a pro-British writers also asserted, "It is reasonable to argue that payment on account of the military expenses of conquering India and interest payments on the debentures of East India Company taken over by the Crown after Mutiny ought never to have been charged to the Indian revenues."

India also paid profits on foreign capital which was invested in India. To ensure maximum profits the foreign capitalists did everything possible to discourage the growth of Indian industries which they feared could pose a challenge to them and result in reduction of their profits.

4. Banking, Insurance and Shipping Charges. In addition to the above, India also paid huge amounts in the shape of banking charges, insurance and shipping which were wholly managed by the foreigners. We can form an idea about the quantum of the strain on this account from the fact that during the year 1921-22 alone India paid a sum of £2.7 million as freight and passenger charges to the foreign shipping companies, while another amount of £10 million was paid as commission to the banking companies.

Consequences of Drain of Wealth. The drain of wealth from India left a deep impact on England as well as India. It shall, therefore, be desirable to examine its impact on two countries.

The drain of wealth from India naturally resulted in flow of vast amounts of resources and capital into Britain which greatly contributed to the improvement in the standard of living of the people. The wealth thus, made available in England was invested in agriculture and industry and greatly contributed to the agricultural revolution as well as the industrial revolution. It is well-known that the rich officials and merchants who retired with huge amounts and pensions after serving in India, devoted the leisure and money at their disposal to the construction of roads, canals, railways and even new inventions. In short, they brought about rapid changes in various sectors of the economy. Thus, we can say that the drain of wealth from India to Britain contributed to the economic prosperity of England.

On the other hand, the drain of wealth from India left disastrous impact on the people and economy of India. In the first place it deprived the country of the enormous resources, which were taken away to England in the shape of profits, which could have been fruitfully invested in India. Secondly, as a result of the public debt policy of government which involved annual payment of interest on the loans taken by the Government of India, the tax burden on the people of India considerably increased. What is still worse that as most of the tax proceeds were transferred to the British creditors, the social services and welfare activities were completely neglected. Thirdly, the transference of tax proceeds to England contributed to the impoverishing of India's trade, agriculture and industries, and greatly contributed to the stagnation of the Indian economy during the eighteenth and nineteenth centuries. It may be noted that if the tax proceeds remain within the country and the money circulates among the people it automatically creates demand for various types of goods and services and helps in the progress of trade, agriculture and industry.

Fourthly, Dadabhai Naoroji held the drain of wealth as the sole cause of India's poverty. He said, "It is not the pitiless operation of economic laws but it is the thoughtless and pitiless action of the British policy, it is the pitiless eating of India's substances in India and further pitiless drain of England. In short, it is the pitiless perversion of economic laws by the sad bleeding to which India is subjected that is destroying."

Fifthly, the drain of wealth produced a harmful effect on employment and income. R.C. Dutt argued, "When taxes are raised and spent in a country, the money circulates among the people, fructifies trade, industries and agriculture, and in one shape or another reaches the mass of the people. But when the taxes in a country are remitted out of it, the money is lost to the country forever, it does not stimulate her trade or industries or reach the people in any form."

Sixthly, drain of wealth also left a deep impact on the industrial development of country. The capital shortage which resulted from the draining of wealth greatly retarded industrial progress of India. As one writer has rightly observed, "No nation can stand such a drain and yet hold its own in the industrial field."

Seventhly, the drain of wealth also adversely effected the foreign trade of India and obliged her to take to large-scale exports. In fact, India had only two alternatives, *viz.* to export or to perish. In other words, she had no choice but to export. Often she had to persuade the foreign buyers to purchase her goods and even reduce prices of her goods. This caused additional loss to her.

In short, we can say that while the drain of wealth from India to British proved immensely beneficial for the English, it virtually wrecked the Indian economy and the Indian people.

Growth of Modern Industry and Rise of Capitalist Class

After the destruction of the handicraft industries for some time the Indians continued to depend on the goods imported from Britain. No doubt after the enactment of the Charter Act of 1883 the Company wad divested of its commercial character and the European settlers and other British capitalists were permitted to invest their capital in India, but no significant investments were made in India till after the Revolt of 1857. In the wake of the uprising the British Government realised that the people of India were encouraged to extend support to the native rulers due to their economic hardship and increasing unemployment. It realised that unless something was done to improve the economic condition of the people the Indians would also go the American way.

Consequently, soon after the assumption of power by the Crown in 1858 the British took a number of steps to improve the economic condition of the people and win them over. One important step in this regard was that it paid special attention to the industrial development of the country. A beginning in this regard was made in the sixties of the nineteenth century when cotton mills, jute mills and mining industries were set up. By 1865, thirteen cotton mills were set up in the Bombay Presidency alone. The cotton mills were under the control of the Indian Parsees. After 1875, there was a boom in the cotton industry and mills were set up at places like Ahmedabad, Sholapur, Nagpur, etc. In 1877, the total number of cotton mills rose to 51. The jute mills were mainly located in Bengal while the mining industry was located at Raniganj. These industries were mainly owned and managed by the British and Scottish capitalists. This period also witnessed the beginning of the railways. In 1865, there were 3000 miles of railways which linked the inland regions with principal ports. The railway mileage increased to 8000 by the end of 1877.

Opposition from British Interests. It may be noted that the establishment of these industries was not a smooth affair and the government had to encounter lots of opposition from the British manufacturing interests. Maximum opposition was offered to the establishment of the cotton textile industry. In fact, in 1853 when the cotton textile factories were started in India, the Manchester Chamber of Commerce appealed to the Government of India to identify itself with "the cause of civilization, justice and Christianity" and destroy the new industry. Subsequently, when the Government of India was forced to enhance import duties on the Lancashire taxtiles to meet the growing financial liabilities on account of the Indian Mutiny and other military activities, the Lancashire interests accused the government of according protection to the Indian cotton mills. This plea of Lancashire interests was accepted by the British Parliament (which still held belief in the principle of the free trade) and it directed the Indian Government to abolish import duties on certain varieties of cloth in 1879. In 1882, all the import duties were totally repealed. Similarly, towards the last quarter of the nineteenth century there was an agitation in Dundee against Indian jute manufacturing. However, the agitation did not succeed because Dundee was not very strong. Further, the jute manufacturing in India was in the hands of the Scotts. As regards the coal industry the government extended full support to it in view of the growing demand of the railways for coal.

Swadeshi and Industrial Development. The industrial development in India received a further impetus following launching of Swadeshi Movement in 1905. The Indian nationalist leaders like Dadabhai Naoroji and Ranade felt that the poverty and sufferings of the people of India were due to industrial backwardness of the country. They accused the British Government of deliberately hindering the industrial development of India. To encourage the growth of Indian industries they appealed to the people to buy indigenous goods and to boycott the imported goods. This imparted new enthusiasm to the industrial activities. Not only the number of cotton, jute industries, etc. showed a tremendous increase, but a number of small industries like manufacture of pencils, cutlery, matches, glass, etc. also came into being, even though they could not operate successfully. In 1907, the Tata Iron and Steel Company (TISCO) was set up, which marked the beginning of the modern iron and steel industry in the country.

First World War and Industrial Development. The development of modern industry in India received a new impetus during the First World War. Soon after the outbreak of War the imports from foreign countries, specially enemy countries, stopped to India, which exposed the pitiable dependence of India on foreign imports even for the necessities of life. The inability of Britain to send military supplies over the long overseas route gave a serious setback to the British fighting strength in the East. Therefore, the British leaders were obliged to develop industries in India as a matter of military necessity for the protection of their Eastern empire. Another reason which prompted the English leaders to promote industries in India was that they were keen to gain whole-hearted support of the people of India in their war efforts. They were convinced that they would be able to secure the co-operation of the people of India only if they conceded certain political and economic concessions to them. In the economic sphere they promised to promote industrialisation by all means. Yet another reason which promoted the British to encourage industries in India was that they looked at the Indian industries as a better substitute for the foreign goods, which were fast displacing the British imports.

In 1916, the government appointed an Industrial Commission under Sir Thomas Holland "to examine the whole question of industrial development of India, and to indicate new openings for the profitable employment of Indian capital in commerce and industry and the manner in which the government could usefully give direct encouragement to industrial enterprise." Even before the Industrial Commission could submit its report the government set up an Indian Munitions Board in 1917. The Board was expected "to control and develop Indian resources with special reference to the needs created by the war" and to apply India's manufacturing resources to the purpose of war with a view to reduce demands on shipping. The measures taken by the Board such as (a) direct purchase of India-made articles and materials to meet the needs of army, the civil departments and railways; (b) diversion of all orders from the United Kingdom and elsewhere to manufacturers in India; and (c) assistance to Indian forms in importing industrial plants and technical experts from abroad, greatly contributed to the promotion of Indian industries. The Board also recommended that the measures taken by it to meet the war demands should continue, with some modifications, during the peace times as well. The Board warned that the failure to do so would deprive the Indian capitalists of a number of profitable enterprises, "whilst in the event of war which renders sea transport impossible, India's all-important existing industries will be exposed to the risk of stoppage, her consumers to great hardships and her armed forces to the gravest possible danger."

The Industrial Commission appointed in 1916 submitted its Report in 1918. In its report the Commission recommended that the government should help large-scale organised industries by conducting research and providing economic data and services of experts. For this purpose, it recommended that imperial and provincial industrial and commercial services should be created and an Imperial Department of Stores be set up at Calcutta to control the placing of government orders and contracts. It also recommended establishment of Imperial and Provincial Department of Industries. Above all it insisted on betterment of factory and industrial conditions as well as improvement in transport and freight facilities.

However, the recommendations of the Indian Industrial Commission for rapid industrialisation of the country did not find favour with the government. The process of industrialisation received a further setback under the Montague-Chelmsford Reforms of 1919 which made industries a provincial subject. This naturally hampered the adoption of a comprehensive industrial policy.

It is true that during the war period the cotton and jute mills worked at full capacity and made huge profits. The steel production also considerably increased on account of the cutting off of imports from abroad. The production of some consumer goods also showed a marked increase. Some of the articles like chemicals, mineral acids, cement, cutlery, fertilizers, etc. for which India had so far relied on foreign markets also began to be manufactured in India for the first time. But this industrial progress was only short-lived because soon after the War when threat to the British Empire in Indian disappeared, the British withdrew the concessions from the Indian industries. Thus, we can agree with Prof. Lokanathan that the First World War "beyond affording temporary gains to a few established industries did nothing to set the country firmly on the road to industrialisation". In fact after some time when the industrial competition from England and other Western countries and Japan revived, the Indian industries could not successfully withstand the competition. As a result, the Indian political leaders and businessmen exerted increasing pressure on the government to assist Indian industries. This led to the appointment of the Fiscal Commission in October 1921. The Commission in its report submitted in 1922 recommended 'discriminating protection' to Indian industries.

In accordance with the recommendations of the Fiscal Commission the government set up a Tariff Board to examine the claims of various industries for protection and decided to extend discriminatory protection to thirteen industries such as iron and steel, cotton textiles, paper, matches, sugar, heavy chemical industries, etc. However, even now the government lacked genuine sympathy for rapid industrialisation of the Indian industries. It merely rendered perfunctory assistance to certain industries to enable them to withstand foreign competition for the time being. It certainly did not adopt the policy of protection as an instrument for general economic development. No wonder thereafter the country witnessed only haphazard development of certain industries and there was no general economic development of India as such took place.

Export of British Capital to India. In view of the enormous profits made by the British controlled jute mills during the War (they showed profits of nearly £42 million during four years from 1918-1922) the British capital started flowing steadily to India. This is borne out by the fact that the total British capital investment in India which stood at roughly £400 million before the War reached £1000 million by 1933. This posed a serious threat to some of the vital Indian industries. The things became still worse when the Tariff Board turned down the application of number of Indian industries for protection. In case of iron and steel industries also the protective duties were lowered and subsidies abolished.

The introduction of imperial preferences gave yet another damaging blow to the Indian industries. As a result of the imperial preference the British goods were given an advantage over non-empire products in the Indian market. Likewise the Indian products got an advantage over the non-empire products in the empire market. This policy was adopted with a view to accelerate the process of Indian industrialisation, but actually helped the British industry to compete in the Indian market. India was merely given favoured rates for her raw materials and semi-manufacturers in the British market. This was greatly resented by the Indian industrialists and they succeeded in getting an advance vote from the Legislative Assembly of India against the Trade Agreement. However, despite this the British Government thrust the Trade Agreement regarding Imperial Preferences on India.

Despite the various difficulties and setback, the Indian industries made a considerable progress between 1922 and 1939. As a result, the production of cotton piece goods increased by two and a half times; production of steel ingots increased by nearly eight times; paper production also increased by two and a half times. With regard to sugar India attained self-sufficiency and the production rose by almost twelve times. Similarly, India made considerable progress in other industries like cement, matches, glass, soap, vanaspati, engineering industries, etc. There was an overall four-time increase in the number of factories. What is more significant India became independent of foreign countries for the supply of machinery and other capital goods without which new industries could not be established in India. Despite all this progress and modernisation of industries, India was still far away from the goal of industrialisation.

Second World War and Industrial Development of India

At the commencement of the Second World War the British Government continued to follow the same policy of industrialisation of India and opposed development of heavy industries, owned and managed by the Indians in the country. But after the bombing of British ships and penetration of Japanese in the South Pacific a serious threat was posed to the British Empire. Even the British supply line faced a serious threat of being cut off. As a result, the British and her allies became increasingly dependent on India for supply of their War needs. With this objective in mind the Government of India took a number of measures which provided a fillip to industrial development in India. In 1940, the government set up the Board of Scientific and Industrial Research to tide over the shortage of technicians and skilled workers which were badly needed for further industrial expansion. The Board not only helped in raising necessary technical personnel but also helped in the development of industries like drugs, dyes, lubricants, plastics. As the Indian industrialists could not obtain new plants from Britain and other developed countries due to War, they tried to make optimum use of the existing plants. In other words, though new industries did not spring up the existing industries worked to their full capacity.

The period of war also witnessed the establishment of a number of new industries like ferro-alloys, non-ferrous metal and metal fabricating industries like copper sheets, wires, cables, etc.; mechanical industries like diesel engines, pumps, bicycles, sewing machines, etc.; and chemicals like caustic soda, chlorine, superphosphates, etc. As the raw materials for these industries were not available in the country India had to resort to import of necessary raw materials from foreign countries. Thus, India once again started importing raw materials for its industries after a gap of over a century.

Impact of Industrialisation. Whatever industrialisation of country was permitted by the British during the Second World War was sheerly due to the pressure of circumstances. The British could never reconcile with the idea that India should cease to be a supplier of raw materials and a market for finished products. Hence, they permitted the establishment of only those 'key industries' in India which the needs of War dictated. It deliberately hindered the development of certain industries in India on the plea that what one country was doing the other parts of the Empire should not do. It tried to safeguard the future interest of the British industrialists in India and prevented the development of certain basic industries in India even at the risk of sabotaging the War effort. This period also witnessed further strengthening of the grip of British finance capital over India and a number of giant concerns like Lever Brothers, Dunlop, Imperial Chemicals, etc. set up their subsidiaries in India. The British offered every possible discouragement to the establishment of automobile industry as well as ship-building industry in India.

The industrial growth in India during the War resulted in overuse of existing industrial equipments and plants, which shortened the life of the machinery and presented the problem of replacing the same at an early date.

Again during the War, on account of scarcity conditions, no attention was paid to factors like location, optimum scale of operations, adequate market, availability of raw materials, financial and technical organisation, etc. while setting up new industries. This produced disastrous results in the post-World War period. Yet another adverse effect of the industrial boom during the Second World War period was that the resources of the country were mainly diverted to the production of goods for defence purposes, which inevitably led to fall in the production of consumer goods. This resulted in sharp rise in the prices of consumer goods. The inflationary tendencies set into operation by the War finances further aggravated the problem of high prices. This immensely benefited the industrialists who made fabulous profits while the common people suffered on this account. The scarcity of the various consumer goods and their continuously rising prices forced the government to take necessary measures to check the rise in prices and ensure their fair distribution. However, the government could not implement its policies effectively leading to wide corruption and great hardship to people.

Rise of Capitalist Class

The rise of the capitalist class in India coincided with the establishment of modern industries in the country, even though the process of this rise was quite slow. No doubt even in the earlier period certain large-scale industrial organisations existed in certain localities but the production was carried on by the artisans without superior capitalist direction. In other words, the production was chiefly in the hands of the artisans who directly dealt with the consumers. A strong middle class which forms the backbone of the capitalist system was conspicuously absent.

With the establishment of the rule of the East India Company the indigenous traders and financiers offered their services to the Britishers in various capacities and made enormous profits. These traders obtained necessary financial support from the native merchants and landlords. In other words, they did not face any scarcity of capital till the introduction of modern industries which needed huge capitals. Further, the lack of necessary talent and incentive for investment of money in industries amongst the Indian landed aristocracy also hampered the growth of the capitalist class. The Indians also did not possess necessary credit facilities and lacked organisational skill concerning modern industries. Above all the privileged position enjoyed by the British capitalists and manufacturers which prevented the Indians from setting up industries also obstructed the growth of the Indian capitalist class.

No wonder the English who possessed a good knowledge about the working and the advantages of the capitalist organisation took a lead in investment of capital. In the main they were encouraged to invest capital in India on account of two considerations. Firstly, they hoped to make high profits through these investments. Secondly, they wanted to produce and provide goods necessary for export to foreign countries. During the initial period these investments were confined to plantation industry like tea, coffee, rubber, etc. Subsequently, they invested their capital in jute mills, woollen mills, tanneries, coal mines, big engineering works, banking, shipping and other trading enterprises.

These capital investments by the English left a deep impact on the emergence of the capitalist class in India. Those Indians who came in contact with the foreign entrepreneurs and technicians and watched their working from close quarters were encouraged to fall in their line and they took lead in establishing a number of modern industries like cotton textiles, paper, cement, sugar, jute mills, etc. But it was as a result of the industrial boom during the First World War that the capitalist class in India gained strength and the total Indian capital showed a stupendous rise. The Indian industrialists and capitalists who made huge profits during the War pressed for further industrialisation of the country and looked for new avenues for the investment of their capital. The British did not want the Indian capitalists to flourish and put every possible obstruction in the way of the growth of new Indian companies. It even tried to strangle those Indian industries which had already come into existence. For example, the European owners of collieries forced a number of Indian coal miners in Bengal and Orissa to close down their collieries.

Thus, we find that a strong Indian capitalist class could not develop in India during the British rule on account of the discriminatory policy pursued by the British towards the Indian capitalists. But a small class of capitalists which emerged in the country developed a very hostile attitude towards the British. They extended full support to the nationalists in the hope that they would get better treatment after the country gained independence.

The Indian Economy in the Eighteenth Century

19

We get plenty of information regarding Indian Economy in the 18th century from the works of R.C. Dutt, Burke, P.E. Roberts, R.K. Mukherjee, Dodwell and Sir Richard Temple. We also get valuable information for the same from the 'Report of the Royal Commission on Agriculture in India', 'Report of Famine Commission', 'Imperial Council of Agricultural Research' and 'Report of the Indian Cotton Committee'.

Economic Organisation. The economic organisation of the beginning of the eighteenth century did not differ much from that of early twentieth century India. It was divided into two parts—rural and urban economy. It was a simple domestic form of economic organisation in the rural society; in urban centres it was more of a capitalistic form of economic organisation. It had considerably a better shipping network and much favourable trade balance. It would not be an exaggeration to say that at time India was the "workshop of the world".

Taking into consideration this fact, it cannot be accepted without reservation that "Almost everywhere in India it would appear that from time immemorial, the people have lived in small villages, the mud houses of which are huddled together in a more or less compact area situated in the midst of the fields which provide the means of livelihood to their occupants."

By maintaining low level of the population, it is also argued that though the area available for cultivation per head was greater in the British era, the people did not attempt to add to its wealth by producing more than what they required for their immediate needs. They were apt to rest content with the production of sufficient to eat and drink and the wherewithal to clothe themselves. With this apathy to better life or (ignorance of the value of the wealth) "there could be no agricultural progress and large scale farming was impossible". However, it is difficult to accept the view that the people of India were not rich and they produced the barest needed by them. In fact it was the wealth of India which brought about the influx of the people, including the British, from outside India.

Abul Fazal reports in *Ain-i-Akbari* that "India as a whole, with all its magnitude of extent and the magnitude of its empire unequalled in its climate, its rapid succession of harvest and the equable temperament of its people. Notwithstanding its size it is cultivated throughout. You cannot accomplish a stage nor indeed travel a kos...without being gladdened by the sight of sweet-waters, delightful verdure and enchanting downs. In the autumn and throughout the depth of winter the plains are green and the trees in foliage.... The soil is for the most part arable and of such productive power that the same land is sown each year and in many places three harvests and more are taken in a single twelve months and the vine bear fruits in its first year." It is also supported by European travellers.

Nikitin who visited Bidar in 1470 notices "that the land was laid out in fields, and the ground was well tilled" and the country generally "exceedingly fertile, yielding much food and with great traffic."

De Page remarks that the southern "dominions are well cultivated and very fertile and are provided with quantities of cattle, such as cows, buffaloes, and sheep...the land has plenty of rice and Indian, corn, grains, beans and other kinds of crops which are not sown in our parts; and also an infinity of cotton. Of the grains there is a great quantity because besides being used as food for men, it is also used for horses since there is no other kind of barley and this country has also much wheat and that good."

Barbosa also adds that the Coromandal coast "is very fruitful and abounds in rice, fish-meat, wheat and all vegetables of other kinds are found there", and that "this is best supplied of all the lands in this part of India saving only Cambay".

Palm tree was the, 'dhenu cow' of Malabar and, as Barbosa tells us, kept the people "from any dearth". They produced ten or twelve things needed by the people within the country and had a great demand in foreign markets.

Gujarat was the mine of "indigo" and also "great store of food; scilicet, abundance of wheat, barley, millet, rice, karmes grain, chick peas, lentils and many other kinds of pulses."

Similarly, Sindh was also a "great store of wheat, barley and fish" and Barbosa observed that "this land is luxuriant, fertile, and full of victuals".

Father Monserrate also accounts the same thing: "This Mughal empire is very beautiful and healthy.... On account of the diversity of the climate in different parts it produces many and various types of crops...the farther one goes towards the north, the more similar does one find the staple products to those of Europe.... Rice, wheat, millet and pulses are produced in great quantities.... In many places in the neighbourhood of the Indus flax and hemp are sown.... Indigo and opium are largely grown in the south and bring no small profit to the royal revenues."

The above accounts are not in keeping with the opinions given by the administrators in late nineteenth century. According to them until the British developed "communications and organised trading", the commercial communities had not arisen. The cultivating classes had no incentive beyond what was furnished by a local demands, to produce foodgrains and other agricultural products in excess of their own needs. Though the famine in the later half of the reign of Aurangzeb followed by the revolts might have reduced the quantum of production but not the fertility. We cannot establish for want of statistics of agricultural production but the trade goods indicate that the agriculture was not an unproductive sector of Indian economy. The agricultural production and the vugas' old industry had made India the "workshop of the world" and Indian economy was draining bullion out of foreign economy to make India wealthier. It cannot be denied that the British had inherited a rich country and reduced it to pauperness within a century. Bernier, for example, reported that "the Kingdom of Bengal had a hundred gates open for entrance (of wealth), but not one for departure".

No sooner the Company got political edge in 1757, the prosperity of Bengal declined and the "kingdom" became, in the words of the Court of Directors of the East India Company, "a scene of the most tyrannic and oppressive conduct that ever was known to any age or country". This fate was met by the people of the principalities immediately after these came under the political hegemony of the Company.

The trader, the cultivator, the bureaucrat, the State every one suffered after the establishment of the reign of force of the English traders. A letter written by Warren Hastings to the then Governor of Bengal, Vansittart, is revealing. He wrote, "Many complaints were made against our sepoys on the road, and most of the petty towns and serais (inns) were deserted on our approach, and the shops shut up from the apprehension of the same treatment from us." The petty young clerks of the Company who spent £1500 to £2000 annually and were clothed in linen and fared sumptuously everyday starved the people and made their lives miserable. It was this oppression and not the situation obtaining in the British era which led to the situation where "the cultivator cannot be certain that he will be left in possession of the harvest he had sown, the incentive to put more labour and capital into the land or to cultivate a larger area than is required for the maintenance of himself and his family is looking".

The activities of the Company effected a grievous injury to the manufacturers, and in turn the producers of raw material. The attempt of Mir Kasim to remove the groaning disability over the Indian manufacturers and producers by universal abolition of inland duty was defeated alongwith his removal after the Battle of Buxar. Mir Jafar was again enthroned and exacted presents and the indemnity which, in fact, were the incomes of the people.

Edmund Burke's criticism is self-revealing. He observed, "In all other countries land revenue following the natural course and order of things arises out of commerce. Here, by a mischievous inversion of that order, the whole foreign maritime trade arises from the revenues; these are carried out of the country without producing any thing to compensate so heavy loss."

This devastation continued in spite of severe criticism. The wealth drained out of India brought decadence in the Indian economy. As stated in the chapter on Industry, the British policy made a deadly assault on the Indian handicrafts which had not only been famed the world over and formed an important source of income but also an avenue of employment to the surplus labour. The handicraft was undoubtedly a small enterprise in terms of figure, but it was the spirit of whole economy. It provided the jobs to the surplus and averted pressure on the land.

The protective policy doomed the cloth industry. The *laissez faire* witnessed the decay of Indian metal industry. Industries of salt-peter, glass-making and paper-making were the worst hit. The Indian shipping industry was discouraged by many restrictions imposed by the Court of Directors of the Company. India, whose ships had once sailed fair and wide, ceased to have a good merchant fleet. Therefore, the reverse trade had taken place after the beginning of British rule. The industries started declining, the cities started shrinking and the pressure on the land was increasing. It was this policy which put the vicious circle of poverty operating in India. "Of the pressure of population as the soil, of poverty and its concomitant indebtedness, of illiteracy, of conditions unfavourable to health", were the natural outcome. This is the true story of sub-holdings, small holdings and indebtedness, the two great evils of the agrarian economy in the modern times which continued unabated.

Britain was not prepared to make the cultivation economical lest the consumer in Britain pay for that. The Industrial Revolution and the independence of colonies in America forced

Britain to depend upon India for the raw materials as well as foodgrains to feed the rising industrial population. The recurring feature of food and raw materials in Britain and revenue of the government on the other hand, increased the unrest among the masses. The great resurgence of 1857 had already made them cautious. The political agitations taking an organised shape in the form of the Indian National Congress (1885) further scared them. These were the reasons which inaugurated a new era in the agricultural development. It was a "great contribution" of the British regime to agrarian economy. This can be understood from the British Revenue Policy.

British Revenue Policy

From the ancient times, as mentioned earlier, agriculture was the most vital economic activity. It provided food to the society and land revenue to the government. There were varied kind of systems prevailing in India. When the British obtained Dewani in 1765, they found that the peasantry, *i.e.* ryot cultivated their land. They paid a fixed share (which varied from time to time) to the collectors of revenue. The collector, in turn, deposited the collected revenue with the Central Government after deducting his approved expenditure. After the Central Government had weakened and the regional officers established themselves as the *de facto* rulers of their respective jurisdiction, their junior officers also behaved in the same way. As a result of the continuing chaotic situation, the collectors of revenue became Zamindars. They continued to collect the revenue and maintain law and order after the Company became Dewan. The Company simply appointed British supervisors in different Zamindarees.

In 1772, Hastings designated them as Collectors and assigned a district to each of them. The District Collectors of present originated first time in his system.

In 1774, the European Collectors were, however, replaced by provincial councils, set up in each district.

A Revenue Board was also instituted in 1780 which regulated the revenue collection.

In 1772, after taking over the administration in his hands, Warren Hastings farmed out the land to the highest bidders for five years. This system was called "quinquennial settlement". But this system failed because the bidders could not recover the paid amount and the peasantry was put under tyranny.

Romesh Dutt observed that as a consequence of this policy "the country grounds were put under the economic tyranny; the revenues failed once more; the system was introduced not to ameliorate the economic conditions of the rural people rather to squeeze out the last drop which left behind it a dark trail of misery, insurrections and famines in Bengal, Benaras and Awadh". It was the exploiting spirit which threw the farmers into chronic indebtedness and the "descendants of old houses found their eatables pass into the hands of moneylenders and speculators from Calcutta; widows and minor proprietors saw their peaceful subjects oppressed by rapacious agents appointed from Calcutta". The land was deserted by the peasantry and the bidders lost courage to speculate in the farming. The British agents who were appointed with a hope to derive increased revenue also did not prove successful. As P.E. Roberts has pointed out there was great loss of revenue due to the misappropriation and mismanagement of the British agents.

Unrest in the Rural Areas. Contrary to it, this inflamed serious disturbances in the various parts of the Dewani. It was confessed by Warren Hastings, who said that "the administration of the province (Benaras) is misconducted and the people oppressed, trade discouraged and the revenue in danger of a rapid decline from the evident appropriation of its means". This squeeze and misery of the peasantry was one of the bones of bitter contention between the executive and the Supreme Court set up under Regulating Act of 1773.

Macpherson, the successor of Warren Hastings, tried to avert this situation. In 1786, he divided the Dewani into 35 (reduced to 23 in 1787) districts. He made the Collectors responsible for making the settlement and collection of revenue. They were controlled by the Board of Revenue. The Chief Saristadar was appointed to ensure proper maintenance of records. Though the District Collectors "laboured to establish a just and humane collection of the land revenue" the corrupt machinery failed to derive desired results. The corruption of the Company's servants had created an alarming situation in political spheres in Britain. Influential leaders like Edmund Burke exhorted that a check was necessary on the Company's activities in India to save democratic institutions in England. Concerned with the falling volume of land revenue, and anxious of curbing increasing discontentment among the farmers, the Company instructed the new Governor General, Lord Cornwallis that the land revenue "be handled leniently, a moderate tax, regularly and punctually collected". It was also necessary to encourage cultivation and make available grain to the rising industrial population in Britain, as also to divert the artisans from manufacturing to the farming.

Land System. Before the British rule in India, the land belonged to the peasantry, and the government received a proportion of the produce.

According to Radha Kumud Mukherjee, "The soil in India belonged to the tribe or its subdivision—the village community, the clan or the brotherhood settled in the village—and never was considered as the property of the King."

The king had the right to share the produce as was fixed from time to time. So far the British were collecting this revenue and they had introduced modification in the procedure and share of collection. The squeezing nature had created both political and economic hazards. As Buchanan reported about the district of Dinajpore in Bengal:

> The natives allege that, although they were often squeezed by the Moghal officers, and on all occasions were treated with the utmost contempt, they preferred suffering these evils to the British mode that has been adopted of selling their lands when they fall in arrears, which is a practice they cannot endure. Besides, bribery went a great way on most occasions, and they allege that, bribes included they did not actually pay one-half of what they do now.

In those conditions, "neither native nor European agriculturist", reported Bishop Heber, "can thrive at the present rate of taxation. Half the gross produce of the soil is demanded by Government."

Lord Cornwallis was least concerned with the problems of the peasantry. He introduced reforms in land revenue to achieve twin aims of the Company policy. As discussed in the chapter on Trade, the Company aimed at increasing demand of British manufactures in India and export of raw materials such as raw silk, wool, cotton, indigo, etc. to British. Their policy had made the commerce the pivot of all the activities of the executive and Indian economy. It is clear from the fact that the "commercial department" had become more important than the "general department". It was the reducing importance of the general department which brought a steep fall in the collection of land revenue and increased the chances of the agricultural economy.

Permanent Settlement. Cornwallis sought to bring about a stability in the agricultural economy. He tried, first, to bring a continuity by making decennial (*i.e.* ten years) settlement in place of annual settlement. In March 1793, he introduced the famous "Permanent Settlement". It was not as benevolent as Romesh Dutt said that "if the prosperity and happiness of a nation be the criterion of wisdom and success; Lord Cornwallis' Permanent Settlement of 1793 is the wisest and most successful measure which the British nation has ever adopted in India". Though the "permanent settlement...helped to make the province the wealthiest and most flourishing in India". It was temporary and at the cost of millions of peasantry and Indian economy. No step can be considered good if it does not hold good for general people. Rather it was the perpetuation of exacting spirit of the Company Government. The land revenue collection had become the severest and exceeded in volume from all times of the past. It had increased from Rs. 14,245,461 in 1728 to Rs. 26,800,989 in 1790-91. "The British administrators with an eye over their investment, oblivious of the interest of ryots, preferred this peak collection and make it final and permanent."

Landed Aristocracy. The "Permanent Settlement" also created a landed aristocracy which was untraditional to the ethos of the Indian society. It was to carry not only the "dirty work" of the economic imperialism, and to become the pillars of the strength of that imperialism, but also to be the bulwarks against the tides of revolts against the foreign rule. It was to play the role in the rural community which the business community played in the urban centres. It may be noted that it was the business community mainly Jagat seths—who helped not only in establishing but also perpetuating the pax Britannica over the Third World. It was this Permanent Settlement which obtained much needed "popularity and stability to the British Government"—which made the impoverishing rural community's future in India uncertain. It created "the landed institution of England among the natives of Bengal". As the landed aristocracy had withstood against the surging revolutionary thought in Europe, these landed institutions in Bengal were to be the bulwarks against the nationalist thought in India.

Impoverished Rural Community. The "Permanent Settlement" led to the grant of lands to those who could afford to invest money, effect realization of exorbitant rents and then pay the revenue regularly. They were given free hand by the government in realising the land rent. They proved more unscrupulous than the British agents. They realised more than £13 million as land rent while they paid only £3-3/4 million as land revenue to the government. There was no measure for the relief of the peasantry. They continued to suffer for more than six decades when the indigo-labour revolts attracted the government to the impoverished ryot and the Bengal Land Act was passed in 1859. Its abusive character is substantiated with the fact that "Permanent Settlement" was confined to Bengal and in other provinces the land reforms were affected with a view to raise the revenue.

William Bentinck and Revenue Settlement. Next to Cornwallis, Bentinck's name is important in bringing a change in rural economy. The East India Company had ceased to be a commercial company with the revision of its Charter in 1833. It was henceforward to be concerned with only administration and providing "Law, order and good government". Bentinck was "the true representative" of the "era of Catholic emancipation and Parliamentary reforms". He brought a revenue settlement in North-Western Province. In that Province, the revenue system had proved a complete failure. Romesh Dutt observed that the inquiries sought for preparing a record of rights to land in the Province could not be obtained. The revenue officers could not assess the correct volume of produce and, therefore, the government demand of over 80% of the (land) rent was severe and impracticable. Bentinck was not prepared to put up with this harshness. Therefore, he made new settlement by enacting the Regulation in 1833. The government demand was fixed at 66 per cent or two-thirds of the gross rental. The settlement was done for thirty years. The new regulation was, however, somewhat harsh in granting arbitrary powers to the settlement officers. Since the company was more interested in increasing revenue, the over zealous settlement officers defeated the aim of being humane in making the demands. They also tried to eliminate the intermediary to avoid expenses on them. This abuse was rectified in 1844 and he issued "directions for settlement officers" to be more humane.

The excessive and impracticable demand of 66 per cent, however, remained in force. It was only in 1855 that these demands were reduced to 50 per cent through "Saharanpur Rule". In this way, the peasantry got relief from exactions of over-assessment after almost a century and the demands were limited to one-half of the rental or the net produce of the soil. This revenue system was later on extended in all the provinces outside the areas of "Permanent Settlement".

Inhuman Revenue Policy. The revenue policy was not, however, as humane as has been described. The increasing demand of revenue had made cultivation uneconomical. As a result, the desertion from agriculture was not only improving the rural economy but also intensifying the political danger. Besides, the Company could not export much needed foodgrains to Britain. Therefore, the Revenue Policy was formulated to achieve twin objectives. Firstly, the policy should not make the revenue static. Secondly, the revenue should not be much exacting that they should make the agriculture uneconomical. It was necessary for preventing spreading discontentment among the rural masses and also encourage agricultural production to meet the rising demands of the industrial population of Britain.

We can say that Bentinck and his successors had foresight than a "true representative" of liberalism.

Inhuman Administration. The collection was the most barbarian. The following observation of Romesh Dutt explains the barbarian approach of the administration:

> Keeping a man in the sun; preventing him going to meals or other calls of nature; confinement; preventing his cattle from going to pasture; quartering a peon on him; the use of kittee anundal, *i.e.* tying a man down in a bent position squeezing the crossed fingers, pinches slops, blows with fist or whip, running up and down; bursting the ears; making a man sit with brickbats behind his knees; putting a low caste man on his back; striking two defaulters heads; or tying them by the back hair placing in the stocks; tying by the hair to a donkey's or a buffalo's tail; placing a necklace of bones or other degrading or disgusting materials round the necks: and occasionally, though rarely more severe discipline....

This approach brought about a drastic change in the approach of the landlords as well. The community feeling was replaced by materialism and individualism which did a great harm to the rural society than good. It was not also good for the government. The resurgence of 1857 was intensified due to this exacting revenue policy and but for other "loyalists", the suppression of peasantry might have been difficult. The revenue reforms of Bentinck and his successors had already alleviated the grievances of peasantry to a large extent.

As a result of this, a great change took place.

Firstly, the anti-industrial policy had increased the pressure on land and the people were left with no other alternative but to on agricultural yields. As a result of this pressure, the land-plots were divided into smaller holding.

Secondly, it led to stagnation and deterioration of agriculture. There was low yields and the labour was going waste.

Thirdly, the increasing burden of the land-rent, had also made the cultivation of lands uneconomical. Therefore, a major part of cultivable areas turned into jungles.

Fourthly, the landed aristocracy gave birth to a class of non-cultivating rent receivers which was contrary to the social ethos of Indian society.

Fifthly, the small holdings and landlordism was the direct cause of increasing indebtedness of the rural population. The agricultural debt was estimated at £675 million in 1931. Another report of the Agricultural Credit Department found the debt exceeding Rs. 1800 crores or £1,350 million by 1937. This indebtedness was the crux of the agrarian economy and presents the true picture of the impoverishing rural population.

Sixthly, the indebtedness made the moneylenders all the more powerful. The speculators had their heyday. It was the latter's dominance that the pieces of agricultural products started slumping down to the uneconomical level during the harvesting period and touched the highest limits during the lean years. The peasants super-imposed by the debt burden had to sell their products at the cheapest rates and later on to purchase at exorbitantly high rates.

This situation was favourable to the traders as also the food products could be made available to the British population at cheaper rates. It was the desertion from the cultivation and low yields which forced the British to think about the agricultural improvements, which in fact was the real contribution of the British to the agricultural economy.

Irrigation. One of the issues which is intimately connected with agriculture is that of irrigation. The importance of irrigation for Indian agriculture is tremendous because the Indian agriculture is mainly dependent on monsoons or rainfall. During the rule of the East India Company, the British paid very little attention towards irrigation. No doubt, the old irrigation works like the Eastern and Western Jamuna canals and the Ganga canals and dams in the South were repaired and kept in working order, but no new irrigation projects were undertaken. It was only in the wake of the repeated famines towards the close of the nineteenth century that the British were compelled to pay attention to the irrigation projects. In 1901, Lord Curzon appointed a Commission on Irrigation. This Commission not only recommended the extension of the productive and protective irrigation, but also prepared a scheme of irrigation works for the next twenty years. The Commission also recommended the setting up of the Irrigation Department, which was actually created.

Under the Government of India Act, 1919, irrigation was made a provincial subject. As a result, the provinces paid great attention to the extension of irrigation works. A large number of canals, wells, tubewells, dams, tanks, etc. were constructed by the different provincial governments within their jurisdiction. Some of the prominent irrigation works which were created during the next few decades including the Sutlej Valley Project, the Sukkur Barrage in Sindh, the Kaveri Reservoir and Mettur Project, the Sarda Oudh Canal in Uttar Pradesh, the Lloyd Dam in Bombay, etc.

After the dawn of political independence in India the Central Governement co-operated with the State Governments in the extension of the old irrigation projects and the construction of many new hydroelectric works.

Famine Relief. In the first order, famine relief was the contribution of the modern times. Agriculture in India from unknown times to this day is dependent on the monsoons. The failure of the monsoon has been causing as much devastation as the overraining destroys the crops. This recurrent havoc, overtaking the rural population, was not as severe in ancient times.

Rather Megasthenes, the Greek Ambassador at the Court of Chandragupta Maurya records that Famine has never visited India and there has never been a general scarcity in the supply of nourishing food.

But from the medieval times we have been knowing the severe famines. There was a severe famine in many parts of the country during the reign of Mohammed Tughlaq. That famine had almost destabilised the Tughlaq dynasty itself.

The next appalling famine occurred in the reign of Shah Jahan. Deccan and Gujarat were hard hit. "The inhabitants of these regions were reduced to direst extremity. Life was offered for a loaf, but none would buy; rank was to be sold for a cake, but none cared for it...." It was this famine which went a long way in weakening the Mughal Empire.

Thereafter, we find a cycle of these famines. It is on record that during the first quarter of the nineteenth century six famines occurred which took a toll of 50,00,000 persons. In the last quarter of the same century, there were almost eighteen famines which took a toll of lives between 1,50,00,000 and 2,60,00,000. In addition to these losses due to famines the epidemics which followed in the wake of the famines also took heavy toll of life. The severity of the sufferings of the people was nonetheless great. The Mughal State had not made any systematic and long-term planning to provide relief in the event of these horrible famines. The British, on the other hand, were more interested in revenue and dividends. Therefore, the rural population had to suffer out of the State apathy towards them.

As stated earlier the recurrence of famines was a great danger both to social harmony and political stability. After the British established their empire the commerce became the source of their strength, the famine was to be gravest danger to this commerce. Therefore, the British sought a long-term strategy to overcome this "plague" for the commercial activities which was eating both the raw materials and the labourers. Rocked by the continuous famines, the British Government appointed a Famine Commission in 1880. The Commission made valuable suggestions to deal with such situations. It recommended that during the times of famine the taxes should be suspended or remitted; food and medicines should be distributed; work should be provided to the able-bodied men; the aged and the infirm people may be provided with doles.

On the basis of these recommendations of the Famine Commission, the Government adopted Famine Code of 1883. Under this Code, a Famine Relief and Insurance Fund was created. After the introduction of decentralization under the Government of India Act, 1919, it was specifically enjoined on the Provincial Governments to contribute a definite sum for the expenditure on famine. This practice is still followed and it has become one of the cardinal duties of the modern government. However, this was not the solution of the problem. The British were serious about bringing a permanent solution. It was on this context that the British started scientific experiments for the improvement of the agricultural economy.

Agriculture and Scientific Methods

The eulogy about themselves that their rule brought about agricultural development is, however, meaningful only in the application of scientific knowledge. It was the British Government which applied the fundamental sciences of agriculture to soil. It was the inauguration of that policy which ultimately ushered in the era of "Green Revolution". Year 1898 is the landmark in this development.

Lord Curzon became the Viceroy of India in 1898. It was during his viceroyalty that scientific experimentation emerged as a major source of agricultural development. The intensive and painstaking efforts of the agricultural scientists revolutionized the entire agricultural outlook. The process of creation and adoption of new technology through the agency of research and education brought to light a whole set of new inputs in the form of equipment, fertilizers, improved crop varieties, and better seeds. These new inputs had a great impact on the area and yield of crops during the British regime in India. It was not all for welfare of the rural population of India. Rather it was, as has been explained below, for the welfare of the population of Britain.

Position before 1898. Earlier agricultural research was hampered in every way for want of funds and men. The Crown Government of India had been encouraging agricultural production to meet the increasing demand in Britain. F.G. Sly, the acting Inspector General of Agriculture in India in 1905 noted:

> The large dairy industry of western India is the result of the Kirkee Dairy Farm; Assam can claim to have introduced the very important Potato Crop of the hill tracts; the result of Poona experiments has been to introduce certain cheap oilcakes as manures for sugarcane; the Central Provinces

have helped Messrs Shah Wallace and Co. to extend cotton cultivation in one tract, with the result that the local purchases expended from 625 to 25,000 bales in 6 years; they have also introduced important market gardening under sewage at Nagpur; a good American variety of maize has ousted a bad local variety over a considerable tract in Punjab; the potato crop around Burdwan is the result of experiments at the Burdwan Farm; the Agricultural Department of the United Provinces has introduced a good variety of wheat into Oudh which is now grown on a very large scale; the very important garden cultivation around Cownpur is the result of teaching the value of sewage; the Department has also popularised iron roller sugarcane mills.

He also expressed the hope that "hundreds of more and larger results will be obtained, if the Department is equipped on a scale adequate to deal with the problems presented to it".

Though the occurrence of famines highlighted the necessity for an improvement in agricultural methods, the agricultural departments were generally more concerned with statistical work and also to develop a machinery to withstand the hazards of famines. The government did not care for training the personnel enabling them to apply scientific methods.

Organisation of Agricultural Research. The successive Famine Commission in 1880, 1898 and 1900 stressed upon the need for agricultural research to overcome the mounting problem. The Commission of 1901 emphasized that "the steady application to agricultural problems of expert research is the crying necessity of the time". It led to thorough reorganisation of the Department of Agriculture.

Establishment of an Agricultrual Research Institute at Pusa in the Darbhanga district, Bihar in 1903 marked the beginning of systematic agricultural research in India. It was equipped with laboratories, an experimental farm and a cattle farm. An agricultural college was also attached to it in 1908. The Pusa Institute was expected to:

(1) initiate programmes of agricultural research;

(2) evolve better methods and better varieties of crops; and

(3) serve as model for extension of agricultural education in different parts of the country.

An All India Board of Agricultue was also set up in 1905 to co-ordinate the research and extension programmes. But the Board ceased functioning after agriculture became a stae subject. As a result, a Department of Agriculture (now evolved into Ministry of Agriculture) was created in each province, and colleges were instituted at Poona, Kanpur, Lyallpur, Coimbatore, Sabour and Mandalay. Each province was divided into circles, each circle headed by Deputy Director of Agriculture. He was primarily responsible for the management of the experimental research, seed and demonstration farms. He was also responsible for educating the farmers and distributing seeds and implements among them. These Departments and Institutes went a long way in applying scientific research in increasing agricultural production in India.

After the All India Board of Agriculture had ceased functioning there was no co-ordinating body. The Royal Commission on Agriculture, 1928 emphasised that "agricultural development is so vital to the prosperity of India that it is inconceivable that the Government of India should divest themselves of all responsibility for it". The Commission observed that the Central Government should continue encouraging research and supply of information to the State Departments of Agriculture. In the absence of co-ordination, there would not only be duplication but also their efficiency would be seriously curbed.

Therefore, the government constituted a new organisation known as Imperial Council of Agricultural Research. The Council was to promote, guide and co-ordinate agricultural research in other parts of the British Empire and in foreign countries. The Council did not exercise any administrative control over the imperial or provincial research institutions. It was an advisory body. But it played a very important role. It provided sound information about soils, crops and animals on the basis of which solutions to the confronting problems were found. It also subsidised a number of village projects applying the results of research in actual farming practices as far as possible. These were the efforts which increased acreage under improved varieties. The government, however, was more concerned for those items which were of great need of the Britons rather than the poor of the country. The area under improved varieties for the crop which produced for export, such as cotton, wheat, jute, groundnut and sugar cane increased by 22.7, 11.9, 14.1, 10.3 and 7.2 per cent respectively; whereas in case of those crops which met the needs of poor in India such as rice, gram, jowar and barley it increased only by 1.1, 0.8, 0.5, 0.4 per cent respectively.

The Council also encouraged investigation in different varieties suitable for high and low lying areas, resistant to flood, draught and saline conditions or to the attacks of particular insect pests and resistant to particular diseases, were produced. The evolution of purple-pigmented variety solved the menace of wild-rice weed which was indistinguishable from rice. It helped in controlling wheat rust, which causes widespread devastation to the wheat crop in the country. Above all, this research set the ball moving for better prospects in agriculture. Again, however, the emphasis was more on crops of commercial importance.

Crop Committees. A number of self-contained commodity committees were constituted for intensive research, marketing and development of important commercial crops. The Indian Central Cotton Committees was constituted in 1921 on the recommendation of the Indian Cotton Committee. It was concerned with the improvement of cotton marketing and the prevention of malpractices both by legislative measures and by constructive action. It also acted as an advisory committee for promoting the development of cotton growing in different provinces. Agricultural and technological research on cotton was its special care performed under its direct control and at its own technological laboratory in Bombay. The Indian Central Cotton Committee was, in short, concerned with all questions arising out of cotton growing from field to factory. The marked success achieved by it encouraged the government to constitute another committee known as the Jute Committee in 1936. Other committees like lac, sugar cane, tobacco, oilseeds, coconut and arecanut were also formed to improve production of these important goods.

The intensive research helped in improving varieties of crops and new methods of cultivation as well as fertilizers, implements and seeds. Intensive soil analysis and measures for the protection of crops against insects and pests were also successfully undertaken.

Agricultural Production. The practical achievements of the research can be judged only in the light of progress in agricultural efficiency and production. Besides, the British policy had already converted Indian economy into agricultural, *i.e.* agriculture had become the base of all economic activities. The crops of India mainly fell into two groups: (i) food crops, *i.e.* those which were primarily for human consumption and (ii) non-food crops, *i.e.* primarily intended for industrial and commercial purposes. The following table shows the area under food and non-food crops between 1898 and 1946-47.

Area under Food and Non-Food Crops in India

(in million of acres)

Year	Under Food Crops	Under Non-Food Crops	Total	Percentage Food Crops	Percentage Non-Food Crops
1901-02	188	57	245	85	15
1913-14	190	42	232	82	18
1927-28	192	45	247	81	19
1938-39	152	122	281	56	44
1940-41	198	50	248	80	20
1945-46	168	114	292	60	40
1946-47	182	117	299	55	45

The above table shows crops falling under non-food group were given high priority from the beginning of the twentieth century up to the dawn of independence of India. The increase in area under food-crops during the year 1940-41 had been due to the increased demand created by the war. The government formulated its policy for meeting the immediate exigencies of the war-time demand and adjusting the agricultural sector to the overall requirements of a war-time economy. In this way, it were once again the war conditions which stressed the need for improving food crops.

The New Pattern of Trade 20

In his *Industry, Trade and Currency,* U.N. Ghoshal has given a clear picture about the new pattern of trade in India in an excellent manner. Added to this *A Historical Disquisition Concerning India* by Dr. Robertson, *Commercial Relations between India and England* by Balakrishna, *History of England in the Eighteenth Century* by Lecky, *The Economic Development of India under the East India Company* by K.N. Chaudhuri and *Some Aspects of India's Foreign Trade* by Durga Prasad are very useful to know more about the 'New Pattern of Trade'.

Principles and Trends of Trade. The Indian trade, even in the Mauryan times, was based on very sound principles. They had determined that "only after clothing and feeding your own people, then of your surplus abundance give to the foreigners and import free to toil useful articles and seeds not easily available while shutting out articles which are harmful".

Indian export since then consisted of cotton manufacturers, dye stuffs, silk, muslin, spices cutlery, metal wares, sugar, perfumes, cosmetics, sandalwood, teak, ivory work, animal skins, etc.

The chief articles of import were bullion, precious stones, wooden goods, wines, horses and minerals.

India was also engaged in re-export after working on silk and ivory imported from China and Africa respectively.

Therefore, the Indian traders and manufacturers also linked the East and West. Since India was mainly the exporter of manufactured goods, it would not be an exaggeration if we say that India was the "workshop of the world". It enjoyed all the benefits such as employment opportunities to its people and favourable balance of trade. Though accurate figures are not available but remarks in the book such as by Pliny substantiate that there was "no year in which India did not drain the Roman Empire of 550 million sesterces (equal to one and half crores of rupees) giving back her own wares in exchange, which were sold at fully 100 times their prime cost".

Dr. Robertson also made the same assessment, "In all ages, gold and silver particularly the latter, have been the commodities exported with the greatest profit to India. In no part of the earth do the natives depend so little upon foreign countries, either for the necessaries or luxuries of life. The blessings of a favourable climate and a fertile soil augmented by their own ingenuity, afford them whatever they desire. In consequence of this, trade with them has always been arrived on in one uniform manner, and the precious metals have been given in exchange for their peculiar production, whether of nature or art."

Invasions from the times of Mahmud Ghazni and internecine warfare among the principalities within the country created political instability. This political instability might have affected the trade, at times even might have come to a naught, the commercial activities, however, never suffered irreparable loss by such political instability.

Marco Polo who visited India in 1271-1274 wrote that India had the reputation of one of the chief markets of Asia.

Ibn Batuta, Nicolo De Conti (1420-1444), and Athanasins Nikitin (1468 A.D.) also contributed to the same opinion.

Besides, the Southern India remained almost unaffected when there was political instability in Northern India. Southern India came under the guns only after the Muhammaden rulers had established themselves in Northern India. Therefore, it cannot be said that Indian trade could have come to a standstill.

The establishment of Mughal rule created the atmosphere for accelerated growth of trade but they gave in this opportunity to the Europeans. Till then, Balkrishna tells us that "India was the repository organ for the circulation and distribution of moneys and commodities of the commercial system of the world; it was the sea wherein all the rivers of trade and industry flowed and thus profusely enriched its inhabitants." Powerful merchants like Hamilton observed that the commerce of India is the commerce of the world and "they knew that he who can exclusively control it is the dictator of Europe". The British policy not only controlled Indian commerce, but also systematically, made the commerce of Britain, the commerce of the world. This policy changed the nature of trade of India.

Indian goods also had a great demand in the European markets. The Europeans had rather become "addicted" to those goods. Besides, trading in Indian goods had been a source of huge profit to the European traders. Rise of Ottoman Empire and "crusades" between the Christianity and Islam blocked the land routes between Indian and European markets. The export of Indian goods got suspended harming both European traders and consumers. Besides religious and political considerations, it were the material considerations which prompted with European merchants to finance the adventurers to discover sea-routes to India. Therefore, the commerce was one of the principle motives which brought British to India and it was their entry which finally affected a revolutionary change in the pattern of Indian trade.

Trade with Europe. The Portuguese adventurers were the first Europeans who came to India to re-establish trade relations between India and the European markets which had suffered after the rise of the Ottoman Empire. They discovered the sea-route to India and replaced the Arabs who had the monopoly of commerce with India. The Dutch, the French and the British followed them to reap the huge profits of the Eastern trade. Mughal Emperors granted them concessions which gave them an edge both over the Arabs and the Indian traders. Thereafter, the Europeans in general, and the British in particular, became the only link between the Indian manufacturers and the foreign buyers. It was the first opportunity to be utilized not in the interests of the Indian manufacturers or Indian economy but in the interests of European manufacturers. They started replacing the Indian goods by selling their own goods, of course, with

Indian mark. It was the first trade tactics which was going to change the pattern of foreign trade of India.

After 1707, India again faced a phase of serious political instability due to the decline of Mughal Empire. The European merchants though helped in increasing the volume of Indian trade but Indian fabrics had "plagued the British and European market".

As Lecky writes, "At the end of the seventeenth century great quantities of cheap and graceful Indian calicoes, muslins, and chintzes were imported in England, and they found such favour that the woollen and silk manufacturers were seriously alarmed." It was not conducive to the British manufacturers who had started emerging by selling their products in different countries due to the replacement of the Arab and Indian traders by the Europeans, including the British. They forced, as Lecky says, "Parliament to pass in 1700 and in 1701, absolutely prohibiting, with a very few specified exceptions, the employment of printed or dyed calicoes in England, either in dress or furniture, and the use of any printed or dyed goods of which cotton formed any part." "It was made", he further informs, "penal for any woman to wear a dress made of Indian calico. In 1779, a lady was fined £200 at the Guild Hall because it was proved that her handkerchief was of French cambric." Fearing this glut of the best quality of Indian fabrics available then at cheap rates, the emerging textile manufacturers in Britain pressed also on the East India Company to bring about a change in their policy which could be conducive to the growth of British Textile Industry. In 1720, the British Parliament also prohibited the use of Indian calicoes in Britain and even its re-export from Britain in third country. Reversing their earlier policy, the Company instead started flooding the Indian markets with bounty-fed exports of cheap machine manufactured goods so as to deprive the Indian industry of even the domestic market. This could be possible for the Company because it had got a monopoly of foreign trade due to misconceived policy of the Mughal Emperors who had granted concessions exclusively to the Europeans. The Firman of 1713 had exempted only the Company from the duties on the goods it traded within and without the country. It was also this policy which enriched the Company and enabled it to obtain political power in India and invest in their metropolitan industries.

Policy of the East India Company. After the Company obtained authority in 1757, its government increased export duties on Indian goods and decreased that duty on the imported goods from Britain. The table on the next page is self-explanatory.

The high duties imposed upon the Indian manufactured goods were sufficient to push them out of the competition. It was made easier after "the import duties on the British manufactures has been reduced to 2½ per cent *ad valorem*, and many of the staple articles admitted free of duty" in India. As the last figures in the following table indicate, the export duty was minimum only on the raw materials. Therefore, the traders could easily purchase the cotton and export it to their country and import manufactured goods. It was this policy which ruined Indian industry and the industrial workers fell back upon the agriculture. As a consequence, the foodgrains were going to replace the manufactured goods in the Indian foreign trade.

"The corn of India has been transported at innumerable rates upon government lines, in order that the food of the (British) people might be cheapened." It was not an act of a welfare state. Rather it was a deliberate attempt to make Indian economy subservient the British economy. Otherwise they should have adopted "the older policy of the(ir) country", as Lecky tells us, which prohibited "absolutely the exportation of corn, but with the increased production of agricultural interest...free exportation was permitted as long as the home price did not exceed fifty-three shillings and four pence a quarter". Thus, British corn was exported only in the times of abundance to avoid ruining of agricultural interests in their country by the violent fluctuations of prices in good and bad harvests. In India, there was no surplus food. Therefore, the brunt of high prices of food was borne by the Indians because export of raw materials and foodgrains from India was encouraged firstly, to feed the rising industries of Britain stimulated by the industrial revolution and secondly, to fill in

TABLE: Duty Imposed upon the Goods Exported from India

Articles	1812			1813			1814			1819			1832		
	£	s	d	£	s	d	£	s	d	£	s	d	£	s	d
Canes	68	6	3	81	2	11	62	10	0	50	0	0	30	0	0
Coir Mats	68	6	8	129	16	8	125	0	0	75	0	0	30	0	0
Cotton Goods on Every 100 of Value	27	6	8	35	9	2	32	10	0	37	10	0	37	10	0
Calicoes	68	6	8	81	2	11	62	10	0	67	10	0	10	0	0
Manufactured Articles of Cotton	27	6	8	32	9	2	32	10	0	50	0	0	20	0	0
Hair and Goat's Wool Manufacture	68	6	8	81	2	11	62	0	0	67	10	0	30	0	0
Wool or Cotton Wool	0	16	11	0	16	11	0	16	11	0	8	7	0	5	10

the blank in exports created by a fall in the exports of manufactured goods. Special attempts were made to encourage the production and export of commercial crops such as tea, jute, wheat, and rice, etc. The nature of agriculture changed from subsistence farming to the growing of money crops such as jute, cotton, tea, etc. Thus, their policy brought about fundamental changes in the pattern of trade after having retained its undisturbed character for thousands of years. The policy of the Company systematically replaced the traditional export of manufactured goods to raw materials.

Ruin of Industry. Though the volume of Indian exports and imports more than quadrupled, yet as a result of the policy of the Company Government the commodity composition and direction of trade had undergone a phenomenal change. British influence, both political and economic, appears to have played a vital part in the transition of India's trade from a traditional to a so-called "modern pattern", and to have introduced the features which it was going to retain for more than a hundred years.

Precise figures are not available for the trade volume of whole of India from 1757 onwards. The table below indicates the volume of trade in merchandise only from Bengal.

It reveals nevertheless many a points. The Indian exports registered a rise of about 300 per cent within 40 years after the monopoly of the Company over trade with India was repealed by the Charter Act of 1813. But this was not conducive to the Indian interests. It negated the ancient principle of India's foreign trade. It can be understood only after taking into consideration the fluctuation in the share of the goods exported.

TABLE: Merchandise

(in million rupees)

Year	Export	Import
1814-15	68.3	11.3
1821-22	109.4	59.2
1828-29	111.29	53.63
1839-40	170.6	66.5
1845-46	170.0	91.0
1850-51	181.0	115.0
1854-55	183.0	124.0

In the year 1814, the Indian exports consisted of indigo (an industrial dye), piece goods, raw silk, raw cotton, opium, sugar, spices, oilseed and cotton. The following table indicates the declining share of the manufactured goods and increasing share of the raw materials exported from India.

TABLE: Indian Exports during 1814-1857

Year	Indigo	Piece Goods	Raw Silk	Cotton	Opium	Sugar
1814-15	20	14.3	13.3	8.0	N.A.	3.0
1828-29	27	11.0	10.0	15.0	17.0	4.0
1834-35	15	7.0	8.0	21.0	25.0	2.0
1839-40	26	5.0	7.0	20.0	10.0	7.0
1850-51	10	4.0	4.0	12.7	34.1	4.3
1857-58	6.1	2.9	2.9	15.6	22.71	4.3

The change in the commodity composition of Indian trade was brought about by arbitrarily fixing low prices of raw materials and high export duty on the manufactured goods. The prices became innumerative and discouraged their manufacturing within the country. Contrary to it the export of raw material, though there also the prices were fixed arbitrarily to provide them at cheap rate to the British factories, was more profitable. Therefore, as Durga Prasad opines, "Indian trade was stimulated in an unnatural way, its growth and development being treated as an 'end' rather than as a 'means' of the economic welfare of the country." This was the Company Policy which helped Britain replace India as the "Workshop of the World". The character of Indian exports consequently underwent a drastic change. The export composition got transformed to the primary commodities. The defence of the Company Policy in the British Parliament is self-explanatory. Before the Parliamentary Select Committee it was argued that:

> ...this company was in various ways encouraged and assisted by our great manufacturing ingenuity and skill. Succeeded in converting India from a manufacturing country into a country exporting raw produce.... The peculiar state of the relation between this country and India and the necessity of extracting from the later three millions of money for Home Charges...and the altered State of Indian

Industry in its being converted from a manufacturing country into a country exporting raw produce....

The violent fluctuations in the prices superimposed by heavy export duty can easily reveal the uneconomic effects of the foreign trade over the Indian economy.

Dependence on Britain. Besides, the direction of trade also underwent a similar change. By 1828, Britain claimed almost half (48%) of the total of Indian exports, China imported 25 per cent, Persian Gulf 7 per cent, France 8 per cent, and the rest of the countries notably Mauritius, Burma, Indonesia, New South Wales, Sweden, and Portugal claiming only 2 per cent of exports from India. British share increased to more than 60 per cent in 1840, whereas the Chinese share came down to about 10 per cent. Thus, Indian trade was made dependent on the demands by the British markets. It was not a healthy sign. Though the scholars have doubts yet it is a reality of the facts that such economic dependence takes away political independence. Loss of political independence deprived the country of the opportunity to get rid of economic dependence. Secondly, the economy also remains always within the zone of red-mark, *i.e.* such trade proves always superfluous. It did happen in India. After Britain got involved in the First and Second World Wars, as will be discussed later, it was India which had to bear the real brunt of economic destruction in Britain caused by the European wars.

Draining Out of Indian Wealth. Imports indicate another side of the same coin which negated the ancient principles of trade. The imports registered a rise of more than 1100 per cent, in between 1814-1855. It simply meant that wealth was drained out of India and filled into the British coffers. As per an estimate about £100 million was drained in Britain from India in between 1757 and 1815 only. It was this wealth which facilitated the industrial revolution in Britain and further affected the composition of Indian trade. It was not, however, an end to the sad story. Draining out of the wealth eliminated the savings of the people and shortage of savings eliminated the possibility of investment. It was Britain which was in a position to and it did invest. The Indians were thrown out of the ownerships and jobs and a vicious circle of poverty had set in. Therefore, poets like Nazeer wept over the declining grandeur of Agra. Above all, the import was also not a stable one and not according to the needs of Indian economy. Again, Britain claimed the greater proportion of this increased import into India. Its share was 34.8 per cent in 1828-29 and increased to 42.9 per cent in 1939-40.

China was the next country. It supplied raw silk in exchange of opium. This raw silk was re-exported to Britain, and India was deprived of those billions which she was getting by independent re-export. Secondly, since the opium trade was monopolized by the British, the Indian cultivators, traders and her economy were deprived of the benefit of this intermediary role as well. British imports consisted of cotton yarn, cotton, piece goods, wearing apparel, metal goods, various other miscellaneous manufactures, and at least half of the total of imports of wines and spirits. The percentage of increase in imports of cotton goods was indeed remarkable. The import of cotton goods in Calcutta only increased from just Rs. 90,000 in 1813-14 to Rs. 26 lacs in 1819-20, Rs. 160 lacs in 1828-29 and Rs. 260 lacs in 1839-40.

India as Exporter of Raw Materials. It was a retrograde development in Indian foreign trade. For the first time, perhaps, in the history of trading relations with the West, India was forced to be a buyer of goods whose traditionally low-cost products were being pushed out both of the domestic and foreign markets. As late as 1858, "India was chiefly known as a dealer in drugs, dyes and luxuries." The Company surrendered its administrative powers in 1858 to the British Crown. Thereafter, India became known as the supplier of foodgrains, fibres and other staples.

After the Crown took over the Government of India in 1858 the imperial control on India was further tightened. Industrial revolution had by this time attained maturity in Britian and a "nation of shopkeepers" had become "workshop of the world". Now, the industrial interests predominated the commercial interests, and the phase of economic imperialism had set in. The economic imperialism necessitated regulation of the use of the resources both in men and materials of a dependent country in the economic interests of the imperial country. Trade was the chief tool to implement this policy of economic imperialism.

Laissez Faire. Britain was free from the fear of competition of the European countries in the 1850s and 1860s. In Vienna Settlement (1815), Britain had already occupied all the strategic points on the ocean. Germany and Italy were still struggling to undo the Vienna Settlement and bring about their national unification. The French were again struggling to establish the democratic set-up in their country by throwing the "imperial yoke" upon them by their own Emperor Napoleon III. After 1859, the foreign policy of Napoleon had started facing disaster and he was not in a position to challenge British hegemony. Rather, he was collaborating with Britain in further imperial expansions. Austria and Russia were still predominantly feudal countries deriving their strength from the land. Therefore, majority of the European powers were lagging behind in industrial development and could not compete with the new pattern of trade dominated by the manufactured goods of Britain. It was Indian industry which was still having a lingering existence. The complete destruction of this lingering industry was possible by allowing "free competition" popularly known as *laissez faire*. It was best suited to compete with the European countries. But in case of India it was not *laissez faire* in its true sense.

Rather, as Horace Hayman Wilson called it, it was strangulation of Indian industry. He says:

> The history of the trade of cotton cloth with India affords a singular exemplification of the inapplicability to all times and circumstances of free trade which advocates the unrestricted admission of a cheap article, in place of protecting by heavy duties a dearer one of the home manufacture. It is also a melancholy instance of the wrong done to India by the country on which she had become dependent. It was stated in evidence, that the cotton and silk goods of India upto this period 1813, could be sold for a profit in the British market, at a price from fifty to sixty per cent lower than those fabricated in England. It consequently became necessary to protect the latter by

> duties of seventy and eighty per cent on their value or by positive prohibition. Had this not been the case, had not such prohibitory duties and decrees existed, the mills of Paisley and of Manchester would have been stopped in their outset and could scarcely have been again set in motion even by the powers of steam. They were created by the sacrifice of the Indian manufactures.

This policy was pursued by Britian in its colonies like India for the sake of British industrial interests even when colonial finances were in almost hopeless plight.

The official support for British industrial interests in India is evident from her policies since beginning. When the supply of the US raw cotton to Britian, for example, was threatened by the American Civil War, the Secretary of State assured the Cotton Supply Association of Manchester that "No measure which is within the power of the Government to adopt for ensuring an increased supply of such an essential article of consumption of a suitable description suitable to the English market would be neglected." On the demand of this Association, the Government of India was asked to comply with the wishes for "the establishment of the Departments of Agriculture in each of the several provinces of India and the more active employment of collectors in matters connected with the cotton cultivation".

The government also abolished export duty on the wheat to encourage its export though there was no real surplus to export from India. In his pamphlet written by Syed Mohammed Hussain the policy was put up in its real perspective. Though it is somewhat lengthy yet needs reproduction. The pamphlet reads:

> It is a pity that our well wishers, without considering the circumstances of the people and the density of the population, conclude that the engagement of trade, and increasing the means of communication will do good to India. They ought to consider that England with a population of only 390 per square mile, cannot produce enough for the consumption of its people, and has to depend upon the produce of other countries. In 1882, of wheat alone no less than 64,171,622

> cwts. were imported from other countries into England, and of these 8,477,479 cwts. came from India; while India, with a population of 416 per square mile, is expected to enlarge her trade by exchanging her food for mere fancy articles and luxuries which were being produced within (India) for thousands of years. We should go further in detail on this point, and contrast briefly the agricultural condition of both countries. According to the Census Report, the North-Western Province, for example, contains a cultivated area of 540,420 square miles which is equal to 34,586,880 acres, and the population being 44,107,869, the average cultivated area per head is .78 acre. The cultivated area of the United Kingdom is 50,432,988, and the population is 35,278,999, or 1.42 per acre per head. Now, with all her improved and scientific agriculture, with the outlay of large capital with artificial manures and the aid of machinery, with an average yield of only 30 bushels per acre England cannot support her people yet India, with her miserable modes of farming, with such insignificant farms and implements, with an average yield of only 13 bushels (per Famine Report) or 18.7 bushels (per "Oudh Gazetteer") per acre, is expected to prosper by her trade, *viz.* exportation of grain and by the increase of the means of communication. The result of this trade is that when the quantity of rainfall reduces, famine threatens the country, thousands of people helplessly die, and the whole affairs of the country are disturbed. In ordinary season, during four months of one year—May, June, December and January—the lower class of peasants support their existence by living on wild herbs and wild grass seeds, the Mango and Mohwa fruit, or taking loans of grain from grain dealers.

He further refuted that its trade brought any material benefit to India:

> Owing to the railway (for example) being made with foreign capital our country derives very little benefit from what we pay for carriage.

Therefore, he said that, "the reader should judge for himself, and consider whether this sort of trade has a tendency to increase the material prosperity or to cause the underfeeding of the people."

This trade policy of underfeeding the people of India continued despite all the criticism, protests, etc. by the Indian leaders and liberal economists even in Britain. Wheat export increased from the value of Rs. 73.6 million in 1901-05 to Rs. 76.8 million on 1905-06 to 1909-10; Rs. 142.8 million in 1910-11 to 1913-14. It came down to the value of Rs. 103.3 million in 1914-15 to 1918-19 not because of change in the policy but because of the break out of the First World War which hampered the exportation to Britain and other European countries. It further came down in terms of value to Rs. 36.7 million in 1912 to 1923-24 because of world famous depression. Therefore, the quantity in real terms might have increased. The increasing population, long innings of famines and rise of militant nationalism could only slow down the export of wheat only. Therefore, Professor Varshney opines that "foreign trade has not served the real interests of the Indian nation. The development of our foreign trade was forced to follow wrong lines. While the people were being impoverished by a foreign administration, foreign trade figures mounted up presenting a false picture of prosperity. What is more important in the nature of articles exchanged. The gain from foreign trade would have been immensely greater under a national government. In fact, it was the U.K. which benefited most from our foreign trade. Almost all the plantations, modern industries and auxiliary services were owned by Britishers and the profits had to be remitted to England by an export surplus". Whatever fringe benefits of the surplus foreign trade were going to the Indian Nation were neither stable nor conducive to the growth of Indian industry which could provide jobs and money to quench their hunger.

The above policy destroyed the indigenous industrial infrastructure. The volume of the foreign trade of India also increased by leaps and bounds. The imports of merchandize, which stood at Rs. 243 million in 1858-59 rose to Rs. 414 million in 1879-80; Rs. 730 million in 1895-96 and Rs. 1,910 million in 1913-14. During this period, exports rose from

Rs. 289 million in 1859-60 to Rs. 692 million in 1879-80, Rs. 1,186 million in 1895-96 and Rs. 2,490 million in 1913-14. India still had a favourable balance of Rs. 580 million in 1913-14. On the basis of increasing volume of trade with a favourable balance, the British boasted that India was sharing the increasing prosperity under the aegis of British imperialism. But it does not present the true picture.

Reversal of Trade Pattern. The main items of imports through the period were cotton textiles, cotton yarn, machinery, mill stores, mineral oils, and a variety of other manufactures. The chief items of exports were foodgrains, raw cotton and jute, hides and skins, tea and indigo. The structure of India's foreign trade fully reflected the colonial nature of her economy. It was no more that India whose trade "in all ages", as Dr. Robertson jealously wrote, "has been the same; gold and silver have uniformly been carried thither in order to purchase the same commodities with which it now supplies all nations; and from the age of Pliny to the present times, it has been always considered and execrated as a gulf which swallows up the wealth of every other country, that flows incessantly, towards it, and from which it never returns". Now India was supplying raw materials and foodgrains and importing, in exchange manufactures of all kinds.

It was being done by Britain where 'owling' or transporting British wool or sheep to foreign countries was treated with special severity as it was supposed to assist the rival of woollen manufactures of the continent, and the penalties against this offence rose to seven years' transportation. A country in which, he further informs, penalties but little less severe were exacted against those who exported machines employed in the chief English industries, or who induced artificers to emigrate; and any skilled workman who carried his industries to a foreign market, if he did not return within six months, after being warned by the English ambassador, was declared an alien, forfeited all his goods and become incapable of receiving any legacy or gift. That country had forced its dependent country, as Major Basu questioned, "in years of drought and famine, instead of foodgrains (to export), other raw materials from India which are also detrimental of India's interests. These raw materials consist of bones and hides of cattle which die in large numbers in times of scarcity. This export trade in hides has greatly affected the leather industry of India. The export of bones takes away out of the country one of the best manures available". "Then again, the export of cotton, has the tendency of making it dear in this country, and thus, its export hampers the development of the cotton industry in India. Cotton seed (binola) yields a valuable oil and is good food for cattle. Its export, therefore, involves great loss."

It was the industry which could provide the jobs to the unemployed and underemployed but as stated above the trade policy was ruining the industry and thereby increasing the unemployment. The loss was making even the cultivation uneconomical and it was this policy which was making a "country of gold" the "poorest of the poor". Contrary to the reality, the British authors like Pearson were describing it as high standard of national character, in spite of telling the truth that "the corn of India has been transported at unremunerative rates upon Government lines, in order that the food of (British) people might be cheapened".

Trade as Centre of Economic Activity. The favourable balance of trade did not help our economy. The trade was monopolised by the British; it was a source of revenue to run the administration and profit to the British entrepreneurs. "India has done everything for us, everything that has made these islands, as insignificant on the face of the globe as the islands that made up Japan, the greatest empire the world has ever known, and for this we owe undying gratitude to India", accepted one authority. What the British Government was doing, Ramesh Dutt aptly puts it this:

> The British nation had spent millions of their own money in acquiring dominions, but in India an Empire had been acquired, wars had been waged and the administration had been carried on, at the cost of Indian people, the British nation had not contributed a shilling. Empire was transferred from the Company to the Crown, but the Indian people paid the purchase money.

Foreign trade became the centre of gravity of the State activities. The internal economy was transformed accordingly. Expanding foreign markets brought about a phenomenal change in our agricultural economy. Development of agriculture had become the criteria for the continued rule of Britain. The era of money crops had set in. It was the commercial policy and foreign trade which had led to the development of railway system, industries, medical facilities, etc. It was going to realize the wish of the Company that even if India at any distinct future got independence, the Company would like to "see millions of Indians" its permanent customers. The foreign trade had sealed the fate of Indian economy and dimmed the welfare of the people. Increased volume of foreign trade establishes the prosperity whereas the British guided trade was impoverishing the Indian population. The foreign trade and impoverishment of the mass increased unabated till India got independence. In so far as the benefits of a favourable balance of trade were concerned, they were no more coming to the Indians rather, as the poet Thomas Campbell versed: "Rich in the gems of India's gaudy zone: And plunders piled from kingdoms not their own."

Dependence upon Britain. The direction and composition of foreign trade, however, underwent a little change. Though the percentage of the manufactures in the total imports declines, yet in quantity it was increasing enormously. Besides, India was the largest importer of manufactured goods from Britain until 1914. The severe famines compelled the British Government of India to put a break on the progressive ruralization of India as a consequence of the policy of *laissez faire*. Ruining of the indigenous industry correspondingly increased pressure on the agriculture. The revised tariff policy also helped evolution of modern textile industry in India. As a result, the proportion of manufactured goods in total imports declined from 65 per cent in 1879 to 57 per cent in 1892 and 53 per cent in 1907. Though India still remained the exporter of raw materials, its raw materials lost importance in the British market. Its share declined from 9.1 per cent in 1870-72 to 6.7 per cent in 1910-12. It was because of the British imperial expansion in Africa (where the raw materials were being procured and exported by the British nationals), and its concern to develop a viable economy in its white colonies, *viz.* Australia and New Zealand. Thus, India was no more "most-favoured" colony of the British in terms of raw materials. Decline in the export of raw materials of Britain was, however, compensated by the opening of Suez Canal. Reduction in mileage, and thereby in freight, helped in developing our trade relations with France, Germany, Italy, Austria, Turkey, Persia, Egypt and Russia. Eighty-eight per cent of our imports and 60 per cent of our exports passed through the Suez Canal. "The first fourteen years of the twentieth century were marked by great prosperity", said Dr. (Mrs.) Vera Anstey, "and a great increase, but little change, in India's foreign trade."

Above all, as stated earlier, our trade was organised in the British imperial interests. Once the British interests suffered because of her imperial policy, Indian interests suffered more badly. It was the result of this dependence, that the increasing volume of trade suffered a blow by the break out of the First World War. Since Germany was fighting against Britain, export of our raw material to that country was prohibited. Laying of mines made the sea routes unsafe and India could not export to Russia. The War also created a scarcity of ships and their freight rates and insurance charges—it may be noted here that the ships and insurance agents belonged to Britain only—increased considerably. The War benefit went in favour of independent countries like the U.S.A. and Japan. Since it was feared that while Britain was involved in War against it European enemies, Indian markets might be captured by her allies, *viz.* Japan and the U.S.A. Therefore, Britain resorted to a strong protective policy to avoid it. It was bound to affect Indian interests. This wrong foreign trade policy has been severely criticized by Dr. Parimal Ray as follows:

> It passes our comprehension why a straightforward course should be avoided and shelter should be sought behind the blind alley of the balance (of trade), to prove the supposed prosperity. The retrograde tendency of our trade during the war period is true beyond any shadow of doubt and no

amount of sophisticated argument or statistical jugglery can disaprove or conceal it.

War and Industrial Growth. As a result of this British policy, the European markets were blocked to Indian goods for the first two years of War. Indian imports declined by 67 per cent and exports by 34 per cent. Imports which stood at 234.75 crore of rupees in 1913-14, declined to Rs. 166.74 crore in 1914-15, and to Rs. 410.84 crore of rupees in 1913-14, to Rs. 354 crore, 20 crore in 1914-15, and Rs. 357.90 crore in 1915-16. In real terms, the loss was heavier to the Indian economy. Prices of the export goods did not increase corresponding to the increase in import goods. However, one aspect of the War was good to the industrial growth in India. Blockade of trade-routes made the British Indian Government realize that self-sufficiency in essential items was strategically necessary. Swadeshi Movement combined with this necessity laid the foundation for modern infrastructure of industries. India's trade again picked up and imports and exports stood up at Rs. 251.93 crore and Rs. 524.25 crore in 1918-19 respectively. Though the growth rate was not as fast as it had been in the pre-War years, but the production of necessary items within the country reduced our demands on foreign markets. It increased trade surplus. It was the result of this development that India could take full advantage in the Second World War and repaid her loans within a short span of five years.

Economic Depression and its Impact on Indian Trade. The position did not improve after the cessation of the First World War. The uncertainty during the post-war period proved more disastrous than the actual war. Economic self-sufficiency had also picked up by the nationalists in India. India was not, however, fortunate enough. Inflection had taken the world. Britain resorted to deflationary measures to improve her economic conditions which could enable her to restore the Gold Standard. (Britain had to surrender the Gold Standard due to destruction of her economy during the War.) It was done at the expense of India.

The Government of India raised the rupee-sterling exchange, *i.e.* devalued the rupee. The rupee-sterling ratio was raised from

1s.4d to 1s.6d. It led to fall in the prices of raw material exported by India, and the prices of imported goods correspondingly increased. It caused hardship to the workers. They went on strike. Their strike further slackened the trade. It was, therefore, for the first time in its life that the Indian trade faced an unfavourable balance by Rs. 79.80 crore in 1920-21 and Rs. 33.94 crore in 1921-22. Exports could increase only after those war-period restrictions were removed in 1923-24. In 1928-29, the imports stood at Rs. 263.40 crore and Rs. 339.15 crore respectively with a surplus balance of Rs. 75.75 crore.

This trend, however, could not be maintained. The pace of economic self-sufficiency could not maintain an adjustment in production and demand.

Products started accumulating in the factories. India suffered a great jolt because of shortage of finished goods. Her imports came down from Rs. 249.71 crore in 1929-30 to Rs. 117.28 crore and exports from 318.99 crore to Rs. 150.23 crore during that period. It does not, however, mean that the Indian consumers could benefit by the contraction of export. Rather the reality was contrary to it.

Exports' figures came down much more because of catastrophic fall in the prices of raw materials. This left little money with the people to purchase goods and their reduced purchasing power brought down the figures of imports.

The depression started receding after 1934. Economic improvement in European countries increased demand for raw materials; consequently the prices of these raw materials also increased. But our trade could not again touch that high mark. The contracting export surplus, as the table on the next page shows, further increased our debt, because that trade surplus could not pay even the high interest on capital borrowed for Indian railways, high salaries and pensions of British civil servants in India. As a result, India became a debtor country and it had to export gold out of country—a complete reversal to the position as it obtained when the British became policymakers.

TABLE: Contracting Export Surplus during 1929-1939

(in crore of rupees)

Year	Imports	Exports	Balance of Trade
1929-30	249.71	318.99	+69.28
1933-34	117.28	150.23	+32.95
1934-35	134.59	155.50	+20.91
1935-36	136.78	164.59	+27.81
1936-37	127.72	202.49	+74.67
1937-38	173.33	189.87	+16.44
1938-39	152.51	159.97	+17.46

During this period the composition and direction of foreign trade also underwent a change. India also started importing foodstuffs and raw materials to satisfy the growing needs of our industries; at the same time growth of industry also led to decline in the exports of foodstuffs and raw materials and capital goods. It could be possible because of emergence of Swadeshi Movement which boycotted imported goods. The Movement forced the Imperial Government to impose increasing duties on imported finished products. Therefore, this protective policy could give impetus to industrial growth. Still it was not progressing to the desired stage.

Cotton and cotton goods still remained the most important items of imports. Manufactured goods such as jute goods, oilseeds products, tanned hides and skins and many other semi-processed raw materials had become important items of exports. India, however, remained one of the greatest exporters of raw materials and foodstuffs and provided the largest market for manufactured goods.

Emergence of New Economic Powers. The post-First World War period also brought about a change in the direction of trade. The United States of America had emerged a powerful nation and could no more be bullied by the dominant commercial nations of pre-War era. They had to accept the Wilsonian principle of equal opportunities to all. Obviously, equality granted to free countries, America and Japan forced upon Britain a tough competition for the first time in her colonies. Britain could not maintain her edge over the U.S.A., Japan and

Germany. They considerably improved their position in the Indian markets. As a result, Britain's average share fell from 41.2 per cent, during the War period to 39.5 per cent, in the inter-War period to the advantage of Japan, U.S.A. and Germany. Japan improved her share from 5.5 per cent to 10.4 per cent; U.S.A. from 5.8 per cent to 10.4 per cent and Germany from 8.5 per cent came down to 4 per cent. (It may be noted that Germany's percentage had come down to only 0.8 per cent during the War.)

The above change, however, did not bring any material change in the Indian dependence over Britain and drainage of former's wealth to the latter. Under the Policy of Imperial Preference imposed upon India by the Ottawa Agreement in 1933, Britain purchased almost all the exports of tea, tanned hides and skins, raw and woollen manufactures. "Even in the jute manufactures and raw cotton she was not an unimportant buyer." The competition between the free countries affected the direction of Indian imports. British share had already come down from 61 per cent in 1920-21 to 36 per cent in 1931-32. Even the dichotomy of Imperial Preference could not improve that situation much. After the Ottawa Agreement, British share increased to 41 per cent by 1934-35, but again declined to 39 per cent in 1935-36, 38 per cent in 1936-37, and 34.5 per cent in 1937-38. Thus, Indian dependence for imported goods on Britain significantly dwindled again to the advantage of U.S.A., Japan and Germany. Japan became "the principal competitor in cotton manufactures, and other piece goods, iron manufactures, etc. Due to the adaptability of her trade and industry, she was able to undersell Britain in spite of the tariff barriers". Her share increased from 7.5 per cent in 1925 to 9.2 per cent, in 1929, 11 per cent in 1933 to 15 per cent in 1935 and 16.2 per cent in 1936.

Second World War and Inflation. This diversified character of Indian trade again was hit by the outbreak of the Second World War. Imperial Government imposed belligerency upon India. Thereby India was prohibited from having trade relations with Britian's enemies. Rather it had to make available all its resources to Britain and her allies, popularly known as Allied

Powers. With the joining of Japan the enemy powers, popularly known as the Axis Powers, Britain dragged India also to the actual theatre of war. India was converted into a war bastion against Japan, and as a result, Indian economy was out on war footing. This put a great demand on Indian industries, especially that of cotton textiles and jute and gave a great impetus to exports. India's dragging into war theatre was, however, opposed by the nationalists in India. Non-cooperation movement left no alternative but to resort to currency mechanism to meet the war demands. By the mechanism of currency only, the Imperial Governemnt in India could utilise the services of men and purchase the resources. This economic mechanism consequently created, on the one hand, scarcity, and on the other hand, infused inflation in Indian economy. Though it increased the trade volume and provided phenomenal trade surplus, only at the cost of people's sufferings. Indian exports increased from Rs. 198.70 crore in 1940-41 to Rs. 252.89 crore in 1941-42 due to heavier war demands. Similarly, the imports also increased from Rs. 166.97 crore to Rs. 173.14 crore. However, India had obtained a significant trade surplus of Rs. 79.83 crore after a long time. This trade surplus increased from 84.53 crore in 1942-43 to Rs. 93.07 crore in 1943-44. The huge trade surplus came down to Rs. 24.17 crore in 1944-45 because of increased imports of goods in larger quantities to redress the peoples' sufferings due to extraordinary inflation which was intensifying political agitation against Britain. Second change which this War brought about in foreign trade was that of diversification. Since the free nations had got divided into blocs, therefore, British dependent countries like India were forced to change the direction of their trade in favour of Allied Powers and the trade was confined to the Allied Bloc. This bloc-trade was inherited by the independent India n 1947.

India gained from the War in other respects. First of all, the fabulous trade surplus helped India to repay her entire amount of external public debt within a few years after the outbreak of War. Sir Jeremy Raisman's remarks are self-deceptory. He said in his budget speech in 1943-44, "India has completed the transition from a debtor to a creditor country and extinguished within the brief space of about three years, accumulations over decades of its public indebtedness to the United Kingdom." It is undoubted that India repaid the loans, but the boasting that India had "ceased to be a debtor country, and there can be little doubt that she will find her creditor position a distinct advantage in the post-war world was far from reality." According to the survey of Reserve Bank of India, the total private foreign investments on June 30, 1948 amounted to Rs. 596 crore. It was very doubtful estimate since the foreign investors did not give correct information about their investment. Still taking into consideration the total balances amounting to only Rs. 700 crore, it cannot be accepted that she emerged as a creditor during the course of Second World War. Rather, independent India inherited a highly inflationary economy and she was forced, immediately after independence, to devalue her money.

Impact of Second World War on India's Trade. The War brought about a diversification in India's trade. Our trade came to a nil after 1940-41 with France, Italy, Netherlands, Belgium, Germany, Austria and Japan. Our exports to the U.S.A. increased from just a share of 8.5 per cent in 1938-39 to 21.2 per cent by 1944-45. Similarly, the share of the imports from the U.S.A. also rose from 5.4 per cent to 25.7 per cent in that period. Thus, trade balance was favourable to the U.S.A. and this drainage of wealth from India to the U.S.A. was a significant phenomenon which the Independent India inherited. Rest of the exports and imports were limited within the British Empire. Its share rose to 61.37 per cent in exports and 78.12 per cent in imports. Since the War had created obstacles in the long distance routes, our trade was more concentrated with the countries bordering the Indian Ocean, *i.e.* the Middle East including Egypt. Before there could have been a reversal to this direction, India got independence. Therefore, the trade pattern had also brought the Middle East nearer. It was this pattern which, in the immediate years after independence, dominated the foreign trade of India.

Impact of World War I on Indian Economy

21

The development of modern industry in India received a new impetus during the First World War. Soon after the outbreak of war the imports from foreign countries, specially enemy countries, stopped to India, which exposed the pitiable dependence of India on foreign imports even for the necessities of life. The inability of Britain to send military supplies over the long overseas route gave a serious setback to the British fighting strength in the East. Therefore, the British leaders were obliged to develop industries in India as a matter of military necessity for the protection of their Eastern empire. Another reason which prompted the English leaders to promote industries in India was that they were keen to gain wholehearted support of the people of India in their war efforts. They were convinced that they would be able to secure the co-operation of the people of India only if they conceded certain political and economic concessions to them. In the economic sphere, they promised to promote industrialisation by all means. Yet another reason which promoted the British to encourage industries in India was that they looked at the Indian industries as a better substitute for the foreign goods, which were fast displacing the British imports.

In 1916, the government appointed an Industrial Commission under Sir Thomas Holland "to examine the whole question of industrial development of India, and to indicate new openings for the profitable employment of Indian capital in commerce and industry and the manner in which the Government could usefully give direct encouragement to industrial enterprise". Even before the Industrial Commission could submit its report the government set up an Indian Munitions Board in 1917. The Board was expected "to control and develop Indian resources with special reference to the needs created by the war" and to apply India's manufacturing resources to the purpose of war with a view to reduce demands on shipping. The measures taken by the Board such as (a) direct purchase of India-made articles and materials to meet the needs of army, the civil departments and railways; (b) diversion of all orders from the United Kingdom and elsewhere to manufacturers in India; and (c) assistance to Indian forms in importing industrial plants and technical experts from abroad, greatly contributed to the promotion of Indian industries. The Board also recommended that the measures taken by it to meet the war demands should continue, with some modifications, during the peace times as well. The Board warned that the failure to do so would deprive the Indian capitalists of a number of profitable enterprises, "whilst in the event of war which renders sea transport impossible, India's all-important existing industries will be exposed to the risk of stoppage, her consumers to great hardships and her armed forces to the gravest possible danger".

The Industrial Commission appointed in 1916 submitted its Report in 1918. In its report, the Commission recommended that the government should help large-scale organised industries by conducting research and providing economic data and services of experts. For this purpose, it recommended that imperial and provincial industrial and commercial services should be created and an Imperial Department of Stores be set up at Calcutta to control the placing of government orders and contracts. It also recommended establishment of Imperial and Provincial Department of Industries. Above all, it insisted on betterment of factory and industrial conditions as well as improvement in transport and freight facilities.

However, the recommendations of the Indian Industrial Commission for rapid industrialisation of the country did not find favour with the government. The process of industrialisation received a further set back under the Montague-Chelmsford

Reforms of 1919 which made industries a provincial subject. This naturally hampered the adoption of a comprehensive industrial policy.

It is true that during the war period the cotton and jute mills worked at full capacity and made huge profits. The steel production also considerably increased on account of the cutting off of imports from abroad. The production of some consumer goods also showed a marked increase. Some of the articles like chemicals, mineral acids, cement, cutlery, fertilizers, etc. for which India had so far relied on foreign markets also began to be manufactured in India for the first time. But this industrial progress was only short-lived because soon after the war when threat to the British Empire in India disappeared, the British withdrew the concessions from the Indian industries. Thus, we can agree with Prof. Lokanathan that the First World War "beyond affording temporary gains to a few established industries did nothing to set the country firmly on the road to industrialisation". In fact after some time when the industrial competition from England and other Western countries and Japan revived, the Indian industries could not successfully withstand the competition. As a result, the Indian political leaders and businessmen exerted increasing pressure on the government to assist Indian industries. This led to the appointment of the Fiscal Commission in October 1921. The Commission in its report, submitted in 1922, recommended "discriminating protection" to Indian industries.

In accordance with the recommendations of the Fiscal Commission the government set up a Tariff Board to examine the claims of various industries for protection and decided to extend discriminatory protection to thirteen industries such as iron and steel, cotton textiles, paper, matches, sugar, heavy chemical industries, etc. However, even now the government lacked genuine sympathy for rapid industrialisation of the Indian industries. It merely rendered perfunctory assistance to certain industries to enable them to withstand foreign competition for the time-being. It certainly did not adopt the policy of protection as an instrument for general economic development. No wonder thereafter the country witnessed only haphazard development of certain industries and there was no general economic development of India as such.

Export of British Capital to India. In view of the enormous profits made by the British controlled jute mills during the war (they showed profits of nearly £42 million during four years from 1918-22) the British capital started flowing steadily to India. This is borne out by the fact that the total British capital investment in India which stood at roughly £400 million before the war reached £1000 million by 1933. This posed a serious threat to some of the vital Indian industries. The things became still worse when the Tariff Board turned down the application of number of Indian industries for protection. In case of iron and steel industries also the protective duties were lowered and subsidies abolished.

The introduction of imperial preferences gave yet another damaging blow to the Indian industries. As a result of the imperial preference the British goods were given an advantage over the non-empire products in the empire market. Likewise the Indian products got an advantage over the non-empire products in the empire market. This policy was adopted with a view to accelerate the process of Indian industrialisation, but it actually helped the British industry to compete in the Indian market. India was merely given favoured rates for her raw materials and semi-manufacturers in the British market. This was greatly resented by the Indian industrialists and they succeeded in getting an adverse vote from the Legislative Assembly of India against the Trade Agreement. However, despite this the British Government thrust the Trade Agreement regarding Imperial Preferences on India.

Despite the various difficulties and setback the Indian industries made a considerable progress between 1922 and 1939. As a result, the production of cotton piece goods increased by two and a half times; production of steel ingots increased by nearly eight times; paper production also increased by two and a half times. With regard to sugar India attained self-sufficiency and the production rose by almost twelve times. Similarly, India made considerable progress in other industries like cement, matches, glass, soap, vanaspati, engineering industries, etc. There was an overall four-time increase in the number of factories. What is more significant India became independent of foreign countries for the supply of machinery and other capital goods without which new industries could not be established in India. Despite all this progress and modernisation of industries India was still far away from the goal of industrialisation.

Impact of World War II on Indian Economy

22

At the commencement of the Second World War the British Government continued to follow the same policy of industrialisation of India and opposed development of heavy industries, owned and managed by the Indians in the country. But after the bombing of British ships and penetration of Japanese in the South Pacific a serious threat was posed to the British Empire. Even the British supply line faced a serious threat of being cut off. As a result, the British and her allies became increasingly dependent on India for the supply of their war deeds. With this objective in mind the Government of India took a number of measures which provided a fillip to industrial development in India. In 1940, the government set up the Board of Scientific and Industrial Research to tide over the shortage of technicians and skilled workers which were badly needed for further industrial expansion. The Board not only helped in raising necessary technical personnel but also helped in development of industries like drugs, dyes, lubricants, plastics. As the Indian industrialists could not obtain new plants for Britain and other developed countries due to war, they tried to make optimum use of the existing plants. In other words, though new industries did not spring up, the existing industries worked to their full capacity.

The period of war also witnessed the establishment of a number of new industries like ferro-alloys, non-ferrous metal and metal fabricating industries like copper sheets, wires, cables, etc.; mechanical industries like diesel engines, pumps, bicycles, sewing machines, etc.; and chemicals like caustic soda, chlorine, superphosphates, etc. As the raw materials for these industries were not available in the country India had to resort to import of necessary raw materials from foreign countries. Thus, India once again started importing raw materials for its industries after a gap of over a century.

Impact of Industrialisation. Whatever industrialisation of country was permitted by the British during the Second World War was sheerly due to the pressure of circumstances. The British could never reconcile with the idea that India should cease to be a supplier of raw materials and a market for finished products. Hence, they permitted the establishment of only those 'key industries' in India which the needs of war dictated. It deliberately hindered the development of certain industries in India on the plea that what one country was doing the other parts of the Empire should not do. It tried to safeguard the future interests of the British industrialists in India and prevented the development of certain basic industries in India even at the risk of sabotaging the war efforts. This period also witnessed further strengthening of the grip of British finance capital over India and a number of giant concerns like Lever Brothers, Dunlop, Imperial Chemicals, etc. set up their subsidiaries in India. The British offered every possible discouragement to the establishment of automobile industry as well as ship-building industry in India.

The industrial growth in India during the war resulted in overuse of exisiting industrial equipments and plants, which shortened the life of the machinery and presented the problem of replacing the same at an early date.

Again during the war, on account of scarcity conditions, no attention was paid to factors like location, optimum scale of operations, adequate market, availability of raw materials, financial and technical organisation, etc. while setting up new industries. This produced disastrous results in the post-World War period. Yet another adverse effect of the industial boom during the Second World War period was that the resources of the country were mainly diverted to the production of goods for defence purposes, which inevitably led to fall in the production of consumer goods. This resulted in sharp rise in the prices of consumer goods. The inflationary tendencies set into operation by the war finances further aggravated the problem of high prices. This immensely benefited the industrialists who made fabulous profits while the common people suffered on this account. The scarcity of the various consumer goods and their continuously rising prices forced the government to take necessary measures to check the rise in prices and ensure their fair distribution. However, the government could not implement its policies effectively leading to wide corruption and great hardship to people.

Growth of Modern Industry

23

Industrial growth in India corresponds with the ups and downs in the Indian polity. The emergence of a strong polity either under the Mauryas or the Greater Mughals also brought labour-accelerated growth; but after the disintegration and political instability resulting from the fall of the Mauryas or the Greater Mughals, industries also suffered a setback. The industrial structure before the British Imperial Rule was, however, not destroyed. On the contrary, the British Imperial Government of India deliberately destroyed that infrastructure for the benefit of their metropolitan industry and from 1880s onward it was necessary to evolve modern industrial infrastructure rather to complement the growth of their metropolitan industry by creating, on the one hand, a demand for the machinery, and on the other hand, to fill up the gap in the volume of foreign trade which occurred due to disappearance of manufactures in the export from India. Therefore, the Indian industry from the immemorial times continued to grow in spite of the stagnation in the times of political instability.

We know from the Greek writers who admired that "India has many huge mountains which abound in fruit trees of every kind and many vast plains of great fertility—more or less beautiful, but all alike intersected by a multitude of rivers.... And while the soil bears on its surface all kinds of fruits, it has also underground numerous veins of all sorts of metals, for it contains much gold and silver and copper and iron in no small quantity and even tin and other metals. India again possesses many rivers both large and navigable." They also praised that "the inhabitants are found to be well skilled in the arts".

The Indian industry was famous since ancient times in the textiles, wood work, ivory, stone-cutting, fragrant woods, metals and jewellery. Their high standard of arts and crafts had secured a better market for their products throughout the known world, and it continued to be so even when the British colonial rule was imposed upon the country. It was richer than Europe in its arts and handicrafts.

The Industrial Commission itself conceded this fact. Its report states:

> At a time when the west of Europe, a birthplace of modern industrial system, was inhabitated by uncivilized tribes, India was famous for the wealth of her rulers and for high artistic skill of her craftsmen. And, even at a much later period, when the merchant adventures of the West made their first appearance in India, industrial advancement of this country was at any rate, not inferior to those of the more advanced European nations.

Therefore, at that time India was the "workshop of the world".

Rural India. On the eye of the British occupation, the Indian industries comprised of almost two distinct sectors, *viz.* rural and urban industries. The same set of artisans such as the carpenter, the potter, the blacksmith, the stonesman, the weaver, the dyer, the tailor, the shoemaker, the drug seller, etc. existed in almost every village community. Their arts and manufactures were hereditary and they were recognized by the caste of their arts and manufactures. They lacked economic organisation and specialisation. Their goods were of the most primitive and crude character. Therefore, their goods were consumed by and served the needs of the poor within the village. With the increasing poverty during the period of British rule their goods became rather essential for the village community. Since their industry did not pose any danger, if not helped in furthering British industrial interests, that village or rural industry continued to exist unabated and preserved the self-reliance of Indian villages.

Urban Industry. The urban industry of higher crafts were carried in the vicinity of administrative centres under the patronage of the Courts. In these urban centres, industries were organised in the guilds or by middlemen who made advances to the craftsmen. Their manufactures flourished and attained great artistic skill in the reign of Mughal Emperors who loved the Persian culture and like them made an ostentatious display of wealth splendour. Therefore, the textiles and other arts attained more artistic touch. Though majority of the industrial units' output was small, it had all essential features of evolving itself into modern industry. This fact is borne not by any indigenous record but rather from the report of Bernier, a French traveller.

Bernier found that Karkhanas (industries) were in full swing in all the parts of the country. About one such Karkhana he informs:

> In one hall embroiderers are busily employed, superintended by a master. In another you see the goldsmith; in third painters; in fourth, varnishers in lacquer work; in a fifth joiners, turners, tailors and shoemakers; in the sixth, manufacturers of silk, brocade and fine muslins.

As he himself informs us that the artisans were busy on a daylong work. He mentions:

> The artisans repair every morning to their respective karkhanas where they remain employed the whole day; and in the evening return to their homes. In this quiet and regular manner their times glides away; no one aspiring after any improvement in the conditions of life wherein he happens to be born. The embroiderer brings up his son as an embroiderer, the son of goldsmith becomes a goldsmith and the physician in the city educates his son for a physician.

These disciplined activities had made tremendous achievement in the manufacturing. India was the hub of world commerce and the magnet of the world precious metals. These goods enjoyed a good market in the island of the East Indies, on the African Coasts and in England as well. Their textiles flooded these markets and these were treated as "plague" especially in the British markets by the British manufacturers.

Indian muslin and fine cotton fabrics were described "as light as women and as slight as cobwebs". It was this urban industry of India which restricting the industrial growth of Britain. Secondly, flourishing Indian urban industry also deprived them of raw material needed by the expanding British industry. Therefore, the British Government pursued a policy which sealed the fate of industrial growth in India, especially before the First World War.

Decline of Indian Industry. The British war upon Indian industry had already been waged in Britain itself. The British Government passed law in 1701 and 1720 against the use of printed Indian calicos in England to accelerate the growth of British woollen and silk industries. The British industrial interests hecticly agitated the East India Company for inflicting an enjoy on the 'British nation' by exporting out bullion to India. Their agitations in juxtaposition of the political domination by the East India Company, after 1767, accelerated, on the one hand, Industrial Revolution in England, and, on the other hand, led to the decay of Indian urban industry.

India's Contribution Towards Industrial Revolution in Britain

It is necessary here to refer to the illusion among certain sections that the Industrial Revolution in Britain was an independent factor and it would have taken place even without political domination. It is not true. The political domination was the basic factor in bringing Industrial Revolution in Britain. The protective legislation passed in the first quarter of the seventeeth century against the import of Indian goods stimulated the mechanical inventions and discoveries, firstly, in the British textile industry. Parallel to it, the East India Company has utilised the opportunity offered by the declining Mughal Empire to establish their commercial and accumulate wealth by fair and foul means. It was this wealth accumulated by the East India Company which provided the main base for building on industrial infrastructure in England.

R.K. Gopalkrishnan, therefore, rightly says that "Before the influx of Indian treasure and the expansion of credit which followed (the commercial and political hegemony of the East

India Company), no force sufficient for (bringing) Industrial Revolution in England existed; and had Watt lived fifty years earlier, he and his invention must have perished together."

This development, on the one hand, moved the wheel of prosperity of the British industry and, on the other hand, put the Indian economy in the vicious circle of poverty. This could be possible because of the policy pursued by the East India Company.

The Company got an opportunity to establish its commercial hegemony, first in Bengal, Bihar and Orissa. The weak Mughal Emperor granted the Company a Firman in 1713 exempting the British trade from all duties to weaken the recalcitrant Nawab Ali Wardi Khan. This commercial charter helped the Company, especially after the death of the Nawab, in ousting the Indian as well as European traders from the internal and foreign markets. Thus, obtaining the economic strength the "superior to all other European powers in the sea, and supported by the government at home".

R.K. Mukherjee rightly notes, "The English within half a century after the death of Aurangzeb acquired Bengal where riches and geographical position proved of invaluable aid to them to obtain mastery of the hinterland and then gradually over the whole country".

Strengthened with the political authority, the East India Company pursued its policy in tune with the interest of the manufacturers of Britain. The British cotton industry was the first to get revolutionized by the invention of spinning jenny and the steam engine. This development as already stated, got an added strength from the policy of oppression of the weavers pursued by the East India Company.

As stated earlier, the Indian weavers could produce the finest textiles and had a great demand for their goods. Their Company officials followed a policy of ruining of the Indian weavers.

The Company Gumashtas forced the weavers to supply cloth at a very arbitrarily fixed low price. They also prohibited them from entertaining orders from purchasers other than the

Company. The weavers were also treated harshly in the event of disobedience of the commands. Besides, the Company and its servants used their monopoly rights against the interests of Indian industry.

The Company servants monopolised the internal trade in more important commodities like raw cotton. They sold these raw materials to the Indian manufacturers only at higher rates. Thus, the increased cost of raw materials and arbitrarily low fixation of prices of finished goods ruined the weavers and other artisans.

William Bolts describes this "one continued scene of oppression; the baneful effects of which are severely felt by every weaver and manufacturer in the country". He further tells us that "the roughly practised (by the Commerce Department) is beyond imagination, but all terminates in the defrauding of the poor weaver, for the price which the Company's Gumashtas, and in confederacy with them, the fachendars fix upon the goods, are in all places, at least fifteen per cent in some, forty per cent less than the goods manufactured would sell for in the public bazar or market upon a free sale". It was sufficient for the disaster of Indian textile industries. Murshidabad "which flourished under the most despotic and arbitrary Government", a report said in 1769, "is verging towards its ruin". Other centres also met the same fate. But perhaps this was not to the satisfaction of the Company Government.

The Indian producers were also crushed through the policy of duties. The Company increased the inland duties, toll and tariff barriers. The number of taxable goods manufactured in India was increased by 1813 to 67 per cent *ad valorem*. Correspondingly, the import duty on the British cloth by the Charter Act of 1813 was fixed only at 2½ per cent—Export of cotton goods to Britain was already prohibitied; and *ad valorem* duty of over 71 per cent was imposed on these goods imported in Britain for re-export to the European markets. It may be noted here that foreign export of India was already monopolised by the British East India Company and, therefore, the Indian products were being exported only through the English merchants.

It was all done in the British industrial interests. It is clear from the remarks of British historian Wilson. He says:

> It was stated in evidence (before the Select Committee in 1813) that the cotton and silk goods of India could be sold for a profit in British market at price from 50 to 60 per cent lower than those fabricated in England. It consequently became necessary to protect the latter by duties of 70 to 80 per cent on their value or by positive prohibition. Had this been not the case, had not such prohibitory duties and decrees existed, the mills of Paisley and Manchester would have been stopped at the outset and could not have again been set in motion, by the power of steam. They were created by the sacrifice of the Indian manufacturers. Had India been independent, she would have retaliated, would have imposed prohibitive duties upon British goods, and would have thus preserved her own productive industry from annihilation. This act of self-defence was not permitted to her; she was at the mercy of the stranger. British goods were forced upon her without paying dury and the foreign manufacturers employed the arm of political injustice to keep down and ultimately strangle a competitor with whom he could not have contended on equal term.

This policy was successfully carried out in running other industries as well. In 1800, for example, the Court of Directors of the Company accomplished the ruin of the prosperous ship-building industry of India by prohibiting the employment of Indian ships in the trade between England and India. One of the reasons they adduced in support of their unjust decision was as follows:

> The native sailors of India are...on their arrival here (*i.e.*, in England) led into scenes which soon divest them of the respect and awe they had entertained in India for the European character. The contemptuous reports which they disseminate on their return cannot fail to have a very unfavourable influence upon the minds of our Asiatic subjects, whose reverence for our character which has hitherto continued to maintain our supremacy in the East,

> will be gradually changed and the effects of it may prove extremely detrimental....

The British policy was successful. The export of Indian goods declined to the benefit of British goods. For example, the export of Indian cotton piece goods to Britain fell from about twelve million metres in 1814 to only about 3 lakh metres in 1835. The import of British cotton goods increased from only about seven and a half lakh metres in 1814 to more than forty-seven millions metres in 1835. Thus, ruined by the unremunerative prices, oppressed by the Gumashtas, and restricted in the market by the import-export duties, the Indian weavers deserted their profession in large numbers and brought further pressure on the only available agricultural sector. Professor P.N. Chopra has rightly said that "from a manufacturing country India has been reduced to the position of an importer of foreign manufactures for the consumption of her people". Instead India became the exporter of raw materials needed by the British industry. In this way Indian industry was ruined and Indian economy was converted into a colonial economy—market for her manufactures and a source for the supply of raw materials to her industries. This was boastfully conceded while advocating for the extension to the right of administration of India by the Company. It was stated before the Select Committee appointed to inquire into the claims of the Company:

> ...this company has in various ways; encouraged and assisted by our great manufacturing ingenuity and skill, succeeded in converting India from a manufacturing country into a country exporting raw produce.... The peculiar state of the relation between this country (Britain) and India and the necessity of extracting from the later three millions of money for Home Charges...and the altered state of Indian industry in its being converted from a manufacturing country into a country exporting raw produce....

Evolution of Modern Industry

Evolution of modern Indian industry can be dated to the year 1833 when the Charter Act, 1833 was passed. This Act divested the Company of its commercial charter. The European settlers and other British capitalists were permitted to invest capital for the expansion of trade. This Company had also accumulated surplus capital. Until 1857, the capital investment, however, remained insignificant. It as Leyland Jenks says "represented simply portions of Indian spoils and revenue" accumulated by the British officers in India. Though construction of irrigation works and railways—which was basically undertaken to administer the country efficiently and facilitated the growth of trade—afforded almost an unlimited field for profitable investment of capital in India, it could not attract the Company which was interested mainly "in exploiting and not improving the resources of the country". Therefore, there were only about 440 kms. of railway line when the resurgence of 1857 brought an end to the Company rule.

Resurgence in 1857 brought a new landmark in the evolution of modern industry in India. This resurgence focussed the world attention in general, and the British, in particular, upon India. The British Government was not prepared India to go to the American way. The root cause for the peoples' support to the native rulers' leadership was their economic hardship and increasing unemployment with the ruining of industry and withering away the only other avenue of joining civil and military administration of the indigenous rulers. Therefore, the British Government terminated the right of administration by the Company and transferred the Government of India to the Crown. It was necessary for the Crown Government to take economic steps, alongwith the political concession, to ameliorate the economic conditions to win the confidence of the people. The policy inaugurated by the Charter Act, 1813 was therefore, re-emphasised for the industrial development in India.

New industrial activities took two forms: (i) plantation; and (ii) factory industry. The plantation industry was the first to attract the Europeans. The plantation industry could provide jobs at a large scale but in reality it could meet the increasing demands for tea and coffee and indigo by the prosperous British society. Therefore, the plantation industry was the first to attract the Europeans. It was for this reason that plantation industry had started emerging much earlier.

Indigo. After the export of Indian calicos was prohibited to Britain and its export to other markets was curtailed, the East India Company faced the problem of finding a substitute to fill up the vacuum as also to invest the surplus capital is a result of huge profits to the Company as well as its servants. The French had already started the indigo factories in Bengal and Bihar. They took extraordinary interests after the French revolution had created obstacles in the way of capitalists of France. It suffered a great setback in 1801-82. But it again took up after the Continental System imposed by Napoleon did not leave any alternative to the Company to increase its trade outside the continent. This industry got further fillip after the investment in opium plantation failed due to increasing resistance of China. As a result, indigo remained the sole source of private remittance. There was a great attraction to it after the Charter Act, 1833 gave the Europeans ownership of land and full freedom of contract. Its production increased to about 58,000 maunds in Bihar and to about 64,000 maunds in the Doab by 1877. The invention of synthetic dye in 1897 dealt a death blow to this industry. Its export, valued at 3.5 millions in 1895, fell to about 4 lacs only in 1905. Between 1904-05 and 1914-15 the area under indigo shrank to one-tenth of the area in 1894-95. In spite of the peasants' revolts to the policy ruining the indigo industry and Gandhi's Champaran Campaign, the industry could not survive. There remained only 65 plantations in Bihar and Orissa in 1921. Out of these, 56 were owned by the Europeans. "Their baroque buildings stand today in ruins all over the country, the vanishing memory of the first British enterprise in India."

Tea and Coffee. The monopoly on trade-rights of the Company were abolished in 1833. The Company thereafter gave a serious attention to the possibilities of tea in India. Andrew Charlton found the tea plant in Assam and William Bentinck immediately realized its importance. He formed a Tea Committee in January 1834.

After experiments, the Assam Company was founded in February 1839. Tea plantations proved very fruitful. The Assam Company could pay dividends at 12 per cent by 1860. It brought about a great rush. Twenty companies got registered in between 1859 and 1865 in addition to many more unregistered private gardens. Barring the depression in the year 1866-67, the Companies made huge profits. Assam Company paid a dividend of 35 per cent in the following decades.

Railway construction in the area further boosted this industry, and increased the dividends. Coffee plantation also started simultaneously. As the tea plantation was the most important industry of Eastern India, coffee plantaion became the centre of activities in South India.

Jute Industry. The third important plantation, which also gave birth to factory industry, was jute plantation. It was the greatest attraction of the British investment and also became a most significant item of export to the US, Penang and Singapore. It was this increasing demand and huge profit which encouraged the British to set jute industry in India.

However, all these plantation industries, from the beginning, were owned, managed and controlled by the ex-employees of the Company and other people connected with the Company. They were interested in huge profits. Indigo, tea and coffee, and jute offered them easy and high return on their investment. But the plantation industries, except for jute, could not emerge in India and the products of the plantation remained mostly as raw materials as the items of export. Therefore, plantation fall more in the agricultural economy than the industrial economy of India. Real and satisfactory progress in the factory industries began only from 1880s.

Local Manufacture. The Famine Commission held that the import of goods from abroad had ruined the local industry. The artisans and other interests fell back upon the agriculture. The agriculture was dependent on the monsoon. As the monsoon fails the rural distress becomes more alarming since they did not have any other occupations. Therefore, the Famine Commission recommended a policy of encouragement to local manufacturers to decrease the burden on agricultural sector. The British administration in India, however, was not keen in industrial growth than aid to the merchant. Investment in social overheads,

State guaranteed investment in railways and irrigation schemes, extraordinary measures to extent the cultivation of raw cotton, re-modelling of land regulations to suit European settlement and investment, expenditure of public funds to encourage European entrepreneurship were the basic principles of the British Government in India. They were rather against the encouragement in industries which was held in contravention to the principles of *laissez faire*. But the British policy had created two forces which helped the evolution of industries in India.

Firstly, the resurgence of 1857 alarmed the British Government and businessmen alike. After the loss of American colonies, India had become the principal unit of the British Empire. Therefore, they accelerated their efforts in making Indian their secure possession. Railways were considered the touchstone of the consolidation of British rule. The railways also served the imperial interests most. They facilitated rapid movement of troops from one place to another in case of emergency. They also provided profitable investment for British capital, promoted export from British of locomotives, rolling stock, steel, machinery and other equipment, brought extension of market for British manufactures in the interior of India and facilitated collection of foodgrains, raw cotton and other agicultural produce from the markets of India for export to Britain. That is why there was a phenomenal growth in the construction of railways. The length of railways increased from 2,573 km in 1861 to 5,428 km in 1865, 8,170 km in 1871, 11,783 km in 1877, 32,523 km in 1896, 49,207 km in 1908, and 55,773 km in 1914. Opening up of the Suez Canal also shortened the distance between Europe and India by about 4,830 kms. This phenomenal growth in communications not only became the pioneer industry of India but also provided the means of further industrialisation.

Secondly, as Clow maintains, the Indian industries at the time "had flourished round the throne of the rulers and had looked to them for support". These economic centres were responsible for the political instability. They helped centrifugal forces indulged in breaking political unity. The political disintegration thereafter brought about stagnation in the industrial activity as well. The British commercial policy ruined the industries and thus eliminated those autonomous economic *vis-a-vis* political centres. Instead big mercantile towns, *viz.* Calcutta, Bombay, Ahmedabad, Madras emerged. These mercantile towns helped in bringing economic unity to exploit the whole country. The commercial fortunes accumulated in these mercantile towns contributes much in laying down the modern industrial foundations in a big way when the opportunity was offered by the American Civil War, the Crimean War and the two World Wars.

Capital Investment. As mentioned earlier, the above two factors created a good opportunity for investment. Plantation, banking, shipping and trade were the main fields of investments in the beginning. As a result, Rs. 225 crore were invested by 1870. This investment further increased economic activities. Revitalization of the economy brought about increase in the investments at a faster rate thereafter. The investments increased to Rs. 441 crore in 1896, and further rose to Rs. 547 crore in 1910. It was this increased investment which helped in increasing the volume of trade as well. The volume of foreign trade increased from Rs. 69.6 crore in 1859-60 to Rs. 1004 crore in 1869-70; Rs. 122 crore in 1879-80; Rs. 195.7 crore in 1891-92; Rs. 266.49 crore in 1908-09; and to Rs. 441 crore in 1913-14. The investments and foreign trade gave a great stimulative forces to the inland trade which increased by 108 per cent between 1890 and 1909. The circulation of currency notes rose from 127 crore in 1896 to Rs. 181 crore in 1908.

The banks and joint stock companies also increased considerably. India had acquired a place among the most advanced commercial nations of the world before the First World War. Thus, the improved transport and communications, growth of foreign trade and consequent accumulation of commercial fortunes had created an impetus for industrial development. Railway building and its maintenance had their effects more far-reaching than opening up of the interior and exposing agriculture to the winds of commerce. As Sunil Kumar Sen opines that it were these circumstances which released some of the latent potentialities for industrial advance. It was only the

British metropolitan, that is in Britain, industrial interests which kept the industrial growth staggering. Before 1900, the Indians could start 194 mills of cotton textiles with 5 million spindles and 40,000 looms. The jute industry, as stated earlier, was in the hands of the Europeans only. There were 36 mills with over 16,000 looms. The coal production was only about 6 million tonnes, though India had the potentiality to increase its output at a faster rate. In conjuction with the availability of iron ore, India, free of British domination, could have still surpassed in the industrial growth, many of the countries of the world.

Swadeshi Movement. It was the Swadeshi Movement, started in the first decade of the twentieth century, which strived and encouraged the entrepreneurs to counteract against the foreign industrial interest. With the spread of English language, a middle class, consisting of men of commerce, bankers, lawyers, doctors and other professionals, had emerged more powerful than in any time in the past. Taught the European literature, they had also become as ambitious as were their counterparts in the European countries. The commercial activities had also forced the foreign concerns to train the Indian in technical subject to run their activities at junior level. Therefore, encouraged by the Swadeshi Movement, these human forces contemplated development of industrial sector in India itself. As a result by 1914, the cotton mills increased from 194 to 273 with 68 lakhs spindles and 104,000 looms; jute mills from 36 to 64 with 36,000 looms; and coal output increased to sixteen million tonnes. With the establishment of Tata Iron and Steel Company (TISCO) in 1907, Indian entrepreneurs entered the iron and steel industry too before 1914. These industries employed about one million labourers or about 3.15 per cent of the total population. Thus, the potentials from the emergence of industrial sector were present. It needed only loosening of the hostility of the government to get the ball moving.

First World War and Development of Industry. The First World War provided this opportunity to the industrialists in India. The British Government appointed to Munitions Board to control and develop Indian resources, regulate contracts, limit and co-ordinate demands for articles not manufactured in

India, and supply the manufacturing resources to India to war purpose, to reduce especially demands on shipping. India was required to supply articles, medical stores and certain technical stores to the Allied Armies in the East. It increased the demand of textiles to Rs. 2 crore a month and hides and leather to Rs. 1 crore a month. Manufacturers were assisted and encouraged to produce goods earlier procured from Europe. This Board was also functioning as Industrial Commission to recommend the means and ways for industrial development to meet the war demands. Since the arrangements made by the Board proved useful in meeting the emergency, the Commission hoped "that care will be taken to preserve such features" of the war times "as are properly adaptable to peace conditions". The Commission warned that until these industries are developed "on an adequate scale, Indian capitalists will, in times of peace, be deprived of a number of profitable enterprises whilst in the event of war which renders sea transport impossible, India's all-important exisiting industries will be exposed to the risk of stoppage, her consumers to great hardships, and her armed forces to the gravest possible danger". The Commission was also not satisfied with the low scale of import of machinery which was now being manufactured in Britain. Industrial development in India was bound, the Commission argued, to increase the demands of machinery which could help Britain to diversify its trade and help rejuvenate its economy devastated by the First World War.

The War had thus, on the one hand, weakened the imperial hold over India, on the other hand, considerably reduced the dominating status of Britain at international level. The Swadeshi Movement had also strained political atmosphere. The Montague-Chelmsford Report on Constitutional Reforms held that the injury done to the Indo-British political relations was due to the widespread feeling in India that their country was subjected to the Lancashire and other British industrial interests. Therefore, the Secretary of State had to grant, for political reasons, freedom in deciding its commercial polity. As it is popularly called, this 'Fiscal Autonomy Convention' brought an end to the policy of *laissez faire*. Instead, the 'protection' to Indian industries, recommended by the Fiscal Commission (1921) was granted to iron and steel, cotton textiles, paper, matches, sugar and heavy chemical industries.

The "protection" extended to Indian industries gave a great fillip and the industrial production increased phenomenonly. On the eve of the Second World War, the production of steel ingots had increased from 132 lakhs to 10.49 lakhs tonnes (80%); cotton piece goods from 1,567.3 million to 3,672.2 million metres (250 per cent); match boxes from 16 million gross to 22 million gross (38 per cent), paper and paper board from 24,384 to 60,075 tonnes (180 per cent); and sugar cane from 24,384 to 945,000 tonnes (3779 per cent). (In 1913-14, the raw sugar of Rs. 15 crore and the paper of the tune of Rs. 1.60 crore was imported.) With the expansion of the industrial sector the number of industrial workers rose from 869,643 in 1912 to 15,55,387 in 1927 and 16,10,921 in 1935. Thus, India figured among the first eight industrial nations of the world. Still the country was not industrialised to the extent of the availability of resources. Rather it was still an agricultural economy which provided livelihood to 70 per cent of the population.

Impact of Second World War. The Second World War exercised more profound influence on the development of Indian industry. As the war intensified the communication and supply lines of the British and other European powers were cut-off and the Japanese pressure increased. The Japanese success brought a heavy pressure upon the British and the American defence of South and South-East Asia as well as West Asia. The British and its allies were, therefore, left with little option than to depend upon India for regular supply to meet their war needs. The British Government again directed the Government of India to gear the Indian economy to its war needs. The Allied Powers laid increasing demands upon Indian economy. The War thus, offered the long awaited opportunities to the Indian entrepreneurs to expand their industries. They were also assured by the government that in any case, in any form, encourage the development of industries for our war needs. Those entrepreneurs who had come to the assistance of the State would not be left high and dry to take care of themselves after the War was over.

But the Indian entrepreneurs also suffered from those very constraints which forced the British Government to encourage expansion of industries in India. The Indian entrepreneurs could not procure new plants from the British and other developed countries. Therefore, they had to put up with mainly the existing plants only. The only benefit which they could get was to utilise their existing plants, for the first time, not only to the optimum level but also beyond plant capacity. In this way, the Indian industries which were already in existence worked to full capacity and often in more shifts than one. New plants were added in some cases and some basic industries were established. A rapid expansion of small scale industries all over the country created new source of supply. As a result of this impetus, the index of the industrial production increased from 102.7 point in 1939 to 120 in 1945.

This war also resulted in the founding of many new industries which might not have come into existence otherwise. These industries were: (a) Ferro-alloys like Ferro-silicon and Ferro-manganese; (b) non-ferros metals and metal fabricating industries like copper, copper sheets, wires and cables, etc.; (c) mechanical, industries like diesel engines, pumps, bicycles and sewing machines, machine tools and cutting tools; (d) a few items of textiles, tea and oil processing machinery; and (e) chemicals like caustic soda, chlorine, superphospahates, etc. The raw material for these industries was not generally within the country and it was imported from the foreign markets. In this way India started importing industrial raw materials after a lapse of about 100 years. It also gave an added advantage to India in comparison to other British colonies and it could inherit comparatively in advanced industrial base and a source of import of industrial raw material through the efforts of an imperial power.

By the end of the war, the number of the companies rose from 11,114 companies with a total paid-up capital of Rs. 290 crore in 1939 to 14,859 with a total paid-up capital of Rs. 389 crore. Indian industry registered its name in the manufacture of hydrogenated oil, transport and electrical equipments, machine tools, basic chemicals, lower alcohol, synthetic resins and plastic, etc. It was also due to this increased production and manufacture of new items, that increased the surplus in the foreign trade and India could repay its all debts and on the eve of independence the country could have a reserve of foreign exchange.

This industrial growth was not, however, much advantageous to the long term interests.

First of all, the overuse of the plants deteriorated the machinery and its life got shortened. Thus, independent India inherited in these plants a burden of replacing it, which is still unsolved in many sectors. For example, sick textile mills are result of the overuse of its machinery during the Second World War period.

Secondly, after the cessation of war, the demand came down to an abnormally low level and the Indian economy went into red when the inflection was taking over in other sectors. Therefore, the Indian economy started with the much-regretful step of devaluing its rupee.

Thirdly, it was also the result of this war growth that it profited most the entrepreneurs and led to the emergence of 'big industrial house'. They conserved so much power that the future social, political and economic growth of the country was to be decided in their favour. It shall not be exaggerating if we say that this war gave birth to that powerful group of industrial interests in India which replaced the British industrial interests in independent India. And they had to exert the pressure in the same way as the British industrial interests had been playing under the aegis of imperial rule. The latter were exploiting the Indian economy to their metropolitan interests whereas to the former was left for exploitation the non-industrial population.

Fourthly, the emergence of industrial interests also tied the fate of those industrial interests with the developed nations. They had to depend upon them. It is not the place to describe in detail, but it was this factor which preserved the oft-quoted "neo-colonialism" in India.

Middle Class and Indian Economy

24

In his popular work *The Indian Middle Classes*, B.B. Misra has explained the growth of middle classes in the beautiful manner. More information are also available regarding the various aspects of Middle Classes from the works of Jawaharlal Nehru (*The Discovery of India*), Edward Terry (*A Voyage to East India*) and Francois Bernier (*Travels in the Mughal Empire*).

In the Western society, especially after the industrial revolution, the society was divided into upper, middle and lower classes in accordance with their economic strength.

According to Prof. Misra, "In a materialistic society, it is briefly the economic inequality of man that influences, if it does not wholly determine, social differentiation." Therefore, the class definition of modern times "arises from the difference of relationship which a person or groups bears to property or the means of production and distribution". In such a society, it is the ownership of the means of production which raises the social status of an individual rather than the birth which decided the place of human beings in the Sanskritized society.

An individual naturally enjoys a low status in comparison to the owner in whose employment he earns his livelihood. A modern society is, therefore, divided into classes or groups of people joined together from motives of common economic interest, common ways of behaviours, and common traits of character. Each such class forms a hierarchy of status according to the varying quality of social prestige and power expressed through the standard of living, nature of occupation, and wealth.

Thus, modern thinking of the society was different from that of ancient or medieval times. Then it was political and religious power which earned a higher social status. But the emergence of commercial and professional and colonisers in the sixteenth-seventeenth centuries started questioning the dominance of feudal and ecclesiastical leaders. Philosophers like Rousseau echoed "equality, liberty and fraternity". Inspired by the new thought the subjected people, but strengthened with the wealth, earned without land and out of the commercial adventures, started fighting for equality of opportunity on the basis of qualification and ability. They broke the hold of feudal chiefs. Their struggle led to recognition to wealth, education and power attained by one's own individual skill. It was this group of people fighting against the old social order which emerged as middle-class or "bourgeoisie" in the western societies.

Pre-British Indian Society. Taking into consideration, the class character of the military aristocracy of the medieval times, the society can be divided into the following categories: the Brahman and the warriors (Kshatriyas), the business community or the Baniyas, the artisans and craftsmen and the working classes. All of them were strictly confined to their castes and professions and did not have the courage to give up their calling and accept a new one. They did not get any special education or training and were deprived of scientific education and research and were restrained from the advancement of their skills. Training to the professions was more or less hereditary and descended from father to son. This segmentation of the social orders was not at all conducive to the development of a new system. "Because they remained divided into water tight status groups according to the caste to which they belonged", observes Miśra, "they could not form themselves into a unitary middle class social order, comparable to the western countries, cases of caste schism did arise from time to time against the hereditary privileges, but they were rare."

The medieval Indian set-up was entrenched with feudalistic character, therefore, it was always involved in infighting for their selfish ambitions and ego. In the capitalistic system, political and social unity was possible side by side with the growth of patriotic spirit. "This is the reason why not a single British Officer betrayed his country during the phase of Indian conquest while on the other several Indian Rajas, merchants and soldiers proved disloyal to the country and acted as traitors." It was because of the social behaviour towards its members.

In the medieval system, the Kshatriya of the Sanskritized society consisted of the king, his courtiers, governor of the province and other nobles controlled army and administered the territories and owned the lands.

The priestly class, *i.e.* the Brahmana was relegated to second place in the medieval power structure. The Brahmana was still engaged in scholarly and professional occupations, but he was now entirely dependent upon the pleasures of the military artistocracy.

The Vaishya was constituted both by the merchant and the agriculturist.

As discussed elsewhere, the Shudra was reduced to the sub-human status and he had not been given any status in the Indian society. The Shudra of medieval times consisted of not only the Harijan of the present age but also the artisans who were at the most touchable Shudras.

The industrial growth, for a longer time, drew the needed manpower from the medieval Shudra—it was this class which constituted the labour force of modern times. It may be remembered here that though from 1920s onward, the pecuniary considerations also attracted people from higher social strata in the industrial sector, but in majority of the cases they filled supervisory posts. In other words, we can say that the upper classes created here also an upper layer in the industrial labour force pushing down the Shudra to lower scale of the industrial labour force. It was the merchant, professional, priestly and administrative class which wore the shoes of English bourgeoisie in the British Indian society.

Therefore, Professor Misra has divided the Indian middle classes in the following categories:

(i) Merchants, agents, proprietors of trading firsm;

(ii) Managers, executives, supervisors;

(iii) Higher salaried officers of institutions and societies, trade associations, trade unions, educational bodies, etc.;

(iv) Civil servants serving in the different departments of the government;

(v) Lawyers, doctors, professors, writers, artists and priests;

(vi) Class of rentiers, revenue collectors;

(vii) Wealth shopkeepers, hoteliers, accountants;

(viii) Salaried hands and supervisory personnel of landed estates;

(ix) Main body of students engaged in higher education;

(x) Secondary school teachers and officers of local bodies and social political workers.

The emergence of these middle classes can be understood properly only in the context of the emergence and the character of the British bourgeoisie.

Growth of Middle Class in Britain. Since middle class had emerged in India as a result of British contact, it is relevant to know its emergence in Britain. In the pre-commercial era, the British society was a simple society. There, the production and commerce was owned by the same individual. "He was a producer-trader because his industrial and commercial functions were indistinguishably mixed up. The master craftsman was, of course, there but he worked with his men under the same roof without any secular or functional differentiation. Their relationship was personal, and together they formed a single category of brother-labourers."

But the discovery of sea trade routes with the East in the fifteenth century brought a marked changed in whole of the European continent. The trade with India and other eastern countries was thriving. Out of this trade spoil, there emerged a powerful commercial class in Portugal and Holland. Their steps were followed by the British and the French. Small group of insignificant traders in England emerged into a giant East India Company who attained sovereignty in India. In juxtaposition with their political power, the wealth started pouring from India into the coffers of traders and servants of the Company. As a result, the trader and servants emerged as "a separate social and functional category" in the British society. He was not only independent of the landlord and the State, rather he had accumulated economic power to influence both the groups who had been placed, since then very high in the social hierarchy. So much so the landlord and royal aristocracy had also become "sleeping partners" of this trader class. The wealth earned out of this trade, helped facilitate industrial growth. This moved the wheel of prosperity and thus, emerged the entrepreneurs, the professional and the scholar who strengthened the middle class. It will be no exaggerating to say that it was this middle class which finally obtained hold over the political parties and provided strength to outwit the landed aristocracy in retaining the political power in Britain. It is not necessary to go into details it is suffice to say that it was this middle class which became the virtual ruler of Britain and British empire. This middle class of Britain is also categorised as the "bourgeoisie" in the Marxian terminology.

Middle Class in India. The situation in India was quite contrary to the British situation. It has now been authentically established that Indian economy and industry were highly developed from the standards of those times. Rather India was then the "workshop of the world". Its industry had given her an edge over other countries.

Edward Terry (1605-1627) was dismayed to see the wealth pouring into the country. To him "as the all Rivers run into the Sea, so many Silver streams run into this (Mughal) Monarchy and there stay".

Bernier also noted that the wealth "after circulating in every other quarter of the globe came at length to be swallowed up, lost in some measure, in Hindustan". This wealth had enriched urban life all round. The aristocracy—both military and landed—

constituted the upper class of the society; the merchants competing with them. As a result of this prosperity, there existed other professions of recreation, meditation and materialism. There were avenues to earn the livelihood respectfully and their voice had been heard in the government as well as peoples' circles. If that be the criterion then there actually existed a middle class in India when the British were struggling to obtain "equality, liberty and fraternity" in their country.

The Indian society was, however, superimposed by the Mughal autonomy. The Mughal nobility did not enjoy economic stability and psychological security like their counterparts enjoyed in Britain. In fact, the mobility in all circumstances, could enjoy with their wealth only within their lifetime. They did not enjoy the right to bequeath their titles as well as wealth to their descendants. The wealth belonged to the Emperor, and the descendants had to start from scratch.

Writing about the nobility's right to bequeath their property to their descendants, F. Pelsaart, an English traveller, says:

> Immediately on the death of a lord (noble) who has enjoyed the king's jagirs, be great or small, without an exception—some times even before the breath is out of his body—the King's officers are ready on the spot, and make an inventory of the entire estate, regarding everything down to the value of a single piece, even to the dresses and jewels of the ladies provided they have not concealed them. The King takes back the whole estate absolutely for himself except in a case where the deceased has done good service in his life-time, when the women and children are given enough to live on, but no more.... And so you may see a man whom you knew with his turban cocked on one side, and newly as unapproachable as his master, his running about with a torn coat and pinched force; for it is rarely that such men obtain similar employment from other masters, and they go about like pictures of death in life, I have known many of them to do.

Though this practice strangled the growth of middle class in India, still they had not been ordinary mass. Their status could have a grave danger only for the foreigners, who had been respectable guests to all the highest posts in the government after the rise of Muhammedan power in India. The descendants of the nobility can be equated with the civil servants in the Eastminsterial model. A son of a Secretary in the Westminsterial administrative machinery had to compete with others to join the "elite service" and he might not be able to come in the selected list, but rarely he would be joining at the lowest of the uncovenanted jobs of this system. It was only during the British rule which created circumstances for the emergence of middle class as a counterpart of the "Bourgeoisie" in Britain. The middle class first of all emerged in commercial sector, and was followed in administration and industry at the last stage.

Emergence of Commercial Middle Class. After the Mughal Emperor, Shah Alam granted exemption of duties on the goods traded by the English, through his Firman of 1713, it went against the interests of the existing commercial people in India. With the systematic policy enjoined with political authority of the East India Company (after 1757), the Indian commercial class were reduced to the status of agents. They could not gain their power till 1833. But in 1833, the monopoly of the East India Company was terminated by the British Crown and it was left with the task of administration only. The country was thrown open to all, especially English, trade interests. But that time India had reached a stage, where, as Professor Misra observes, "the mild and constitutional character of Government and the rule of law, the security of private property and the defined rights of agricultural classes, a national system of education and a period of continued peace, an economy of *laissez faire* and a liberal policy of employment and social reform" had been inaugurated.

Emergence of Agents, Brokers and Middlemen. The Company trade monopoly over trade in India had already created a class having potentialities to become commercial middle class. Clive's report to the Directors of the Company is self-explanatory. He reported that "the sudden, and among many, the unwarrantable Acquisition of Riches, had introduced luxury in every shape, and in its most pernicious excess. Every inferior seemed to have grasped at wealth, that he might be enabled to assume the spirit of profusion which was now the only distinction between him and his superior. In a country where money is plenty, where fear is the principle of government, and where your arms are ever victorious...it is no wonder that corruption should find its way to spot so well prepared to receive it. It is no wonder that the lust of riches should readily embrace the preferred means of its gratification, or that the instruments of your power should avail themselves of their authority, and proceed even to extortional in those cases where simple corruption could not keep pace with their rapacity". This tendency increased the lust for wealth and subverted the social norms. Accumulation of wealth by fair and foul means justified the ends. The wealth had been obtaining respect to the people in the society. Clive himself further reported that the wealth "were so publicly known and vindicated, that every one thought he had a right to enrich himself, at all events, with as much expedition as possible; the monopoly of salt, bettel, tobacco, etc. was another fund of immense profits to the Company's Servants, and likewise to such others as they permitted to enjoy a share, while not a rupee of advantage accrued to the Government, and very little to the Company, from that trade".

The behaviour of the corrupt officials of the Company was not only imitated but also got encouragement for rampant corruption among the Indian agents. But the British did not punish a person for accumulating wealth by foul means as well. This tendency encouraged others also to accumulate wealth by underhand deals. It was the "rule of law operated in the field of free enterprises", (which) contributed considerably to the growth of the commercial middle class. It was this fortune which made it possible for them to build large landed estates. These were thus, able to supplant the old aristocracy and commercial monopolists.

Commercial Class as a Pressure Group. As their economic power increased, the commercial class grabbed all the available jobs as well. In 1835, for example, the total number of Indians on the petit jury list of the Supreme Court of Judicature at Calcutta was 99. Of these, 96 were Bengali Hindus consisting of 54 *banyans* or *sarkars*, 28 writers, 10 *zamindars*, 4 clerks and 3 bankers. The Parsis constituted the dominant parallel interest in Bombay and the Brahmans in Madras. In this way these people had supplanted the power of political patronage earlier, almost exclusively, exercised by the military aristocracy. They organised themselves as a pressure group "not only to safeguard their commercial rights, but also to influence the policy of government in the enactment of measures calculated to encourage free enterprise". Trade Associations, Chambers of Commerce and Indigo Planters' Association had emerged on the political scene of India on these counts. They imitated the role their counterparts playing in Britain. In India also, however, the lead was provided by the British themselves.

The Indigo Plantation, for example, was the exclusive pressure of the British. The Indigo Planters' Association had formed "to collect information on 'the state and wants of the various districts' in regard to public works, including roads, canals navigation, irrigation and bridges; to receive representations on the 'state of the revenue laws' on the 'administration of justice', on the state of police and its bearing on the security of person, capital and industry; to receive suggestions for reform on all these subjects; to watch the progress of legislation, and to communicate with the higher authorities in India and at home, whenever the interest for the advancement (were threatened by any governmental measure)". Their activities inculcated that spirit of furthering their own interest which could be congenial for the advancement of their material interest among the indigenous commercial class. It was their continued pressure that the transport and communication system was improved in India. It was this British vested interests which, in fact, initiated the process of modern industrialization in opposition to the Imperial interest of their home manufactures. This commercial middle class also became one of the major sources of strength to the political movements and they were always in the forefront. These middle class people increased the pace of the growth of foreign trade of India.

The Industrial Middle Class. Industrial advancement of the country withered away with the consolidation of British rule in

India. With it the artisans also fell back upon the agriculture; and those who could not find any other alternative became "domestic servants" of the "saabs". This state of affair continued for long since the British metropolitan industrial interests held up the industrialization of India in the modern times as well. It was this policy which made the industrial occupation "not a respectable one. It was low and demanding in social estimation". Thus, by the systematic British policy, both economic and sociological factors precluded the growth of an industrial middle class in India on the European lines. It was again the British who made the industrial occupation a respectable one and gave birth to the industrial middle class.

Company Servants and Industrialization. The Company had permitted its servants to invest their "savings" into such "industries" which could be useful to the British people and industries. The Company servants, therefore, invested their capital in such industries which could not thrive in their own country and had a great demand. Such an industry was indigo and it was the indigo plantation which became, in the beginning, the most attractive field of investment to the servants. It is, therefore, rightly said that "root of independent British enterprise in Bengal (and in other provinces) is to be found in the civil service". They introduced to maximize their earnings by power-driven industrial plants in India. In this way the process of industrialization had been initiated.

After 1933, the British Government terminated the commercial monopoly of the East India Company. It opened the gates of Indian economy to the private European entrepreneurs. Following the civil servants' entrepreneurship, they invested capital in plantation industry such as indigo, jute, sugar, tea and coffee. The Crimean War had obstructed the import of jute from Russia. Disappearance of this source of supply of strategic goods like jute goods, increased the importance of jute and jute industry, in India. Besides, the government encouraged the construction of railways through private capital. As has been discussed earlier, the railways were the first tangible step towards industrialization. Though it was the greatest source of draining out the wealth of India, but this enterprise also released considerable capital for circulation, created a variety of new openings for employment and set into motion a degree of social mobility that the country had never previously experienced. This phenomenal growth of capital investment also opened avenues for the investment of capital by the Indians in industries.

Indian Investment. Though constrained with the fear of risk in the event of anti-industrial and hostile attitude of the government, a few Bengali and Parsi took courage and invested their capital into industrial enterprises. They initiated the process of developing, first textile industry. It was this investment which created industrial middle class-bourgeoisie of India. As has been analysed earlier, the future development went on providing opportunities for the diversification and growth of industrial activities in India. With it there emerged the great though junior to the British industrialists in India as well, industrial magnates. They were also helped by the free-trader boggey which emerged stronger and the government had to bow down before them. In this was the private entrepreneurs, both Europeans and the Indians, emerged as the most powerful middle class in India. It was this middle class which wore the shoes of British bourgeoisie and in juxtaposition of the commercial middle class increased its weight in directing the internal as well as foreign policy of India.

Management Agency and Middle Class. In the process of increasing commerce of India and industrialization of the country to produce export goods, the Europeans had started investing capital in India. The profit volume and the British policy of building capitalist system, there emerged managing agency system. "Management contracts between British companies and Anglo-Indian merchants—as resident British traders were then called—first became known in the eighteen-thirties when the East India Company's monopoly of trade ended. It attracted a flood of British capital for, first, railway constructions. The merchants had a unique opportunity to branch out from export trading into production for exports if only they could acquire new funds. The London and Liverpool houses readily extended the required capital investment if only they could find reliable management able to cope with alien conditions in India. In these conditions there emerged managing agency system.

It was a very important source of strength not only of capitalist system but also of the foreign power. The managing agency provided the money for investment by a joint stock company raised in Britain. It was a lucrative profit earning enterprise. Its popularity and growth can be understood from the fact that on the eve of the Second World War sixty-one foreign agencies were managing more than 600 rupee companies in addition to a number of sterling ones.

Andrew Yule, who had been referred earlier, was one of these magnates. He managed 59 companies in India. The growth of this type of managing agencies helped in the growth of managing executives joint-stock company raisers, shareholders, directors, *i.e.* all those professions, which are very pecuniary professions, emerged in India. It was this class which gained greater strength than other professions, to pressurize the governmental policies. Therefore, in a nutshell, the commercial class which emerged wealthier during the years of the decline of Indian economy, emerged as agents of the foreign capital and government.

Taking advantage of their system they also accumulated wealth and imitated their practice. They raised their own companies, invested in industries and formed their joint stock companies. All these steps led to the emergence of a powerful business community which became the core of middle class in India. They attained that political respectability which their counterparts had been enjoying in the British Westminsterial system. Outside this middle class, these were landed middle class and the professionals, *i.e.* intellectuals who took up those professions which were respectable. The latter is called the educated middle class.

Labour Force and Indian Economy

25

Labour force played significant role in Indian economy; even today labour force occupies a predominant place in Indian economy.

Labour is not a new phenomenon in modern India. It is considered as the oldest phenomenon in our society.

Meaning

In technical terms, labour is constituted by those who do not possess means of production. They sell their physical labour—skilled or unskilled—to earn their livelihood. Assuming this, it can safely be said that in the Sanskritized society in India Shudra constituted the labour force.

As stated, this Shudra population went on increasing, and by the time the British obtained power, all the professionals, especially at lower level, became touchable and untouchable labourers. They worked for the bureaucracy, landlords and moneyed classes.

Since in the western terminology, the term labour has become synonymous with the factory labour only, these labourers did not fit into modern labour force, because according to the modern concept, industrial and commercial labour force is dependent for wages and employment upon the entrepreneurs. It is not, however, correct to say that workers in the pre-British India did not constitute a labour force as they were "self-employed" in a trade and not available for hire. Though in many instances, extremely difficult to distinguish, the "wage earner" were treated as a labour in statistical inquiry. The modern labour force emerged, after the change in British policy facilitated the growth of modern industry. In this sense we can agree that the labour force, as it is understood in European terminology, emerged only during the second half of the British rule.

Pre-Modern Industry Labour. After the ruin of indigenous industry till the building of new industrial sector, the labour force existed round the pivot of land. In almost all through the entire Gangetic belt, now comprising Bengal, Orissa, Bihar and Uttar Pradesh, the landlords system prevailed. The tenants had definite tenancy rights only at some places. But all the tenants paid revenue to their respective landlords only, who were assessed by the government. Besides, the revenue to be paid by the landlords was fixed once for all in Bengal and Bihar and was revised after every thirty years. In the Punjab and Haryana, there were small holdings and generally the holders cultivated themselves. In western and southern India, it was ryotwari system. The landholders paid their taxes directly to the government. A large minority of these ryots or 'pattadars' did not cultivate the land themselves and employed sub-tenants. In some parts, the landlords acted as Zamindars like those of Bengal. The true cultivators put their services of the whole families including women and children. They also employed extra labour during the sowing and harvesting seasons. This labour was offered by those landholders whose holdings were small in size and their families were obliged to hire themselves out during their spare hours to the more prosperous neighbouring landlords. The ruin of industry and the rapid growth of population brought about pressure on land and led to the emergence of increasing landless labourers. This class of landless labourers was permitted to stay in the villages on the understanding that their services would be available to the cultivators. In majority of the cases they were paid in kind. The economic position of this landless class depended on the agricultural prosperity and the needs of the tenants. They earned good wages in prosperous agricultural sector of the Punjab but extremely low in the eastern Uttar Pradesh and Bihar where the pressure on the soil was great. This labour was designed as agricultural labour and it still exists in India.

Non-Contractual Labour. The second type of labour was provided by the womenfolk of the agriculturists, especially in North India, who engaged their spare hours and slack times in hand spinning and cotton weaving. Raw cotton was obtained by them either from their own fields or on payment of their services rendered by their families in cultivation. This labour still exists in the villages. Besides, fishing in eastern Bengal, gur making in Punjab and Uttar Pradesh, basket and rope making were also done by the peasantry in the villages in all parts of the country.

Labour in Rural Industry. The principal occupation in the villages was agriculture, including subsidiary employment in the agricultural products.

Non-agriculturists pursued their traditional occupations and were known by the caste of their work. The weavers (dhanak) put their labour in handloom weaving, shoemakers (chamar) in leather goods such as bags and shoes; blacksmith (lohar) in cards, wheels and the shoes for the cattle; carpenter (badhai) in house-building and wood-work. The potter (kumhar) made the utensils.

The goldsmith (sonar) worked on gold and silver ornaments.

The washerman (dhobi) washed the clothes.

In this way all those goods needed especially by the poor village community were manufactured by this kind of proprietor-labourer within their respective villages.

The goods such as salt, tobacco, matches, etc. which could not be produced by the village artisans were supplied by a small shopkeeper (bania). This bania was also moneylender or the village banker.

The organisation of the village artisans was quite simple. They produced for the needs of other villagers who supplied the food to them. This system preserved the barter system. Their prosperity depended on the agriculture on which the peasantry, landlord, artisan and even bania all depended. This with no fixed payment in coins, this type of village labourer is not generally included in the labour force. This type of labour force was the product of the modern type of industry.

Urban Labour Force. The urban industries in the pre-British times consisted of cottages and karkhanas which produced variegated muslins, calicoes, chintz, silk goods, saltpetre, etc. This indigenous industry flourished around the courts, the administrative headquarters and the pilgrimage centres. Normally the urban industries produced for the rich and the middle classes living in those urban centres and also for exports. "Catering for a limited and well-to-do class of consumers, the artisans attained wonderful skill and aptitude in their respective trades" but their base was political stability of semi-feudal character having a stake in the soil of India. Once this political stability was disturbed by a commercial nation, *viz.* Britain having a stake in their mother soil, this urban industry was the first to bear the brunt. Ruin of the industries forced the urban population to fall back upon agricultural economy. Only labour that remained in urban centres was mostly in domestic service. The labour force which emerged in India thereafter was different from the labour of pre-British India.

Emergence of Labour on Railways. The growth of modern industries in India remained always on background. It was because of the policy adopted by the East India Company. The Company was more interested in trade. Though, as the Indian Industrial Commission pointed out, attempts were frequently made throughout the period of its domination, and even subsequently, to introduce into India various manufactures with State support and encouragement. The main policy of the Company was to increase its trade. As stated earlier due to their policy, trade had become the hub of all the economic activities of the country during the Company rule. Therefore, in order to increase the commercial activities and also effectively administer the country, the Company initiated the building of road-railway network. (It is apparent from the geography of the railways built during their rule that the railway lines connected the centres of raw materials with the administrative headquarters.) The railways system and peace brought about by the Pax Britannica, even if the British might not have expected, were a *sinequanon* of industrial progress. As a consequence thereof, the jute industry, textile mills, coal mines, iron mines had started growing from 1850s onward. The foundation of these modern type of industries caused the emergence of a new class of labour force in India.

The railways network was the most vital factor in creating a labour force. The growth of the railways system in India was phenomenal. Just 32 kms in 1853, it rose to 7,678 kms in 1870; 39,835 kms in 1900; 57,119 kms in 1919-20 and 66,185 kms in 1947. Each kilometer of railway line covered about 61.9 square mile of area and served about 5,878 people. The expansion of railways not only became instrumental in helping to increase the internal and external trade of India, their construction and maintenance have given employment to a large number of people and have afforded an excellent alternative in times of harvests. Besides, the railways brought about the mobility of labour. Large industrial centres like Bombay, Calcutta and Madras emerged because the railways facilitated procurement of labour which could not be obtained locally. Though the urbanization was very slow, but the increase in urban population was very phenomenal. This increasing urban population facilitated in its own way the growth of industrialization and emergence of labour force.

The growth of factories and the opening up of the mines created an increasing demand for the labour not only of men, but also of women, and children. There are no statistics available for the labour before 1892 in factories and 1902 in the mines. However, the latter statistics tell the volume of the emerging labour force.

Industrial Development and Rise of Labour

The 1850s was the conspicuous decade for the sharp increase in the labour intensive industrial development. It was this decade which saw the successful establishment of jute and cotton mills. The coalfields were connected with the railway junctions to facilitate the supply to the expanding railway system in India. Since India was subjected to British industrial interests, the building of railways system and working coalfields could not give stimulus to industrial revolution. It was not the beginning of a diversified industrial growth, but both a beginning and an ending.

Rather, as Daniel Thorner has observed, the railways system was constructed both to drain out the raw materials at economical rates and also to create the demand for British industrial goods. He said:

> In the economic sphere the railways fostered a measure of regional specialization in both agricultural and industrial production and encouraged the bringing of more land under cultivation. The railways also appear to have helped raise the level of wages and prices and to have helped make them more nearly uniform in the sub-continent as a whole. Yet when we consider the fact that the railways have been the largest and most important enterprise of a truly modern character in India, involving heavy machinery, precision techniques, and advance communications, we have to conclude that they have had surprisingly few constructive results. They helped spread a veneer of modernization over the countryside while doing little to initiate a process of modernization.

In 1946, 70 per cent of the industrial index was constituted by the cotton textiles, jute textiles and coal. All other mining and industrial concerns accounted for about one third of the total industrial production on the eve of independence. The industrial growth up to the First World War was confined entirely to these four basic industries, *viz.* railways, coal, jute and cotton. It was the alarming growth of steel industry in Germany which rather compelled the British Government to develop conciliatory steel industry in India, and the Tata Iron and Steel Industry (TISCO) made its mark on the industrial map of India in 1911.

Coal Industry. Next in importance to the railways industry was the coal industry. It was not only the basic requirement of railways in India, but also of the British industry. The coal production was just one lakh tonnes in the 1840s. It rose to three lakh tonnes in 1860, one million tonnes during the First World War, and thereafter, remained almost static on 250 million tonnes during the period of subjugation of the country to Pax Britannica. Until 1920s, the coal industry was controlled and managed exclusively by the British. After 1920s, small coalfields were developed by the Indian management.

Jute Industry. The jute industry was also started by the British. First jute industry was established in 1854. Three more mills came into existence by 1862. By 1877, 4000 looms were in operation. By the close of the century the number rose to 15,000 looms. It was the military preparations in Europe in the twentieth century, that helped increase the number to 40,000 looms when the First World War came to an end. This mark was sustained by the continued tense situation and wars for the power struggle in Europe.

Cotton Industry. It was the Indian textile industry which was ruthlessly destroyed by the British in India. But it was also the cotton industry which was revived by the Indian entrepreneurs. The Parsi community which traded in the raw cotton were the first to establish a cotton mill in 1854. The growth of cotton industry was rapid. The number of the mills increased from just 8 in 1861 to 271 mills in 1914 and continued to maintain the expanding tempo up to 1946.

Other Industries. It was the First World War which forced the industrial growth at a faster rate and in diverse areas. Marine activities being curbed in 1800, India was left with no merchant marine of its own. The country was also deprived of the marine facility offered by the British merchant fleet during the war. It exposed the grave danger to the British empire in the East since the non-availability of spare parts and machinery brought almost a breakdown even in railway service. British compulsion to place its demands for government stores, so far obtained from England, on Indian resources helped emergence of other light industries. The general and electrical engineering industries which were absent from the industrial map of 1914, had become an important sector by 1919. Similarly, railway workshops, ordnance factories, iron and steel factories, chemical industries and others had obtained a respectable place on the industrial map of India.

It was this industrial growth which provided jobs to an increasing number of people and led to the emergence of a substantial labour force in India. The following table gives a vivid picture:

TABLE: Growth of Industrial Employment in India ('000)

Industry	1892	1899	1909	1919	1929	1939	1949
Railways	25	309	510	713	818	709	901
Coal mines	33	83	129	190	180	227	345
Other mines							
Cotton textiles	121	163	237	280	338	449	653
Jute textiles	66	102	204	276	347	299	332
General and Elec. Engg.				30	53	48	136
Railway workshops		52	93	134	136	104	108
Ordnance		13	15	24	22	32	84
Iron and steel	12	17	24	21	32	41	60
Chemical				2.8	3.5	4.8	18
Other factory employment	55	105	213	404.2	622.5	715.2	1053
Total labour employment	546	844	1425	2134	2736	2824	3354

The above table shows that there was a labour force of about 546 thousand in 1892. The strength increased to 3854 thousand by 1949, *i.e.* it increased 700 per cent during this period. The phenomenal growth was in the railways. It employed the largest number of people. Their number rose from 259 thousand in 1892 to 901 thousand in 1949. Therefore, there was an increase of about 350 per cent in the employment of labourers in the railways. Next to it was the mining industry. There were just 33 thousand miners in 1892. Their number rose to 594 thousand in 1948, *i.e.* the employment opportunities increased by 180 per cent in mining industry. Next to the railways in providing employment was the cotton industry. It employed 121 thousand people in 1892 and 661 thousand people in 1848. Overall, the factory employment was insignificant. There were only 254 thousand people in the factory employment in 1882. The factories in India were providing jobs to about 2580 thousand people in 1949.

As stated earlier, the industrial growth, however, was much below the potentialities of the country. The resources, but for British over rule, could have created more industry and, therefore, more jobs to the people and lessened the burden on land. There was a temporary change during the Second World War but India still remained predominantly an agricultural country. Only eleven per cent of the population remained in the urban centres. Until 1939, over seven-tenths of the export trade consisted of raw materials and foodstuffs and about three-quarters of the imports consisted of wholly or partially manufactured goods. The number of persons employed in organised sector was extraordinarily low for a population of the size of India and the daily average number of hands employed by establishments in British India to which the Factories Act applied only 1,553,169. It was mainly because of this tendency that the country could not have a substantial labour force, which could leave its impact on the socio-economic development of the country during this period.

Character of the Indian Labour Force. The real labour force, however, exists in a country only when the workers obtain a permanent employment in factories and when the industrial environment provides them a more adequate fulfilment of personal satisfaction, then they enjoyed in the village or rural society. This aspect has been analysed in the following pages. Here it is sufficient to say that there was no such growth of industrial sector in India. In 1881, only 9.3 per cent of the Indian population lived in urban centres, while by 1941 it increased to 12.8 per cent and by 1951 it rose to just 17.3 per cent. This increase was also more because of the partition of India which had forced dispossessed rural inhabitants to urban centres. These figures, however, do not tell the truth Industrial employment becomes quite insignificant if we look at occupational distribution of Indian population. According to the Statistical Abstracts for British India, the occupational structure before the World War II is given in the table below:

TABLE: Occupational Structure before the World War II

Occupation	Principal Occupation			Subsidiary Occupation		
	Males	Females	Total	Males	Females	Total Number %age
Exploitation of animals and vegetation	744	288	1032	74	1107	65.80
Exploitation of minerals	2.5	0.9	3.4	0.6	4	0.24
Industry	10.8	4.5	15.3	21.7	17.5	10.38
Transport	20	2.5	23	4.3	27.7	1.65
Trade	58	21	79	14	93	5.53
Public force	8	0.7	9	1	9	0.56
Professions and liberal arts	20	3	23	4	27	1.61
Public administration	9.6	9.4	10	1.5	11.5	0.69
Persons living principally on their income	9.7	0.5	2.2	0.6	2.9	0.96
Domestic service	21	88	109	18	127	7.51
Insufficiently described occupation	46	31	77	8	75	5.03
Unproductive	10.5	6	16	0	87.5	1.04
Total	1050	488	1539	150	168	100%

As the occupational structure reveals the industrial employment was just 10.38 per cent whearas the domestic employment was to the tune of 7.51 per cent. These two contradictory employment avenues tell the real character of the labour force in India, and that is why the real labour force in British India was really insignificant. It is necessary to know the source of the supply and working of the labour force to understand this aspect of the labour force.

Position of Land. Before the rise of the British power, the Indian rural economy was self-sustaining. The villagers had their own plots of lands. Others could have land on pattadari from the big landlords. The local artisans worked on the goods needed by the peasantry. This was not a feudal system. It was more based on community feeling tempered by the political abuses. But after the British obtained the political authority in Bengal, Bihar and Orissa they resorted to "Permanent Settlement". Big plots of land were allotted to many a farmers at fixed rate. These farmers with the passage of time emerged as Zamindars. The Zamindars allotted the plots of lands to the peasantry and charged the land rent according to his assessment. The land rent was so much inflated by them that it became sometimes uneconomical to the peasantry. But the Zamindar was empowered to confiscate the lands in the case of defaults in the payment of the land rent. Thus, the peasant was forced to work as a labourer on Zamindar's lands to provide for himself and his family. Besides, the Company Government, and later the Crown Government encouraged farming of cash crops such as cotton, jute, oilseeds, etc. The agriculture was commercialized to the advantage of the consumer of Britain. Therefore, the peasantry was left with little surplus to withstand the poor harvest—a normal feature of Indian agricultural economy. Consequently, the farmer had to live at the mercy of village-banker. As the miserable position of the peasantry obtained in the fifties and sixties, in that process the peasantry became permanently in debt.

Social Status of Labour. Their indebtedness increased further after the increasing population could not find another avenue and had to depend upon the available land to his family. This led to subdivision of land into uneconomical small holdings. As the population went on increasing, the rural economy did not expand, there was increasing unemployment. This forced the surplus members of the agricultural family to hunt for job outside the agricultural economy. It was particularly essential for the members of those families who came "from the lower castes, and had less to lose by leaving the security of the village. It was this low caste rural population which came in the urban centres and merged into labour force of modern India". This character is still retained by the labour force in India. "The mass of workers still represent the superfluous elements of India's rural population whom an impoverished land", aptly observed by Shiva Rao, "is incapable of supporting socially and economically. They represent the most backward sections of population." This was also the reason that manual labour could not obtain respectability in the society.

Social Constraints. The industrial and economic policy had impoverished the village community more than the urban economy. After the industrialization offered new opportunities to unemployed and underemployed in agricultural economy, the villagers were not as free to move out as their counterparts in Europe were able to become industrial labour. The industrial labour in India had a strong link with the village. It was mainly because in the late nineteenth century the social system was very much linked with economic activities. A change in occupation was constrained by the social norms. Blunt's observation was a true picture of the society. He observed that in the Hindu society:

> It is the caste and not the individual that counts. A man's social position is that of the caste of which he is a member. The caste chooses his occupation for him, and if he disregards its decision it can take away his social position altogether by outcasting him. Secondly, the caste system is rather a socio-economic unit than a social organization. Almost every caste is closely associated with a particular occupation.

It was for this reason that generally, the industrial labour came from the lower layer of the society. According to a survey of 550 families of Bombay, textile workers in 1937, for example, 43 per cent of them belonged to lower layers of the caste structure. Most of these 43 per cent were Mahars whose hereditary occupation was serving as village menials, performing such services as guarding of crops, scavenging of passages, cutting fire-woods, carrying cowdung cakes and so on. "The development of industries in the city, however, opened a new channel for them for the betterment of their economic condition and for emancipation from the economic and social dependence on the caste Hindus."

This was the position in all the industrial centres. According to another survey of 959 families in eight industrial centres, including Delhi, Nagpur and Indore, conducted in 1950-53, 79 per cent of them were untouchables. Sixty-four per cent of them were landless agricultural labour. The surveyor concluded that 65 per cent of these people migrated from their villages because of economic distress and related reasons. Next to the people of lower layer, it was the peasantry which migrated to the industrial units to lessen the burden on land as well as indebtedness of his family. It is for this reason that we find that the growth rate of population between 1901 and 1951 was 50 per cent; but the population of advanced industrial centres, *viz.* Bombay, Calcutta, Delhi and Madras expanded by 235 per cent. The better prospects in the industrial units comparing with rural avenues improved the social position of their families in the villages also. It encouraged the people of higher castes also to seek jobs in industrial sector.

A survey of 38,000 families in the textiles in Bombay in 1941 revealed that sixty per cent of them were members of respectable cultivating caste. It brought down the percentage of "depressed" people to 16 per cent. Thus, the pecuniary benefits weakened social constraints and accelerated the mobility of rural population to industrial population.

The Labour Investigation Committee observed in 1946:

> In recent years...there has been a greater concentration of the working class population in industrial areas and this has led to the rise of an urban proletariat in most cities, which is prepared to stick to the town to a greater extent than before.... A steady increase in the ranks of landless labourers, moreover, has compelled many to remain and settle in the town and to regard it as their home.

It is, however, an exaggeration. Though the social norms had started crumbling down, but the gap in the proletariat and the elite in the urban centres created new constraints upon the industrial labour to maintain their link with the village where their meagre assets could obtain for them more respect than expected in the urban centres. It was also due to the recruitment and management policy.

Recruitment of Labour. After the British started their jute and plantation industry they looked upon the leaders of the castes in the villages to provide them needed labour. They paid them a commission to bring their people to these industrial units. But after working in these industrial units, the labourers found better conditions than prevailing in the villages. It opened a mad rush of the "depressed" people and even they paid "bribe" to the recruiters, who had by their work become a link between the employer and the labour. These were the two abuses which went against the industrial security of the labourers in India. The Royal Commission also stressed these abuses in the following words: "The temptations of the jobbers' positions are manifold and it would be surprising if these men failed to take advantage of their opportunities. There are few factories where a worker's security is not, to some extent, in the hands of the jobber; in a number of factories the latter has in practice the power to engage and dismiss the worker. We are satisfied that it is a fairly general practice for the jobber to profit financially from the exercise of this power." The jobber's financial position further enhanced after the attraction for factory labour increased beyond the demand by the staggering industrial growth. They could establish not only their control but were also in a position to supervise the labour in a better way.

Radha Kumud Mukherjee has explained it as under:

> It is he who visits the villages of miners and loaders, offers advances to them and brings them to the colliery, maintaining an adequate labour force from day to day. It is he who keeps the labour in village and family gangs, which adds to the amenities of their toil in an uncongenial environment. He is a man of higher intelligence and ability than ordinary mines. He keeps watch over them, sees that they go to pits regularly and reports if they do not obtain proper facilities for work, *i.e.* suitable working faces, and an adequate supply of tubs. He is also responsible for all tools and plant issued to miners and loaders, keeps them under discipline at their work and also remains present when the payment is made to them. He acts in fact as the middleman between the management or the rising contractors and the miners.

Thus, the recruiter of labour became all in all to the labourers. The employers found the job quite easy as they could depend upon these recruiters not only for the supply of labour but also for supervising their work.

Indifferent Management. Assured of supply of labour, discipline and direction of work through these recruiters, the employers became indifferent to the interests of the workers. With better prospects in the industrial sector, the surplus and underemployed labour in the impoverished rural economy had already been induced towards migration. They could ignore their interests since the people being pushed into factories had no other avenues left. They had no difficulty in attracting skilled and unskilled labour at cheap rates since the low wages were more attractive and comparatively higher to the poor returns of the hardwork they were putting in the rural economy. The indebtedness and appalling poverty was rather pushing them into industries. The entrepreneurs, therefore, did not care for providing adequate housing, sanitary facilities or other amenities which could develop commitment in the industrial labour. The revelations in the report of the Labour Investigation Committee in 1946 are not only startling but also expose the very exploiting nature of these entrepreneurs in India. The Report noted that, "On the whole, it may be stated that employers who take a most indifferent and nonchalant attitude towards welfare work and say that no rest/shelters are provided as the whole premises belong to the workers themselves, no latrines are provided because workers prefer the open spaces, no canteens and sports are necessary because they are not likely to make use of such facilities, and soon, constitute the majority. It is apparent that, unless the precise responsibilities of employers in regard to welfare work are defined by law, such employers are not likely to fall in line with their more enlightened and far-sighted conferers."

The housing problem was rather more serious. One third of the industrial labour was not provided with any housing facilities. As a result, one-room hut provided to a meagre percentage of the labourers was shared by about 4.8 persons. These occupants were not members of one family. They belonged to different families and shared the accommodation "to save by starvation" and pay for the living of their families left in their respective villages. It was the exploitation which kept "the village an infinitely better place than the city for the young and the aged, the sick, the maimed and the exhausted, the unemployed and the unemployable". It may be noted here that it was the exploiting nature of the entrepreneurs which had forced the helpless labourers to pay through their nose. The capitalist approach of the British Imperial Government in India was not prepared to intervene unless "the discontentment burst out and threatened their rule". Moved by the miserable plight of the industrial labour in the cities, Mahatma Gandhi and other leaders argued for the revival of rural industry so that the labourers are not pushed into the labour centres and they could be in a position to bargain with the entrepreneurs. With this, the entrepreneurs argued for reducing the wages of the workers in the 1920s after the First World War came to an end and the demand for their goods decreased and the chances of optimum profit by the entrepreneurs disappeared. Their irrational approach gave birth to labour movements and trade unionism.

Labour Movement. It has been often talked that Indian economy is predominantly agricultural economy. About 70 per cent of the population is engaged in the agriculture. The industrial activities engaged only about ten and a half per cent in addition to about five and a half and one and a half per cent engaged in subsidiary occupation such as trade and transport respectively. They were, however, contributing more in the national product. Therefore, they occupied the most important key centres of the economic activities in India. Besides, their concentration made the industrial labour identifiable forces. They could be organised into political weapon in easier way than the huge unorganised rural mass. It may be mentioned here that it was the industrialization of European countries which provided the strength to the politicians engaged in the struggle against the aristocracy for sharing in the government. The revolutions in France were successful because of the combined support of the labour force, and Paris could dictate the vast majority of rual population after 1789. It is for this reason that all the political parties and ambitious leaders took keen interest in the labour and sought the allegiance of organised labour movements to their cause.

Indian Factory Act, 1911. Non-committed attitude of the labour force and their continued attachment to the rural economy and society impeded the chances of organisation of any labour movement in India for a longer time. Besides, the unchallenged British supremacy before the First World War proved bulwark against the penetration of socialistic thought in India. The political movements in India were not those of protest. Rather they were of compromising nature. Before the First World War, the people who believed in obtaining better treatment from the British by winning their confidence, were powerful leaders of the society. It was only the partition of Bengal in 1905 and disappointment created by the Government of India Act, 1909, that this group agreed with the "revolutionaries" that the future of the Indians could not be better with the continued imperial rule. Therefore, the labour protests were sporadic and had little chances of success.

Humanitarian and British Industries Interests. It was the humanitarian and liberal approach, then dominant in British politics, which voiced the labour grievances against long working hours. It echoed that the Indian labour should also be provided with safeguards like regulated working hours, holidays, regular payment, insurance and hospitalisation facilities available to their counterparts in British industries. But there was little improvement in the lot of the Indian labour. The welfare measures were rather forced upon the entrepreneurs in India by the British manufacturing interests. The British manufacturers apprehended that the low-cost of Indian products due to cheap labour would be putting them into "unequal competition". Therefore, they exerted their pressure on the Government of India to enforce welfare measures which could increase the cost of their products. It was their pressure that the first Indian Factories Act was enacted in 1911. The Act regulated the working hours of adult male labour to 12 hours per day. The labourer was still insecure and weak in bargaining for better wages and security.

First World War and Trade Unionism. It was the First World War which increased the hardships of labour to limits beyond endurance. The Indian National Congress was also opposed to the British who dragged Indian into the War. The Congress leaders had already started protesting and organised movements against British rule on being disappointed by the Government of India Act, 1909 which had shattered their hope of getting a "share in the government" by conciliatory approach. It was in this context that the Congress passed resolution in 1918 urging its provincial committees and other associations to organise labour in the country. With this aim the All India Trade Union Congress (AITUC) was formed in 1918. The AITUC, however, could not develop the movement to the expected stages. It was only an unaffiliated unit in Ahmedabad which could do something tangible and became the forerunner of Indian National Trade Union Congress (INTUC).

The Ahmedabad Textile Labour Association (TLA). In 1918, the Ahmedabad textiles sought scrapping the "plague bonus" paid to their labourers for many years. The workers, however, argued that the rise in cost of living must be compensated by paying them 50 per cent rise in dearness allowance. The labourers were led by the sister of the Chairman of the Millowners' Association. Viewing the seriousness and effectiveness of the movement, the millowners sought the mediation of Mahatma Gandhi, who had by then made his debut in Indian politics. The District Collector also urged Gandhi to use his good offices to avoid any untoward incident since the "millowners" had "threaten(ed) to lock out the mills, which will naturally cause great distress and hardship". Consequently, an Arbitration Committee was constituted, consisting of Congress leaders, millowners and the Collector. Apprehended labourers, however, went on strike and the millowners threatened dismissal of all the "absent' labourers. Their approach, quite revealing, is still dominating many an entrepreneur in our country. The millowners argued that the Congress leaders' assumptions were not based on facts. The mills are not "run out of love for humanity and as a matter of philanthropy, that their aim is not to raise the condition of the workers to the same level as that of the employers. In reality mills are privately owned, and are run with no other motives than to make profit. Workers are employed with this aim in view, and therefore, employment of labour and conditions of employment are determined purely on the basis of supply and demand and from the point of view of their efficiency". The millowners' rigid approach worsened the poor workers' conditions.

Before the strike could fizzle out Gandhi went on fast. It gave a fillip to the workers' agitation and aroused public concern. The workers' determination, for the first time won this "righteous struggle" in their favour and strike came to an end. This revealed them the benefit of united action and also developed a new labour ideology, *viz.* "Gandhian" labour ideology. Gandhian way stood for lawful course based on "truth and fairness" and harmonious relations between the owners and the labourers. It did not give political emphasis to trade unionism. In this way, this struggle established a non-violent labour struggle in the history of Indian labour movement. It was this ideology which led to the formation of Indian National Trade Union Congress (INTUC).

Radical Trade Unionism. It was clear from the millowners' attitude that they wanted to take advantage of slow industrialization of the country and increasing labour supply. Since the government was not inclined to unrestricted industrialisation of the country, it was also obliged to extend protection to the labourers working in these factories. The International Labour Organization (ILO) was also stressing the need for harmonious industrial relations. The victory of the "Bolsheviks" in 1917 in Russia had alarmed the western countries. They were not prepared to risk the law and order by letting the scrupulous entrepreneurs free of government control and exploit the workers. As had been established by various investigations the exploitation, impoverishment and concentration of labourer were heaven for the emergence of "Bolshevik atoms" to "throw out the duly constituted and lawful governments". In order to combat the spread of the Bolshevik ideology, the government took initiatives for the betterment of the conditions of industrial labourers throughout their colonies. True to the policy, the Government of India enacted the Indian Factories Act, 1922. It fixed a ten-hour working day. Next year, the Indian Mines Act, 1923 was passed which regulated the timings of the miners for the first time in the country. The Workmen's Compensation Act also provided security measure and compensation in the event of accidents.

Recognition to Trade Unionism. The investigating parties also revealed that unless the workers are provided a platform to air their grievances, there could not be any link between the government policy and the aspirations of the labourers. Lack of this compatibility also leads to serious underground activities and revolutions. Therefore, the investigators suggested formation and recognition of trade unions. It had already been practiced in the European countries. The Government of India also passed the Indian Trade Unions Act in 1926. The Act provisioned that any association of seven persons could get themselves registered as a trade union. The Act also provided immunity from criminal prosecution for any agitation furthering trade union objectives. The trade union could work in the direction of furthering their interests.

The Condition of the Labour and the Rise of Communist Ideology. As stated earlier, the government had legalised the trade unionism as a bulwark against the spread of communist ideology. There was a great gap between its actions and deeds. The entrepreneurs continued, as the Labour Investigation Committee reported in 1946, to ignore even the legitimate demands of the labourers. They were paid very badly. The British Trade Union Congress delegation to India reported in 1928 that "all enquiries go to show that the vast majority of workers in India do not receive more than about 1s (one shilling) per day. In the province of Bengal, which includes the largest mass of industrial workers, investigator declared that as far as they could ascertain, 60 per cent of workers were in receipt of wages not more than 1s 2d a day in the highest instance, scaling down to as low as 7d to 9d for men and 3d to 7d in the case of children and women. Our own inquiries support these figures and, as a matter of fact, many cases have been quoted to us of daily rates in operation which descend to 3-1/4d for women and 7d or even less for men".

The housing was worst. The above delegation reported that: "We visited the workers' quarters wherever we stayed, and had we not seen them we could not have believed that such evil places existed.... Here is a group of house in 'lines', the owner of which charges the tenant of each dwelling 4s 6d a month as rent. Each house consisting of one dark room used for all purposes, living, cooking and sleeping, is 9 feet by 9 feet, with mud walls and loose-tiled roof and has a small open compound in front, a corner of which is used as a latrine. There is no ventilation in the living-room except by a broken roof or that obtained through the entrance door when open. Outside the dwelling is a long narrow channel which receives the waste matter of all descriptions and where files and other insect abound.... Outside all the houses on the edge of each side of the strip of land between the 'lines' are the exposed gulleys; at some places stopped up with garbage, refuse and other waste matter, giving forth horrible smells repellent in the extreme. It is obvious that these gulleys are often used as conveniences, especially by children...."

The overcrowding and insanitary conditions almost everywhere prevailing demonstrate the callousness and wanton neglect of their obvious duties by the authorities concerned. The plantation workers were in worst conditions. The male worker got only Rs. 7-10 per month. The earnings of women and children were less by two to three rupees to those of male workers. They were treated like slaves. It was due to this reason that the entrepreneurs were making huge profits. The Dundee Jute Trade Unions to India reported in 1925 that: "When Reserve Funds and Profits are added together the total gain to the shareholders (in the jute industry) in the ten years (1915-24) reached the enormous total of three hundred sterlings, or 90 per cent per annum of the capital. There are from 300,000 to 127,000 workers employed at an average wage today of £12.10 per annum. A profit of £399 million taken from 300,000 workers in the ten years means £1,000 per head. This means £100 a year from each worker. And as the average wage is about

£12.10 per head, it means that the average annual profit is eight times the wages bill." It was the condition of cotton industry as well. Fourteen mills paid a dividend of 100 per cent, whereas two mills paid over 200 per cent. In some cases the dividend rose as high as 365 per cent.

The justification for decreasing the salaries after the boom of the World War had slumped down was not based on truth. The mills continued to make huge profits. Romesh Dutt informs us that: "The level of profits today, while no longer equalling the orgies of the post-war boom, still abundantly reveals the exceptional exploitation. Thus, in jute, the Reliance Jute Mills Company paid dividends of 50 per cent in 1935, 42½ per cent in 1936 and 30 per cent in 1937. In tea, the New Dooars Tea Company paid dividends of 50 per cent both in 1935, and 1936; the Nagaisuke Tea Company paid dividends of 60 per cent in 1935 and 50 per cent in 1936; and the East Hope Estates Company paid 23 per cent in 1935, 88 per cent in 1936 and 40 per cent in 1937."

In the wake of these mounting profits and draining out the wealth, the workers were impoverished. The labour legislations were also favourable to the entrepreneurs. Shiva Rao reports: "Taking all labour legislation into account, affecting factories, mines, plantations, docks, railways, harbours, etc. it is doubtful whether more than seven or eight millions at the outside come within its protective influence. The rest who constitutes by far the greater majority of the industrial workers are engaged in small or what is known as a unregulated industries." The main factory legislations extended only to about sixteen lacs and fifty thousand workers.

Curiously enough the factories established in the "native states" were completely left out of the purview of these factory acts. It were these reasons that the factory workers resorted to strikes. Protesting against the proposed reduction of wages there were about 200 strikes involving one and a half million workers in 1920. After the Congress leaders professed conciliatory approach and the government was not prepared to amelioration of the impoverished workers, the socialistic ideas came forward.

Encouraged with the successful revolution in Soviet Russia, S.A. Dange started his journal, *The Socialist* in 1924. The people having socialist ideas formed their own Trade Union Congress and Dange became its first Assistant Secretary. The British Government was not prepared to withstand any socialistic ideas. It arrested four prominent Communist leaders namely Dange, Shaukat Usmani, Muzaffar Ahmad and Das Gupta. They were sentenced to four years' imprisonment. It was this repressive approach of the government which rather strengthened the socialist ideas and spread the Communist movement among the working class people. By 1939, they had attained potential power and brought almost a breakdown in the factories. They also co-operated with the political movements. It gave greater strength to the nationalist ideas. It was this reason that the Socialist and Communist leaders were arrested in the Second World War and the Communist Party was banned. Their repression further strengthened their status among the workers. In this way the industrial labour in India was baptized with the radical ideas.

Indo-British Economic Relations

26

The history of Indo-British economic relations and their various aspects have been clearly indicated and vindicated by K.T. Paul in his work *British Connection with India*, by Goldwin Smith in his book *The Empire*, by Zacharia in his popular work *Renascent India*, by B.B. Misra in his book *The Indian Middle Classes* and by N.V. Sovani and V.M. Dandekar in their masterpiece *Changing India*.

The British came to India as traders and then they turned as rulers. They finally created the mightiest empire of the world in India.

Competition for Commerce. Relations between England and India originated mainly in commerce. The Indian products created a lucrative trade with Egypt, Greece and Rome—the markets which met the needs of whole of Europe. At that time India was not receiver, rather it was giver of all that what the humanity needed.

K.T. Paul has summarised this in the following words: "The points of interest is that in all those times, pre-Roman, Roman and Venetia, there was little or no contribution from the West to India. India taught or gave, receiving comparatively little in return. The contact was so to say entirely one sided; it was the contact of the West with India and not the contact of India with the West."

Out of this trade there flourished a prosperoús market in Europe and the merchants earned a lot. European nations, establish their monopoly in trade with this country. It was one of the bitterest bones of contention between the Roman Empire and the Arabs. The Roman Empire sent many naval expeditions to seize Aden from the Arabs and wrest the Indian trade out of their hands. If we go into the past, we will be surprised to know that this struggle was as fierce as in the eighteenth century between the British and all other European nations.

The Roman ascendancy was successfully contested by the Arabs who emerged as the most powerful Islamic nation of the medieval times. They controlled old trade route via Egypt, Red Sea, Aden and the Indian Ocean. The Europeans then started trading through Central Asia via Constantinople. However, Constantinople also fell to the Turkish in 1453. Entrenched in the crusades, the Islamic world would not allow the Christians to obtain their necessities and products from India and other eastern nations. It compelled the European commercial houses to discover sea-routes still beyond the control of the Islam. This led to the emergence of various nations of Europe on the economic-political life of India. This resulted in a long drawn out struggle between these nations.

After Aurangzeb annexed Golkunda and Bijapur in Southern India, which had so far served as "breakwaters against the spread of the Maratha insurrection", the Mughal Empire got entrenched in a prolonged confrontation with them. This confrontation dislocated both civil and military administration. The European factories also came under heavy pressures. They utilised this excuse and opportunity to fortify their settlements on the eastern and western coasts, since as they argued, they were "convinced themselves, after much anxious discussion" that the success and comparative security of the Dutch, as formerly of the Portuguese, lay in their armed strength. It was this accumulation of arms strength which proved quite favourable to the British in the struggle for supremacy in Europe which got extended to their commercial enterprises in India which coincided with the struggle for supremacy in India also.

Struggle for Supremacy. France and Holland were involved in war in 1672 which continued up to 1713. It was this struggle among these two European nations which affected India first time in 1603. The Dutch captured Pondicherry, and driven out the French from their factories. Though the settlement was returned to the French in 1699, but the French trade suffered heavily during the period of Dutch control. This skirmish established a point that the rival's trade could be affected by seizing its settlement in India. It was this example which prompted Dupleix, in 1748, to take sides in the struggle for power among the native rulers to bring them under French influence and drive out their enemies, including English, out of India trade. This challenge was courageously taken over by Watson and Clive.

In the three famous Carnatic Wars (1740-1765), the British defeated the French and also subjugated the native princes to their dictation. During the course they also established their hold over the Mughal province of Bengal through two military transactions at Plassey (1757) and Buxar (1765). Administration of Bengal, Bihar and Orissa was taken over from the Nawab by Warren Hastings in 1772 and it inaugurated the era of British rule in India.

By acquiring a territory on the Indian soil, the Company came into direct confrontation with the Indian contenders in the power struggle. The Company subdued all of them and became the supreme political power of India by 1818. All the States and the people were subjected to Pax Britannica by suppressing their last attempt to win back the independence in 1857.

The British continued to rule India for next 90 years and transferred the power to Indians in 1947.

The modern period (1757-1947) under study is the period of British rule over India. In this period the Indo-British relations were those of the rulers and the ruled. As will be discussed later, it was the rule of Britain and all the rules and regulations had derived their legality from the British Government. However, the British maintained a facade of "trustee" of the "uncivilized" people. (To them all the subject nations, including India, were inhabited by the uncivilized people.) It is this facade which can have any sense in describing the Indo-British relations.

Political Relations. The British rule in India can be divided into two distinct parts. From 1772 (the year in which Hastings took over the government from the Nawab) to 1857, the country was ruled by the East India Company, under the Charter granted to it by the British Crown. After 1857, the Charter of the Company was terminated and India came under the direct control of the Crown. But it is a difference of legality, otherwise the power was always exercised by the same kind of British people.

The Government of India was first regulated under an Act of 1773 passed by the British Parliament. This Act brought the administration of the Company under the direct control of the Crown. The Governor General, Governors, other important executives and the judges were to be nominated by the Crown. The Governor General-in-Council could enact rules for the "law, order and good government" only with the approval of the Home Government. The Crown also established a Supreme Court to which, in fact, the executive was subordinated. In this way the country was controlled indirectly by the Crown. Since the British Crown could act only on the advice of the British Parliament, therefore, the Indian people were also ruled by the British Parliament and thereby were affected by the British party politics. There were many reforms in the provisions of administrative framework, but the supremacy of the British Government continued to increase and the Government of India would have gone under the direct control of the Crown even if there would not have been any resurgence in 1857.

When the Company obtained political power there emerged a great controversy in Britain. The conflicting interests of the political parties of Britain led to the appointment of a Select Committee and Secret Committee by the British Parliament. On the recommendations of these Committees the Parliament passed the famous Regulating Act (1773) which introduced Parliamentary supervision over the Company Government of India. Consequently, the governing machinery of the Company was modified.

The Act provided the "Directors (of the Company) in England should before the Treasury (*i.e.*, Government) all correspondence from India dealing with the revenues; and before a Secretary of State everything dealing with civil or military administration." From 1781 onward they were also obliged to have concurrence of the Secretary of State to all the despatches sent to the Government of India. In this way, the Parliamentary supervision—in reality the control of the British Government was established and India became a subject country of Britain.

Though the Company was given the privileges of appointing Governor General and his Council—the *de facto* rulers of India—they were subordinated to a Supreme Court of Justice consisting of a Chief Justice and three puisne judges. All the judges were appointed by the Crown and, therefore, this Court is also called King's Court. In this way the executive in India was also subjected to British Crown through the dichotomy of judiciary. But as discussed under the Legal Sysem in India this system could not work smoothly. Rather, it threatened the continuance of their rule in India itself. "It had neither given the State a definite control over the Company, nor the Directors a definite control over their servants, nor the Governor General a definite control over his Council, nor the Calcutta presidency a definite control over Madras and Bombay." In other words, the Regulating Act had created a multiplicity of masters due to which the Indian people had to live under unknown, and unexpected tyranny. The observation of P.E. Roberts on the execution of Nand Kumar, an important officer of Nawab Siraj-ud-daulah and an accomplice of Clive in conspiring against the Government of the Nawab, who had earned the displeasure of the Governor General, Warren Hastings reveals the cruelty of this system. He observes, "It casts the darkest and most sinister shadow over the reputation of the men who used him for their own purpose and then callously and contemptuously flung him to the wolves."

This system came under severe criticism in British Parliament. Edmund Burke was the greatest critic of the British executive in India. It may, however, be noted here that he was not as much concerned about the oppressed Indians, as he was concerned about the "Naboobs" who would endanger the democracy in Britain. This fact becomes clear from the Judicature Act of 1871 which removed the judicial control over the Company executive. The Regulating Act was amended by the Pitt's Act.

The Pitt's India Act created "Commissioners for the affairs of India" known as the Board of Control over the Directors of the Company. The Board consisted of a Secretary of State, the Chancellor of the Exchequer and four Privy Councillors appointed by the British Crown. They had access to all the papers except purely of commercial nature of the Company. The Board was also empowered to send secret or urgent orders to the executive in India. In this manner, the Government of India went under the *de facto* control of this Board. It was this Pitt's Act which maintained the political relationship between India and Britain throughout the Company rule. There were further stipulations about the subordinate status of the country.

The Charter Act of 1813 stressed upon "the undoubted sovereignty of the Crown" over the country.

In 1853, the Crown was given the authority to nominate "three" out of eighteen Directors of the Company; all future appointments—through competitive examinations—were to be made with the express approval of the Crown.

In this way these Acts had been gradually transferring the power and authority from the Company to the Crown. The abolition of the Company and the transfer of its powers to the Crown were inevitable even if the resurgence of 1857 would not have terminated that process in an abrupt manner. Therefore, we can say that the British Government was responsible for all the acts of Indian Government which were in the British interests more than the welfare of the people of India.

It was only in Queen's Proclamation of 1858 that there was an effort to assure the subject people in explicit terms. It is described as the Magna Carta of the Indian people. In that Proclamation, the Queen promised to respect the rights, dignity and honour of the native princes and to pay due regards to the ancient rights, usages and customs of India...and proclaimed a policy of justice, benevolence and religious toleration, enjoining the government to "abstain from all interference with religious belief or worship" of the subjects. The most important aspect of the Proclamation is considered that it admitted to offices in our service, the duties of which they may be qualified, "by their education, ability and integrity, duty to discharge". But the growing racial discrimination between Indian and the British the "trusteeship" of British Crown and as Russell, the *Times* Correspondent in India, reported, "The mutineers have produced too much hatred and ill-feeling between the two races to render any more change of the rulers a remedy for the evils which affect India, of which those angry sentiments are the most serious exposition.... Many years must elapse before the evil passions excited by these disturbances expire; perhaps confidence will never be restored; and it so, our reign in India will be maintained at the cost of suffering which it is fearful to contemplate."

Thereafter, the Crown assumed the direct control over India. An Act was enacted on 2 August 1858 which provided that "India shall be governed by, and in the name of, the Sovereign through one of the principal Secretraries of State, assisted by Council of fifteen members." The Governor General concurrently became the Viceroy of the Crown. The Crown's rule, in fact inaugurated the era of using India for the British imperial interests.

After 1858, the Secretary of State became the virtual ruler of India. The Act of 1869 reduced the power of his Council and term of the members to ten years "renewable at the pleasure of the Secretary of State". His powers were further strengthened with the opening of a telegraph line in between India and London in 1870. Henceforth, the Secretary of State exercised a far mere effective control over the administration of India than was the case before, and the Viceroy really rended to be a mere "agent" of the Secretary of State. It was at the same time the Secretary of State under whom the constitutional development took place which has been interpreted that the British Government was sincere in granting the self-government to Indians and they had been taking the steps in this direction since they took over the government. It is a question of great reservation. We cannot go into details, but will refer how this development took place which will also analyse the future political relations between the British Government and India.

Movement. From 1840s onward there were many staunch advocates of revoking the imperial rule and grant the colonies independence. It has created a confusion about the British policy towards the colonies; and many believe that the British were having liberal attitude towards the colonies. This was not, however, the case. In fact, all those who argued for the grant of independence to the colonies referred to those colonies which were settled by the British, such as Canada, South Africa, Rhodesia, Australia, etc. They had advocated separation of the colonies from the empire with the increase *laissez faire* approach; but there was no support to this move in colonies inhabited by non-European people.

Professor Goldwin Smith who did his best to establish himself as an anti-imperialist and spoke provocatively, in case of India said that: it stands on a footing of its own, apart from the other dependencies of our Empire. There we have not only placed ourselves in a position from which it is hard to retire, but taken upon us duties which we are bound for the present to perform. If we were to leave India we should leave it to anarchy.

Though India was, in his opinion, now economically or militarily more "advantageous to Britain", it was a conquered territory, and it belonged to the conqueror country as "providence puts the stolen purse into the pocket of the thief". Following this line of thinking, Goldwin Smith opined that "the principal of Colonial Emancipation does not apply to India". Similarly, Disraeli was though averse to continue control over "colonial dead weights", *i.e.* those colonies by settlement where Britain had given up the right to govern themselves, but he advocated that "power and influence should be exercised in Asia". All these people did not favour withdrawal from lands like India and Ceylon since it would, they argued, lead to anarchy and "would cease at once to export their goods to us and to consume out manufactures". Rather they resented that instead of holding "India for the acquisition of prestige and trade", Britain "decided that we are to govern India in the interest of the people of Hindoostan". For them non-European was not fit for self-government or elimination of imperial control, but, what British Governor of New Zealand pointed out, they need enlightenment which could render them "a valuable consumer of British manufactured goods" and dependencies formed, as Dilke argued "a nursery of statesmen and of warriors".

It was this view which was strengthened by the Act of 1892 which declared that "Nothing in this Act shall detract from or diminish the powers of the Governor-General-in-Council at meetings, for the purpose of making laws and regulations." The reforms were introduced to combat the increasing discontentment among the Indian mass. Therefore, Pradhan observed, "The Indian Council Act of 1892 was an attempt at compromise between the official view of the Councils as pocket legislatures and the educated Indian view of them as embryo Parliaments." It were the violent movements which compelled the British to present a liberal approach rather than granting self-government to India even within the British Commonwealth of Nations. While introducing the Act of 1909, the Secretary of State for India, Lord Morley unequivocally declared, "If I were attempting to set up a Parliamentary system in India or if it could be said that this chapter of reforms led directly or necessarily up to the establishment of parliamentary system in India, I for one, would have nothing at all to do with it."

Change in the British Approach. It was only the First World War which forced the British to issue a statement which would reconciliate the growing discontentment among the Indian nationalists. Montague, the Secretary of State for India, declared on 29th August 1917 that, "The policy of His Majesty's Government with which the Government of India are complete accord, is that of the increasing association of Indians in every branch of administration with a view to the progressive realisation of responsible Government in India as an integral part of the British Empire. I would add that the progress in this policy can only be achieved by successive stages. The British Government of India, on whom the responsibility lies for their welfare and advancement of Indian people must be the judges of the time and measure of each advance and they must be guided by the co-operation received from those upon whom new opportunities of service will thus be conferred and by the extent to which it found that confidence could be reposed in their sense of responsibility."

But when the War was over, the British introduced not only dyarchy which was to create obstacles in the economic advancement, as will be discussed later, but it also introduced communal franchise which finally led to the strengthening of two-nation theory and establishment of Pakistan. Alongwith it, "Instructions were issued from London that henceforth the Reforms were to be worked with a view to not how much but how little, self-government for India they could be made to yield." It disappointed not only the radicals but also the liberals who had been considering the British rule as providential.

They started Non-cooperation Movement which almost paralysed the working of the governmental machinery in India, while this Movement was going, Labour Party won the elections and formed its Government in 1929. It was the first declaration by the British Prime Minister, Macdonald who said at a conference, "I hope that within a period of months rather than years, there will be another Dominion added to the Commonwealth of Nations, a Dominion of another race, a Dominion which will find respect as an equal within the Commonwealth. I refer to India."

It was in these changed circumstances that the British administrators started re-interpreting the past declarations and motives of the British Government. Governor General of India, Lord Irwin announced on 31st October 1921, "I am authorised on behalf of His Majesty's Government to state clearly that in their judgement it is implicit in the declaration of 1917 that the natural issue of India's constitutional progress, as there contemplated is the attainment of Dominions Status." Not contented with these wild promises, the Congress Party started Civil Disobedience Movement in 1930.

Forced by the successful movement, the Government enacted the Act of 1935. In this Act, the British recognised federal structure, a reference to which has already been made. Professor

Keith, therefore, rightly observes, "It is difficult to deny the justification of the contention in India that federation was largely evoked by the desire to evade the issue of extending responsible government to the Central Government of British India. The proposed federation was likely to fail due to the assertion of the controlling power of the Governor General backed by the Conservative elements of the states and of British India." Therefore, the federal structure was so envisaged as to make any real advance impossible and no loophole was left for the representatives of the Indian people to interfere with or modify the system of British controlled administration. The nationalist movement in India, however, had got that momentum which could not be diffused by such tactics. Above all, the world was overtaken by the Second World War. This war broke the British hegemony—and after war, the people of British again voted Labour Party to power. Therefore, the Labour Party accelerated the transfer of power to Indians but only by dividing the country on religious grounds and giving "in legacy perpetual conflict between the two brothers". In this way, we can summarise that the Indo-British relations were dictated by the British Government as an imperial power. The policy was not for the welfare of the people of India, but for the people of Britain. But the British had created those institutions, through which the transfer of power was inevitable even if it would have come at a very late stage. It was that "vehicle which after started moving could not be stopped".

Foreign Policy. The foreign policy of India was dictated by the British imperial interests in the international sphere. Therefore, the Indian foreign policy was nothing but British foreign policy. There was no cognizance to the Indian interests. It is one of the strongest cases for the colonial status of the country in the modern times. Therefore, India was dragged in the wars which were waged for British imperial interests; and the resources of the country were utilised to meet those ends.

The conflict between Britain and Russia is the best example of this nature of foreign policy. After the European powers had been busy in expanding their "spheres of influence" over the "uncivilized world" there emerged a hostility between Britain and other European powers. We have seen how the country was subject to Britain in that struggle for supremacy in the European continent. After 1815, there was a cordial relationship between the European countries and Britain. However, the Russian expansion towards the Black Sea and the Central Asian regions caused a great anxiety among the British statesmen. In order to combat these moves, British Government forced upon India resources the burden of war with Afghanistan. The threat of the Russian expansion in Central Asia was, however, met with an agreement of 1844 which accepted that Bukhara, Khiva and Samarqand would be kept "as a neutral zone between the two empires in order to preserve them from a dangerous contact".

The Crimean War (1854) again brought the two Powers against each other and the cordial relationship came to an end. The British Government summoned Indian troops for use in the Crimean War. (It was one of the causes of resentment among the Indian soldiers which contributed towards the resurgence of 1857.) Thereafter the British Government suffered until Anglo-Russian Entente (1907) was concluded. Until then the British Government suffered from the fear that the Russian "Bear" humiliated in the Crimean War would be restless and endanger British Indian Empire. It was in the fit of this Russo-phobia that the Indian resources were used time and again to secure British imperial interest to thwart Russian expansion in Central Asia.

In 1864, the Russian again started marching into Central Asia. By 1868, they captured Samarqand; in 1873 Khiva was also annexed. In this way the "neutral zone" had passed under the Russian control. It created an alarm to the British. They sought keeping the Amir of Afghanistan by sending arms and money from India. This subsidy was continuously paid by the Viceroys of India to secure "British interests" (it was suspended only for the brief period of Gladstone's Ministry who did not view the Russian expansion in Central Asia as a threat to the safety of British Empire in India).

But by 1874, the situation underwent a change. Disraeli, one of the staunch imperialists, became the Prime Minister of Britain and Lord Salisbury became the Secretary of State for India. In 1877, Russia defeated Turkey and imposed upon her the Treaty of San-Stefano (it was at this juncture that the Indian troops were stationed in the Mediterranean—cost of which was met out of revenues of India). By this treaty, Russia had completely changed the balance of power in the Dardanells and the Black Sea—a grave risk to the British Empire dreaded by the British Government. It created a great anxiety for the British Government. Therefore, Disraeli Government accepted the forward policy; accordingly Indian Government was asked to complete that objective. As a result of this forward policy, India had to wage a war against Afghanistan. Similarly Burma, East Africa were also annexed by deploying Indian troops. These wars brought no benefit to Indian people. India was thrown into two World Wars in spite of opposition of the Indian people. There is no such study so far, but the expenditure incurred on the wars waged for British imperial expansions was beyond imagination.

Staffing Policy. These British imperial interests were met by devising a staffing policy. Sir John Lawrence, Viceroy of India, explained this policy in the letter to the Secretary of State, dated 17 August 1867:

> The chief objection to a change (in the manner of recruitment to Indian Civil Services) is that of policy. We conquered India mainly by force of arms though policy and good government have largely aided us. In like manner we must hold it. The Englishmen must always be in the front rank, holding the post of honour and of power as the condition of retaining our rule.

It may be noted here that no Indian ever rose to the rank of even Governor of a Province. To keep the Indians at subordinate level, competitive entrance examinations for the Civil Service in India were held exclusively in England until 1928. The Royal Commission on Public Services (1912) recommended that Indians should also be provided opportunity to run the government; but these recommendations were kept in cold storage. The Montford Commission's (1919) recommendations to open up one-third of ICS posts to Indians and of the Lee Commission (1924) to allocate one half of the posts to the Indians by 1939 were delayed deliberately. By 1939, there was no potential Indian bureaucracy which could have taken over from the British; it was this policy which prolonged the British rule. However, the Second World War worked against this policy. Britain was forced to devolve that task of administration upon as many Indians as possible. Maurice Zinkin tells us about this: "The land was scoured and scoured again, to find army officers, purchase officers, officers of a hundred and one different sorts. The arena of power were made public, and Government gave itself over to what was in effect one of the greatest training programmes in history."

The subjugation of the country was not sought only through administrative supremacy. Rather, this policy was extended into financial affairs as well. In fact it was this economic policy which not only created the strongest forces favouring the continuation of British rule, but it was this policy which kept the Indian economy under British control even after independence. It is this economic subjugation which is called neo-colonialism.

Trade Policy. Commerce was the cause and means of British rise to power. The British Parliament had passed the rules in 1720 to stop import of manufactured goods from India. Thereafter, the British Government systematically diverted the trade of India from manufactured goods to the raw materials. It was clearly in favour of the British interests rather than the interests of the subject country. The policy was clear.

Lord Salisbury explained this policy in clear terms:

> ...the question of administration interests us very much, and we hope that great advantage may be conferred upon the natives by the introduction of English Government, and the enforcement of the case which accompanies English rule; but the administration of the country is not the sole or main object that should interest us. It is our business in all these new countries to make smooth the paths for British commerce, British enterprise, the application of British capital....

Another Prime Minister, Joseph Chamberlain also stressed upon the commerce as the means and end of the British policy.

These cardinal features of the British towards the subject countries which were the bases of Indo-British relations are reflected in all the policies they adopted in this country.

The British Government was clear in its goals which were (i) economic development of the country should be complementary to the interests of British metropolitan interests; and (ii) there should be developed capitalist system owned by the private British entrepreneurs which could be a source of power to the foreign rule in India. The first example for the British policy towards India is clearly reflected in the tariff policy. As mentioned earlier, the British Parliament had passed laws against the import and re-export of Indian goods, especially calicoes. After the British attained political power, they raised, in connivance with the British Government, export duties on manufactured goods (to the extent of 70 per cent in case of textiles), and reduced the import duties to the barest minimum of two and a half per cent, on British manufactures. In this way, the Indian indigenous industry was ruined.

After this successful implementation of policy injurious to Indian industries, the British Government advocated policy of *laissez faire*. *Laissez faire* became "secular religion of the British middle class". The *laissez faire* was not conducive to Indian interests. As discussed earlier, the country at that time needed state protection to encourage industrialization. But India was not free like Germany or France who resorted to "protectionist policy" to compete with industrialization in Britain. Above all, the British Government itself was the staunch supporter of the Free Trade advocated by *laissez faire-ists* since it helped furtherance of British manufacturers' interests. It becomes clear from the remarks of Lord Hardinge, Governor General of India during 1910-1916. He writes in his Memoirs: Lord Morley (then Secretary of State for India) came up to us and taking me aside asked if I would like to succeed Lord Minto as Viceroy of India.... What struck me as curious at the time was that the only question he put to me was whether I was a free-trader, and I was honestly able to say that I was then always had been a free-trader. He told me that I might regard the matter as settled...."

Ruin of the industry threw the artisans and other people living on the business of goods were rendered unemployed. They fell back upon the agriculture. The increasing population could not find a job and also resulted in diminishing returns on the fields. There was a series of horrified famines in which millions of people died. The Famine Enquiry Commission (1880) recommended encouragement to industrialization of the country and sponsor technical training to mitigate the famine hardships and ameliorate the conditions of the vast mass of the people of India. But these recommendations were completely ignored. When the Madras Government, supported by the then Viceroy Lord Curzon, set up a Department of Industries, it "aroused the opposition of local European commercial community, who interpreted them as a serious menace to private enterprise and an unwarrantable intervention on the part of the State in matters beyond the sphere of the Government." The subject was not approved by the Secretary of State, Lord Morley, and the Department of Industries in Madras Province was instantly disbanded by the Madras Government. Anti-industrial policy was pursued solemnly in other provinces as well. Instead of encouraging industrial advancement, the British Government was shocked when the First World War necessitated encouragement to industrial growth. On the recommendations of the then Governor General, the Secretary of State's note is quite revealing.

As discussed earlier, the British had no alternative to put up with this favourable attitude towards industries. But the British Government was perhaps averse to appreciate any economic advancement which should be a competitor rather than complementary to British metropolitan interests. In the Reforms of 1919, the subject, industry, was transferred to State Governments, while the Centre kept fiscal, tariff, transport and general economic policy. It was aimed at slowing down the industrial growth which had become inevitable by the war and spread of transport-communications' network in the country.

Though the Government of India founded an Imperial Department of Industry in 1921, but by 1931, Anstey reported, "It had not yet undertaken any foregoing constructive functions."

Many a plans were taken up to develop heavy industry, but they remained just plans on papers. The policy continued up to the Second World War itself.

Currency and Exchange Policy. The slow and complementary oriented industrial growth was achieved through the currency and exchange policy. As in the case of political authority, the Currency Act also derived authority from the British Parliament. We have seen that the British policy had diversified the foreign trade which was favourable to metropolitan (British) interests than the Indian interests. Besides, the Indian economy had got centred upon foreign trade. The evolution of production both in the agricultural and industrial sectors was not export-oriented but also diversified to make them supplementary rather competitive. This is reflected in their policy towards currency and exchange of India.

Up to 1835, as we have discussed in detail elsewhere, there was almost a complete chaos due to multiplicity of currency. It was beneficial to British commercial interests who believed in exploitation of the Indian commercial interests by virtue of the former's monopoly over the trade in India. But as a result of this chaos, it had been a hindrance in the optimum exploitation of Indian resources. With this aim, the British Government prescribed silver standard for Indian currency. By keeping face value to its intrinsic value, the Act of 1835 gave the Indians a right for free coinage of rupees. It was not, however, to their advantage. The fluctuation in the price of silver brought about correspondingly a fluctuation in the prices of raw materials as well as finished goods. It had an adverse affect and caused a severe inflation and forced devaluation of rupee. As a result the burden of debt, which mainly came from Britain, also became heavy. Though the silver standard was abandoned in 1893, but the currency was subjected to the sterling interests. Instead gold exchange standard was gradually introduced. Under it, the rupee became a token coin. It was inconvertible into gold for internal purposes; but for external purposes it was convertible, at a fixed rate, into a currency which was on the Gold Standard. The exchange value with sterling pound was not only more favourable to the British than the Indian, it also facilitated the drainage of gold out of the country. It remained stable for a long time but, nonetheless, it was an insurance to draining out the wealth of India.

Banking and Public Finance. Banking is closely linked with currency. A good banking system can strengthen the monetary mechanism; an inadequate one hinders it. Both contribute to the money supply of the country and banking helps to economise the use of currency. Because of the close connections between the two, a Reserve Bank was instituted by the Reserve Bank of India Act, 1934. But the Reserve Bank was not in full control of India's credit mechanism. It was done especially to safeguard Agency Houses and Joint Stock Companies which had been, in majority of the cases, set up by the British to outwit the indigenous bankers.

Agency Houses. The Agency Houses, first, started operating from Bombay and Calcutta. They extended financial aid for trading activities. But the speculations soon ruined these Houses. Their place was taken by joint stock banking system. They also failed miserably, but they swindled away the money deposited by the Indians. Besides, by not providing a sound banking system the credit facility could not be developed in extending industrial base in India. Instead, the industrial infrastructure came under the domination of British financial houses. It dealt upon Indian resources a heavy burden and the investment in Indian enterprises with services of foreign loans. The volume of the burden is clear from the fact that on the eve of the Second World War, the sixty-one foreign agencies were managing more than 600 rupee companies in addition to a number of sterling ones. Some were well above average; of the ten major British houses or groups, Andrew Yule managed 59, Bird Heilger 37, Martin Burn 34, Begg Sutherland 27, Duncan and Octavius Steel 25 each, Mcleod Gillanders Arbuthnot, and Shaw Wallace 11 each, and Jardine Henderson 20. In this way the Indian economy was controlled by "Houses of Britain" and it was this policy which maintained as is criticised in many spheres, neo-colonialism in the colonies like India even after independence.

Transport Policy. The transport policy was also shaped by the British interests. As the Bombay investors' Year Book depicted:

> British shipping interests have often claimed that they have built up the Indian trade at considerable sacrifice. It is, however, well-known how Mackinon obtained at the breakfast table a subsidy, from Sir Bartle Frere, the Governor of Bombay, in 1863 and turned the Burma Steam Navigation Co. Ltd. into the British India Company of today. Not only did the British India not undergo any sacrifice but it minted tonnes of money by its virtual monopoly of the coastal trade in India.... Moreover, it was almost a scandal when the presence of Lord Incheape as the Chairman of the Retrenchment Committee in India secured for his company, the British India, a contract for the carriage of coal to Burma for a long time period of ten years on very favourable terms—which the Government refused to disclose—without even giving an opportunity to an Indian company to put in the tender despite the assurances given by the Government.... It need not mention the large sums of money which have been paid to the British shipping companies under the Mail Contracts and the exclusive privileges given to them for carrying practically the entire requirements of Government stores and other materials on the coast under the guise of helping the so called "Empire Shipping" which meant in Practice British Shipping only, the Civil and Military Officers enjoying the benefit of Lee passage were practically compelled to travel by the ships of the British Lines. And even today when they want to appoint a Controller of Indian Shipping who is expected to look after the interests of the ships owner, controlled and managed by Indians, the British Government of India cannot find a responsible Indian to fulfil that office but has appointed a Britisher who in his life time has done everything possible to stifle the development of Indian shipping in this country.

In this way, the British policy was systematically superimposing the British economy which actually made the Indian economy its complementary economy. It not only resulted in lopsided growth of industrial and agricultural sectors but also it was responsible for technological backwardness of India. Michael Kidron has explained it in these words, "No family group, however extended, could provide the resources of empires of this size and diversity, the more so as hired management was even less plentiful than it is today. 'Cheque book capitalism' took root, the managing agency system was made to reveal an incredible capacity for financial manipulation and malfeasance, 'selection and promotion...by favour' become the rule, 'sufficient regard...not being paid to efficiency', and technological backwardness fed in itself. Add to this the lack of a machine making industry, the need, therefore, to carry large stocks at the end of a long foreign-dominated supply line, the difficulties of adapting foreign machinery, and multitude of associated factors and the general inefficiency of Indian industry can begin to be grasped. Paper manufacturing might serve as an example, it only, because it was closely scrutinized as late as 1954. Eddison writes, "Most foreign-made equipment was planned and constructed for us under contrasting climatic conditions, and with dissimilar raw materials, differing grades of chemicals, and more highly trained workers than are to be found in India. In consequence, this equipment often gives unexpected difficulties and generally operates at lower efficiency than it would in its native land."

"Additonal problems arise from the fact that many imported units have designed into them automatic devices and mechanical conveyors which are economically justified only in countries where labour cost are much higher than they are in India."

In this way, the Indian requirements not only depended on the foreign, especially of British markets, but also ensured what the Directors of East India Company cherished in their instruction to their Administrative Officers in India in 1832 that they would "not like to rule over millions of natives" but would certainly cherish to have lacs of "permanent consumers" of British goods even if they were independent of British political rule. Therefore, Montgomery Martin rightly put it in 1838 that "so constant and growing a drain would make even England poor, how severe then must be its effects on a poor country like India, where the wage of a labourer was two or three pence a day?" Burke also described the ruinous effects of this contant drain. He said, "The Tartar conquerors made India their home; so their unlawful loot went back to the people, and their own interests lay India's prosperity; trade and industries prospered. But the English rulers were like birds of passage—and of prey—and there was an endless procession of new going out to exploit Indians and to become "nabobs" overnight."

Drain of Wealth. Therefore, we reach to the conclusion that though three administrators like Bentinck, Munro and Wingate who loved Indians and therefore, are remembered by Indians as their well-wishers but the economic policy had not only established institutions which could continue the exploitation of the Indian resources to the advantage of British financial houses. Their policy had also systematically drained out wealth of India. The country in which all the streams of gold and silver were flowing in and there was no gate open for going out of that wealth had been made a pauper houses. In every aspect of their economic activity, the people of India were paying a share, directly or indirectly, to the British financial country. Many a scholars have estimated this, but it is such an aspect which needs thorough study to find out the means and volume of this drainage. Here we are giving various theories and estimates which have been made so far by various authorities.

Montgomery Martin is the first authority who estimated the drainage in 1838. He wrote, "This annual drain of £3,000,000 on British India amounted in thirty years at 12 per cent (the usual Indian rate) compound interest to the enormous sum of £723,997,917 sterling...so constant and accumulating a drain even on England would soon have impoverished her: how severe then must be its effects on India, where the wage of a labourer is from two pence to three pence a day?" He further writes that "For half a century we have gone on draining from two to three and sometimes four million pounds sterling a year from India, which has been remitted to Great Britain to meet the deficiencies of commercial speculations to pay the interest of debts, to support the home establishment, and to invest on England's soil the accumulated wealth of those whose lives have been spent in Hindustan. I do not think it possible for human ingenuity to avert entirely the evil effects of a continued drain of three or four million pounds a year from a distant country like India and which is never returned to it in any shape." It is this constant drainage which is criticised as "neo-colonialism" by the independent countries of the Third World who had been under imperial domination of the European countries.

Growth of Indian Economy from 1947 to 1964 (Nehru Era)

27

Pandit Jawaharlal Nehru was the maker of modern India. He had pushed traditional Indian society into liberal streams and the technological age of the 20th century. He had initiated economic planning to provide the masses with the opportunity to lead a good life.

Indian economists maintain that in India, Britain followed a systematic policy of "planned underdevelopment" which left gaps in the country's economy, that will take a long time to fill. In 1947, India's industrial base was weak. There was too much pressure on land and the standard of living was poor while the opportunities for employment were limited.

In 1949, the annual per capita income of India was 57 US dollars againt 1,453 dollars of the U.S.A., 773 of the UK, 870 of Canada and 100 of Japan. The production and consumption of steel is regarded as the index of a country's economic development. In 1947, India produced one and a half million metric tonnes of crude steel as against 87.6 million metric tonnes of U.S.A., 16.6 of UK and 4.5 of Japan. Her production of electric power was also very low as compared with that of other developing countries. Yet India's resources for producing steel and power have been very considerable.

The poverty of India was reflected in the extremely thin social services provided. In 1950, there was one physician for every 6,000 people in India.

Economic Policy. Jawaharlal Nehru believed that there must be industrial development at all costs. According to him, a country without highly developed large-scale industries could not count in the modern world. On the other hand, Gandhiji was in favour of autonomous villages where the Panchayats should perform legislative, executive and judicial functions. Gandhiji was averse to the idea of growth of cities having large-sclae industries. The economic policy of free India rejected Gandhiji's objection to the growth of cities, but in a way, accepted the reforms of Panchayat Raj. While Gandhiji wanted the village to be independent unit, Nehru desired to make it a constituent unit subordinate to higher organisation and at the same time enjoying sufficient measure of autonomy.

When India attained independence, industries were grouped into three categories.

Armaments, railways, transport and certain other industries belonging to the first category became a government monopoly.

The second category contained a list of basic and strategic industries such as coal, iron and steel, ship-building and mineral ores and the responsibility of their future development was vested with the state.

This third category covered the rest of the industrial field which was open to private enterprise.

The policy was reiterated through the Industrial Policy Resolution of April 1956. This shows that Nehru was in favour of encouraging private enterprise.

The coexistence of public sector and private sector in industry is called a mixed economy. India's mixed economy is a via media between the so-called capitalist system and the socialistic pattern of Soviet Union or China. The Industrial Policy Resolution covered also the investment of foreign capital in India. Nehru made it plain that he wished to encourage foreign capital investment in the industry not for its own sake but because of the industrial and technical knowledge it would bring with it. He said that, as a rule major interest in a new undertaking should be in Indian hands.

The Indian National Congress at Avadi in January 1955, explicitly stated that the object of planning must be the establishment of a socialist pattern of society. In February 1956, at the Amritsar Congress, the goal was defined more clearly. The term "socialist pattern" was replaced by "socialism" as the guiding principle.

Implementation of Economic Policy. In pursuance of the principle of socialism the government nationalised various institutions and industries. The Imperial Bank of India became a publicly-owned and publicly-managed State Bank. Life Insurance was nationalised. In April 1956, the Centre advised the State Governments not to grant any licences for coal prospecting to private parties. Colliery companies were asked to surrender the leases of areas that they had not so far exploited.

The State Trading Corporation was established in 1955 primarily to handle trade with communist countries. This company was given monopoly of trade in cement. The cost of imported cement was higher than that of cement produced in India.

A few years later, the import of cement was discontinued and the State Trading Corporation continued to hold the internal trade. Another factor tending towards socialist state is the control-mindedness of the Government of India. For instance, limited company cannot appoint its managing agent without the approval of the government. Remuneration of directors is also limited by statute. In respect of labour, there is a statutory fixation of minimum wages and award of bonuses. All these restraints were necessitated during Nehru's rule in order to protect the "have-nots" from the exploitation by "the haves".

During Nehru's days economic policy towards foreign companies was appreciated even by foreigners. Foreign businessmen had not suffered serious discrimination. The government believed that the recruitment of foreign technicians and skilled personnel would eventually facilitate the training of Indians. The progress of Indianisation may be seen from the figure of employment in foreign-controlled companies on salaries of Rs. 1,000 per month and above. In January 1954, there were 3,455 Indians and 7,000 non-Indians but in 1959 the number of Indians rose to 7,916 and non-Indians fell to 5,304.

Planning for Progress. The Congress gave evidence of its faith in planning as far back as 1937 when it accepted office in the provinces according to the Act of 1935. The appointment of the Planning Commission in March 1950 marks the beginning of a new era in the economic history of India. India's Five-Year Plans attracted worldwide attention. America and many Western countries welcomed them. They regarded these Plans as a crucial test on behalf of democratic planning. The First Five-Year Plan (1951-56) was relatively modest and exceptionally fortunate in that most of its targets were achieved. The success that achieved the First Five-Year Plan led to the revision of objectives in the Second Plan. It sought to secure doubling of national income by 1967-68 and the per capita income by 1973-74. But the 1961 census showed that the planners had underestimated the rate of growth of the population. To meet the demands of the growing population, the long-term objective of Third Five-Year Plan was to increase the national income at the rate of six per cent per annum as against the average rate of four per cent per annum during the period of the first two plans.

Five-Year Plans. Our national income at 1960-61 prices increased from Rs. 10,240 crore in 1950-51 to Rs. 14,500 crore in 1960-61. Due to an increase in population, there was no significant rise in the per capita income. However, the per capita income at 1960-61 prices was Rs. 284 in 1950-51 and Rs. 330 in 1960-61. Foodgrains production increased from 52 million tonnes in 1950-51 to 7.6 million tonnes in 1960-61. The expectation of life at birth increased from 32.45 years for males and 31.66 years for females during 1941-51 to 41.68 years and 42.06 years respectively during 1956-66.

Strides in Agriculture. During the period of Third Five-Year Plans the government provided facilities for supply of good seeds and fertilizers. Demonstration plots were laid out in the villages and irrigation work was given top priority. "Grow More Food Campaign" was intensified. The deficiency of foodgrains in spite of such attempts is attributable to the increase in population and increase in standard of living. Competent investigations estimated that, for the foreseeable future, India would need to import two to three million tonnes of foodgrains annually. It is a matter of gratification that the U.S.A. undertook to supply seventeen million tonnes of foodgrains to India during the Third Five-Year Plan period. On the other hand, the government abolished the Zamindari system. In agriculture, the middleman was eliminated to give tenancy right to the tiller. Greater security of tenure was given to the tiller. Rents were reduced and ceiling on agricultural holdings was fixed.

During the days of Nehru the Tennessee Valley Scheme of the U.S.A. had caught the imagination of educated Indians. Therefore, there was a demand for the initiation of multipurpose schemes which were executed were the Bhakra-Nangal Project on the Sutlej; the Damodar Valley Scheme, the Hirakund Dam Project (Orissa); Kosi (Bihar); Nagarjunasagar (Andhra Pradesh); Chambal (Rajasthan and Madhya Pradesh); Lower Bhawani (Tamil Nadu) and Tungabhadra (Andhra Pradesh and Karnataka). These projects were meant for irrigation and flood control and also for generation of electricity.

Industrial Progress. India's raw material situation is very favourable for industrial development. It is difficult to describe in general terms free India's industrial progress during the days of Nehru. The official figures show that industrial production in 1959 was twenty per cent greater than it was in 1955 and if the traditional industries such as cotton textiles, tea and jute were excluded the increase would work out to fifty per cent. During the period of the First and Second Five-Year Plans, industrial production as a whole increased by forty per cent. But it must be observed that credit for this increase should go very largely to the private sector. The public sector suffered due to over-optimism in estimating construction time and under-estimation of costs. Therefore, a large number of projects in the public sector had fallen behind schedule. This should not in any way detract from some remarkable achievements in this sector. The first important achievement in the public sector was the

Chittaranjan Locomotive factory. The next most important development was the Sindri Fertilizers and Chemicals in Bihar. This was started in 1947 with the collaboration of the UK and U.S.A. and completed in 1950. Production started in October 1951. This factory is the biggest of its kind in the East. This factory produced over 30,000 tonnes of Ammonium Sulphate annually. Other schemes in the public sector followed in quick succession.

The production of steel increased considerably in the Second and Third Five-Year Plans. The major projects in the public sector are the steel plants at Rourkela, Durgapur and Bhilai. The Rourkela Steel Plant was set up in collaboration with the German firms, Krupp and Demag, in 1955 and completed in 1961.

The Durgapur Steel Plant had been put up with the assistance of a consortium of British firms. Work on the plant started in 1956. It was designed for an initial capacity of one million tonnes of steel. During the Third Five-Year Plan, the capacity was to be increased from one million to 1.6 million tonnes. The Bhilai Steel Plant in Madhya Pradesh was set up with the technical and financial co-operation of the Soviet Union. The general trend in steel production has been one of gradual increase.

During the period of these plans, India made a great headway in the production of crude petroleum. To manufacture the much-needed heavy electrical equipment and machinery, the government had set up a factory called Heavy Electricals Ltd. at Bhopal. The government entered into an agreement with a Swiss firm to set up a machine tool factory called Hindustan Machine Tools Ltd. in Bangalore to make the country self-sufficient on this front.

In respect of cotton industries, the government policy was to see that cotton mills did not hamper the handloom industry. So the government placed restrictions on any increase in the number of looms in cotton mills. Production of mill-made dhotis was also limited. In spite of these restrictions, total production of cotton cloth had appreciably increased. In 1960, production of cloth was 33 per cent higher than it was in 1950. These Five-Year Plans also promoted village industries like handloom, Khadi silk and handicrafts. These industries created employment opportunities for millions of weavers in the rural areas.

Promotion of Co-operative Movement. Under the Third Five-Year Plans, Co-operative Movement got great impetus. Co-operative societies were established for providing credit as well as marketing facilities. The number of primary agricultural and multipurpose societies which was a little over one lakh with a total membership of 4.4 million in 1950-51 doubled and the membership increased over five-fold by 1963-64.

Promotion of Rural Health Services. During the period of Third Five-Year Plans, about 5,000 primary health centres were established in Community Developments areas. These centres provided medical aid, maternal and child health services, including health, education, control of communicable diseases, environmental sanitation and advice in family planning to the village community.

Programme of Rural Electrification. Under the Three Five-Year Plans the programme of rural electrification was implemented. Many villages and towns were covered under this programme. The total number of villages and towns which were electrified rose from 4,687 in 1951-52 to 55,000 in 1965-66.

Community Development. Community Development programme was launched on Gandhiji's birthday, 2nd October 1952. The aim of this programme was that each village should have a plan of all-round development, of increasing agricultural production, organising village crafts, giving health education, and providing minimum health services.

Tangible benefits accrued to the rural population in those villages where there had been a hearty co-operation between the villagers and departmental officials working out the Community Development Project. An official investigating body admitted that the Community Development had failed to evoke popular initiatve.

Economic Development under Mrs. Indira Gandhi

28

Economic Development under Shastri

Shastri at a Press Conference said that the problems that would receive the highest priority were the soaring prices, defence, poverty and unemployment, national integration, evolution of a new social order through peaceful means, envisaging equitable distribution of national wealth.

Shastri as a Gandhian. Shastri was not a socialist. Essentially, he was a Gandhian in thinking and even in his way of life. He believed in self-sufficiency at village level and hard labour. Shastri was opposed to giant mechanised enterprises because they concerned substantial investment, used little labour and delayed benefits. He told his colleagues at the very first cabinet meeting, "I am a small man and believe in small projects with small expenditure so that we get quick results."

Economic Position. The economic climate was depressing when Shastri took over the government. The annual increase in national income between 1961-62 and 1963-64 had barely kept pace with the 2.8 per cent rate of population growth. The price level had risen by 49 per cent between 1961 and 1964. The suffering of lower groups had increased owing to scarcity of foodgrains. The achievements of the Third Five-Year Plan (1961-66) were far below targets—foodgrains by 30 per cent, mill-made cloth by 20 per cent and steel by 5 per cent. Some of the big river valley projects were showing poor results.

He did not want to depart from Nehru's basic policies and neither did he want to follow the beaten track. On 19th September 1964, Shastri emphasised independent thinking while making a statement in the Parliament. He drew the example of Stalin's successor Khrushchev and said, "No real leader ever walked the beaten track. Conditions change and it is for the leader to respond to them."

Planning Commission. Shastri's experience of economic decision-making was rather limited. He had served as Commerce Minister but only under Nehru's umbrella. In fact, he was frank enough to admit at the very first meeting of the Planning Commission on 25th June 1964, that he had no ready answer to the problems of planning and would need time to get to grips with them. However, when it came to the formulation of the Fourth Plan, Shastri accepted tentative guidelines that Nehru had approved but Shastri switched investment priority from industry to agriculture. His dictum in the words of Mahatma Gandhi was, "If God were to appear in India, he will have to take the form of a loaf of bread." Shastri clashed with the Planning Commission over the Plan's size and warned that we should cut the coat according to the cloth.

To Shastri, the Commission was "a talking shop of intellectuals". The first blow on the Planning Commission fell when its members were divested to their long-standing privilege of indefinite tenure. Their contracts were made renewable, this resulted in the departure of Tarlok Singh and M.S. Thakery from the Commission.

During Nehru's time, the pre-eminence of the Planning Commission was recognized because all important decisions were taken at its full meeting over which the Prime Minister as the Commission's Chairman presided. But Shastri started the practice of inviting the Deputy Chairman of the Planning Commission or its member to the meetings of the cabinet or its sub-committees to find a common solution. But whenever it came to a choice between conflicting views of a ministry and the Commission, the former prevailed.

Food Scarcity. Shastri was confronted with food scarcity in the country. The Planning Commission advised State intervention through price controls, procurement and rationing of foodgrains whereas the Food Minister, Subramaniam, advocated the market approach providing incentives for individual investment, higher outlays for yields, increasing inputs and imports under the US PL-480 surplus food programme. Shastri appreciated the committee of experts whose opinions coincided with the views of the Food Minister. Meanwhile, Shastri decided to try for increased US food aid. He sent the then Railway Minister, S.K. Patil to Washington to negotiate for the supply of 20 million tonnes of foodgrains, over a five-year period. An agreement for the immediate supply of four million tonnes of wheat and 3 lakh tonnes of rice came as a relief.

Development under Mrs. Gandhi. For the first time in the history of the Congress Parliamentary Party, there was contest for leadership. Mrs. Gandhi secured 355 votes and Morarji Desai less than half 169 votes. There was no doubt that the party's choice was popular.

March towards Democratic Socialism. It was clearly noted by Mrs. Gandhi that the benefits which free India could confer were shared by the big industrial houses, whereas the common man had to wait to enjoy his due share in these benefits. There was disillusionment among the common people who could not afford to wait for this for a long time. In order to ameliorate the conditions of the underprivileged people, she placed a programme before the AICC Session in Bangalore on 30th July 1969. It was programme of socialism. She suggested:

(i) A ceiling on unproductive and conspicuous expenditure;

(ii) A change in the procedure to lend money from public finance institutions so as to encourage professional and competent persons;

(iii) Allotment of more funds for new entrepreneurs and backward areas;

(iv) Appointment of persons to man the Monopolies Commission;

(v) Greater autonomy for public sector undertakings;

(vi) Building of a cadre to run public sector undertakings;

(vii) A ban on the entry of big business houses into consumer industries which should be in the small-scale and co-operative sectors;

(viii) Avenues of employment to the young and educated;

(ix) Prohibition of foreign capital in fields where local know-how was available; and

(x) Heavy punishment for those indulging is restrictive trade practices.

At this session, she also hinted at the nationalisation of a few banks, creation of service co-operatives in the rural areas and improvement of the lot of agricultural tenants and the landless labourers. It is heartening to note that the Bangalore Congress Session adopted her 10-point programme.

(a) **Nationalisation of 14 Banks.** At the cabinet meeting on 25th October 1967, Morarji Desai, Satya Narayan Sinha and Chenna Reddy, the then Steel Minister, spoke against the takeover of the fourteen banks while Jagjivan Ram, Chavan and Swaran Singh favoured it. Indira Gandhi's own inclination was for nationalisation but she was afraid lest Morarji and his supporters should challenge her before she had consolidated her position. Her basic instinct was for survival and her antenna indicated danger. So she accepted Morarji's proposal for social control of the banks to be operated by a National Credit Council under the Chairmanship of the Reserve Bank Governor to give more aid to agriculture, small-scale industries and exports. As stated earlier Mrs. Gandhi was not happy at the nomination of Mr. Reddy as a candidate for the post of President by the Syndicate. So her struggle against the rightist elements had started. She relieved Finance Minister Morarji Desai of his portfolio. It was a severe blow to the Syndicate. Before the Syndicate could regain its balance, Mrs. Gandhi nationalised 14 banks. This step was taken some time after the end of Bangalore AICC Session (August 1969).

Never had the people applauded any economic step as they did this one. Even the Federation of Indian Chambers of Commerce and Industry, the official organ of business interests, kept quiet and it was left to the Indian Merchants Chamber (with its strong Gujarati affiliation) to protest against the nationalisation of banks and the unceremonious outster of Morarji Desai from the Union Cabinet. In the din of popular response, what little criticism there was of her action against Morarji was drowned.

(b) **Removal of Poverty and Congress Response.** After the split she inducted like-minded colleagues in her Cabinet. They were wedded to the philosophy of socialism. The political climate in her favour encouraged Mrs. Gandhi to give a fresh edge to her "Garibi Hatao" Programme. Bonus for labour was increased from four to 8.33 per cent. There was a new ceiling on agricultural land 10 to 18 acres for irrigated lands and 54 acres for dry lands.

(c) **Take over of 106 General Insurance Companies.** Mrs. Gandhi also took over the management of 106 general insurance companies, Indian and foreign, with assets of Rs. 2,400 million. An ordinance for the nationalisation of these companies was issued on 3rd May 1971. This was applauded by the progressive sections and the people.

(d) **Nationalisation of the Coal Industry.** Another magnificent step that she took was the nationalisation of the coal industry, consisting of 214 coking coal mines and 12 coke-oven plants.

This was done on the insistence of Kumaramangalam who had argued that with an energy crisis in the offing and the talk of a price hike, the coal industry should be developed on a national basis. Nationalisation of coal industry and general insurance did bring applause from progressive circles, but did not accelerate the growth rate which continued to be sluggish.

(e) **Abolition of Privy Purses and Privileges of Ex-rulers.** The Congress Party image had to be refurbished and Indira Gandhi was convinced that it could be done only by adopting some progressive measures. One of them was to abolish the privy purses and privileges of the ex-rulers. Negotiations with them had failed. They argued that privy purses were not grants or conferments but what the rulers had entrusted in good faith in the safe-keeping of the Government of India. The ex-princes were clear that the law was on their side, but it could be changed. The Law Ministry suggested the deletion of Articles 291 and 362 of the Constitution which had guaranteed payment of the purses. It was presumed that Article 363 which barred law courts from interfering in disputes arising out of treaties and agreements with the ex-rulers could be invoked while dealing with privy purses. The government also favoured keeping the door open for negotiations on the mode and scale of compensation. The government proposed to give more compensation to those among the princes whose circumstances were far from princely. It knew that nothing could be done without amending the Constitution. Yet on the advice of the Prime Minister, President V.V. Giri issued an ordinance abolishing the Privy Purses of the ex-rulers. As was expected, the ordinance was challenged in the court, which gave a verdict to the effect that due compensation should be paid to the ex-rulers and appropriate amendment to the Constitution be made for the abolition of Privy Purses. The court's ruling gave full power to the government to determine the extent of compensation payable to the ex-rulers.

The Constitution 26th Amendment Act, 1971, which came into force on 31st December 1971 omitted Article 291 relating to Privy Purses of ex-Rulers and Article 362 relating to rights and privileges of Indian states and inserted Article 363 and thereby abolished Privy Purses and other privileges of ex-rulers of

Indian states with effect from 31st December 1971. According to Indira Gandhi, the grant of Privy Purses to the ex-rulers was an anachronism. The enactment of legislation abolishing Privy Purses was yet another step in the direction of socialism in India.

(f) **Other Steps towards Socialism.** Among the other steps towards the establishment of socialism were the nationalisation of oil companies such as ESSO, Burmah Shell and Indian Oils, the establishment of fair price shops, the Panchayati Raj, the conduct of raids for recovering black money, efforts to check smuggling, measures to arrest inflationary trends, demonetisation of currency notes of one thousand denomination. Restrictions in monopoly of trade and expansion of public sector undertakings.

In 1975, a new project for the socio-economic rejuvenation of the nation was inaugurated by the Prime Minister Mrs. Indira Gandhi. It was known as 20-Point Programme. It was handled as a blue print for national progress. They are:

(1) Reduction of prices and the display of stock positions.
(2) Ceiling of agricultural lands and their redistribution among the poor.
(3) Housing sites for the poor to be provided in rural areas.
(4) Abolition of bonded labour.
(5) Liquidation of rural indebtedness.
(6) Fixation of minimum wages for agricultural labour.
(7) Better irrigation facilities to be provided to ensure greater productivity.
(8) More power to be generated to greater production.
(9) Development of handloom sector.
(10) Better cloth to be provided for more people.
(11) Socialisation of urban land.
(12) Property valuation and punishment for tax evasion.
(13) Confiscation of smugglers' properties.
(14) Liberalisation of investment procedure.

(15) Worker participation industry.

(16) National permit scheme for road transport.

(17) Income tax relief for the middle-classes.

(18) Essential commodities for students to be provided at controlled prices.

(19) Textbooks and stationery to students to be provided at controlled prices.

(20) Training and employment opportunities to be increased.

Internal Emergency (25 June 1975). The most important proclamation was the one that was issued under Article 352 of the Constitution on 25th June 1975. The Shah Commission of Inquiry appointed by the Government of India on 28th May 1977, has in its report described the circumstances that led to the declaration of emergency. It was on June 12, 1975, that Justice J.L. Sinha of Allahabad High Court allowed the election petition of Raj Narain and declared Mrs. Gandhi's election void. On 24th June 1975, Justice Krishna Iyer of the Supreme Court gave a stay order which enabled Mrs. Gandhi to continue to discharge her functions as Prime Minister of India. During the interval of twelve days, the Congress Party's resources were used to demonstrate sympathy and support to Mrs. Gandhi. According to the Shah Commission, the decision to impose an emergency when there was already in existence an emergency proclaimed as early as 1971, was exclusively the decision of the Prime Minister who had not sought prior concurrence of her Council of Ministers for such a step. Though she was not bound to act on the advice of any minister, yet it was desirable to consult the Council of Ministers for such a serious step.

Defending her decision to impose the emergency, Mrs. Gandhi said in the Lok Sabha on July 22, 1975, "Democracy has not been endangered by what Government has done, but democracy was being endangered and would have destroyed, had the Opposition Front been allowed to launch direct action and its plans of sabotage under RSS guidance and to go ahead with its campaign to create dissatisfaction in the army, the police and amongst our industrial workers."

She also said that the country was on the brink of a disaster and the attempt of her government was to put democracy "back on rails". In her letter to the Shah Commission (December 2, 1977), Mrs. Gandhi stated, "As Prime Minister of the country, I could not abdicate my responsibility to stem the impending disaster merely for fear that my motive in proclaiming the emergency could be suspected." She reminded the Shah Commission that "proclamation of emergency by the President was a constitutional step and that it was approved by the Cabinet and duly rectified by both the Houses of Parliament".

The government was armed with extraordinary powers. The law courts could not protect the citizens from the operation of the Maintenance of Internal Security Act (MISA). Indira Gandhi's mailed fist fell heavily on the opposition leaders and she succeeded in crushing the voice of dissent. She believed that the judiciary was creating hindrances and delays in the implementation of progressive programmes of national reconstruction. During the Emergency she had a free hand in the expeditious execution of her 20-point programme. Specially under the family planning many acts of high-handedness were committed by the authorities. Indira Gandhi had the noble intention to have the family planning programme implemented in the overriding interests of the poor, but her officials at the lower level resorted to arbitrary and unscrupulous methods to implement the programme, and they earned notoriety for the government. Unfortunately, due to press censorship, the acts of omission and commission of the corrupt officials could not be brought to light and an undercurrent of resentment and disaffection worked as a volcano which erupted in the shape of debacle of her party in the general elections of 1977. It cannot be denied that the press was gagged and arrests and detentions went on apace.

Effective dissent was smothered and there was excessive use of power by the executive. But we cannot deny the fact that the Emergency ensured efficiency and discipline in all public offices and institutions and corruption was weeded out to a great extent. The operation of emergency powers was restricted to smother the voice of dissent and reclaim the anti-social elements.

The general public benefited from the efficiency of government concerns. What brought about the downfall of the Congress Party in the General Elections of 1977 was people's discontent and dissatisfaction due to the high-handedness of the officials concerned with the implementation of the family planning programme. However, press censorship, arbitrary arrests and infringement of civil liberties contributed to the Congress debacle in the General Elections (1977).

Janata Government

On the economic front, private enterprise was given a great boost. The prices of essential commodities showed signs of a downward trend. Due to stability in prices, the common man felt relieved but man does not live on bread alone. The people were watching with concern and anxiety the infights within the Janata Party. This image of the Janata Party was tarnished as the pulls and pressures within it brought it to the brink of dismemberment.

29 Economic Condition of India after Mrs. Indira Gandhi

After Mrs. Indira Gandhi, Janata Party came to power in the year 1977 under the leadership of Morarji Desai. During this Janata Rule the Planning Commission was reconstituted. The Janata Government announced a new strategy in planning. The strategy involved a change in objective and pattern. The objective was laid down as "Growth for Social Justice"—a distinction without laid a difference. The new pattern was the "Rolling Plan" which merely meant that every year the performance of the Plan will be assessed and a new Plan based on such assessment will be made for the next year—a continuous planning, in fact. The Rolling Plan started with an annual plan for 1978-79 and as a continuation of the terminated Fifth Plan.

Under his leadership many steps were taken to improve the economic conditions of the people.

After Morarji Desai, Charan Singh became the Prime Minister in the year 1979. During his brief period (170 days) he followed the footsteps of his predecessor.

Once again Mrs. Indira Gandhi came to power in January 1980. Her return to power witnessed many-sided developments in the economic field. She continued her economic policies under Sixth Plan (1980-85).

After the sudden and unexpected murder of Mrs. Indira Gandhi, Rajiv Gandhi became the Prime Minister of India on

31st October 1984. He sincerely and seriously followed the footsteps of his mother not only in the economic field but also in other fields.

Then V.P. Singh, Chandrashekhar, P.V. Narasimha Rao, Atal Bihari Vajpayee, H.D. Deve Gowda, Inder Kumar Gujral and Shree Atal Behari Vajpayee occupied the seat of Prime Ministership one after another from 1989 to 2004. The present Prime Minister is Dr. Manmohan Singh. Let us study the economic development or economic history of India during the period.

India embarked on a unique experiment of economic planning in a democratic framework, the largest in the world, at the beginning of 1950s soon after the independence. Enormous strides have been made in every sector of development whether in terms of output, per capita income, reduction of illiteracy and fertility rates, man-power training, building up of infrastructure, urban and rural development and scientific and technological advances.

There have been serious deficiencies as well, especially the slow progress in alleviation of poverty and in generating massive employment opportunities for millions. It is now well recognised that unless India's growth is sustained at 7 to 8 per cent for several years to come, adequate resources cannot be mobilised to tackle the challenges of social development in which India lags behind many developing countries.

Apart from the economy moving to a higher growth path, the 1990s have been noteworthy for the rise in gross domestic savings and investment up to 24.3 and 25.7 per cent of GDP respectively, low current account deficit in balance of payments at below 1.5 per cent of GDP, and taming of inflation to an average of 8.7 per cent till 1997 and 6 per cent in the subsequent two years ending March 1999. The annual rate of inflation by the end of June 1999 was less than 3 per cent.

In the first three decades (1950-80), India was in a low growth syndrome with an annual average of 3.5 per cent in Gross Domestic Product (GDP) but during 1980s (Sixth and Seventh Five-Year Plan periods) the economy grew by an annual average of 5.9 per cent. But there were serious imbalances, fiscal and external.

Unsustainable fiscal deficits of 1980s and excessive external borrowings precipitated the crisis of 1991 when the foreign exchange reserves plummeted to a mere one billion dollars (ten days' imports) and India was on the brink of default on its external obligations. Inevitably, the country had to turn to the International Monetary Fund (IMF) for a large standby credit and accept strict conditionalities in the shape of fiscal adjustment and structural reforms, in order to overcome macro imbalances and set the stage for accelerated growth of the economy. The crisis led to a quiet economic revolution with sweeping changes in trade, industrial investment, fiscal and exchange rate policies, all designed to place India on the path of liberalisation and closer integration with the world economy.

India is one of the few countries which made a successful adjustment bringing down inflation from a peak of 17 per cent, achieving a degree of fiscal stabilisation, and broadening the tax base without any destabilising impact on the economy. While tight demand management initially did sharply reduce growth, the wide-ranging reforms beginning with a devaluation of the rupee by 23 per cent, delicensing of industries, lowering of import tariff and dismantling of import restrictions, opening up of the economy for foreign investments and introduction of market-determined exchange rate system triggered dynamic growth in industry and exports.

In the post-reform phase, especially between 1992-93 and 1996-97—which was the Eighth Five-Year Plan period—the growth rate rose to an average of 6.8 per cent. For three consecutive years, 1994-95 to 1996-97, GDP growth averaged 7.7 per cent a year, though in the two subsequent years, recessionary conditions and adverse global factors limited growth to 5 per cent in 1997-98 and 6 per cent in 1998-99.

Since 1996-97, there has been deceleration in growth in both the manufacturing sector and exports. Industrial growth slumped from 12.8 per cent in 1995-96 to 5.6 per cent, 6.6 per cent and 3.8 per cent in the three following years ending March 1999, when demand for product had declined. Export growth also fell to 5, 1.3 and 3.7 per cent respectively in those three years

(1996-97 to 1998-99). Unstable coalition governments have been in power at the Centre in this period.

The second budget (1999-2000) of the government headed by Mr. Atal Behari Vajpayee, presented by Finance Minister Mr. Yashwant Sinha, and passed by 12th Lok Sabha before its dissolution in April 1999, without detailed scrutiny, had generated business confidence with its incentives for investors and fiscal package for the housing sector. The budget had held out promise of a 'second generation reforms' and set a Rs. 10,000 crore target for disinvestment in public undertakings.

In the first quarter (April-June) of 1999-2000, there were some signs of a pick up in manufacturing activity, increase in output of cement and sales, and a sustained buoyancy in the stock market attracting fresh inflows of portfolio capital from Foreign Institutional Investors (FIIs), the modest rise in exports, a further decline in the rate of annual inflation to below three per cent and maintenance of foreign exchange reserves at around 30 billion dollars despite a widening trade deficit.

The Finance Ministry reported an encouraging improvement in tax receipts, especially indirect taxes denoting revival of economic activity. The GDP growth target for the year is 6.5 per cent. It was expected if strong revival of rural demand for goods in the wake of the record foodgrain production of 203 million tonnes (estimated by the Ministry of Agriculture) materialises, industry would be able to contribute a larger share to the gross domestic output of the year, apart from services which was growing by 8 per cent during the 1990s.

Agriculture remains the bedrock of the Indian economy. Although its share in the total GDP has been declining over the years—from over 50 per cent in the early 1950s to 27-28 per cent in late 1990s, agriculture is of critical importance for economic growth, employment, social justice and balance of payments. With a fourfold rise in foodgrain production from 50 million tonnes in 1950-51 to 200 million tonnes by the end of the 1990. It rose to reach 212.20 million tonnes in the year 2003-04. India has become self-sufficient in foodgrains and provides food security for hundreds of millions of its people.

Economic Development under Five-Year Plans

30

Planning in India derives its objectives and social promises from Directive Principles of State Policy enshrined in the Constitution. The Planning Commission was set up in 1950 to prepare the blueprint of development, taking an overall view of the needs and resources of the country.

In the past, economic planning envisaged a growing public sector with massive investments in the basic and heavy industries. Now the emphasis on the public sector is less pronounced and the current thinking on planning in the country, in general, is that it should increasingly be of an indicative nature.

First Plan (1951-56). The First Plan with a total outlay of Rs. 2378 crore was rather haphazard venture, as the Planning Commission had no reliable statistics to work upon. Besides, the plan had to be correlated to the prevailing activities of various government departments. The result was a patchwork of isolated projects. All the same, the plan had a national character and was based on a rational hypothesis. It laid emphasis on agriculture, irrigation, power and transport so as to provide an infrastructure for rapid industrial expansion in future. The plan turned out to be more than a success, mainly because it was supported by two good harvests in the last two years.

Second Plan (1956-61). The Second Plan (1956-61) was a big leap forward. It laid special stress on heavy industries. The industrial policy resolution was amended so as to shift the primary responsibility for development on the public sector. Private sector was left to handle consumer industries. But the great quantity of imports that the plan envisaged in both public and private sectors, practically denuded IX India's accumulated sterling balances (as much as Rs. 500 crore) in two years and compelled the country to seek extensive foreign aid. Agriculture and small-sclae industries remained sluggish, without addition any momentum to development.

Third Plan (1961-66). The Third Plan rode on a wave of high expectation following overall growth of the Indian economy in the first two plan periods. The Third Plan aimed at establishing a self-sustaining economy. Internal resources having been strained to the utmost the Plan had to rely on heavy foreign aid.

During the Third Plan, national income (revised series) at 1960-61 prices rose by 20 per cent in the first-four years but registered a decline of 5.6 per cent in the last year. Per capita real income in 1965-66 was about the same as it was in 1960-61.

A growing trade deficit and mounting debt obligations led to more and more borrowings from the International Monetary Fund. The rupee was devalued in June 1966 to little purpose, as it soon turned out. The Third Plan had become stuck.

Interim Planning. The Third Plan having one awry, planning itself had become discredited in the eyes of many and demands were made from different quarters to declare a Plan holiday. But neither the government nor the Planning Commission admitted failure. They refused to fall in with the demand for a Plan holiday and proceeded to draw up the Fourth Plan as from 1966-67.

But the economy had so far degenerated that the Fourth Plan could not be started in time, that is to say, in 1966. Instead, as a stop-gap arrangement planning was made annual. The Annual Plans continued from 1966 to 1969—1966-67, 1967-68 and 1968-69.

Fourth Plan (1969-74). The Fourth Plan (1969-74) officially commenced from April 1969 with publication of the Draft Plan.

Growth with stability was the main objective of the Plan. Agriculture was expected to lead the growth with rate of 5 per cent per annum. Such a growth in agriculture would set up a chain reaction in the economy. The target for the growth rate of industry was set at about 9 per cent per annum. Altogether the national income was expected to increase at the rate of 5.5 per cent per annum. Allowing for the increase of population at the rate of about 2.5 per cent, the per capita income was expected to increase at the rate of 3 per cent per annum or about 16 per cent in the Fourth Plan period.

Fifth Plan (1974-79). The Fifth Plan Draft as originally drawn up was part of a long-term perspective plan covering a period of 10 years from 1974-75 to 1985-86.

The perspective plan attempted to co-ordinate various sectors of the economy in terms of the new slogan *Garibi Hatao* (Remove Poverty). The long-term rate of growth which the economy was expected to achieve on a self-sustaining basis was put up at 6.2 per cent per annum.

By the time the Fifth Plan was approved by the National Development Council (September 1976) its promises had become obsolete and the total outlay had to be increased from Rs. 37,463 crore to 39,303 crore.

This belated attempt had an inglorious end in another 6 months, when the Janata Party came to power. They scrapped it unceremoniously.

The Janata Government reconstituted the Planning Commission and announced a new strategy in planning. The strategy involved a change in objective and pattern. The objective was laid down as Growth for Social Justice—a distinction without a difference. The new pattern was the Rolling Plan which merely meant that every year the performance of the Plan will be assessed and a new plan based on such assessment will be made for the next year a continues planning. In fact, the Rolling Plan started with an annual plan for 1978-79 and as a continuation of the terminated Fifth Plan.

Sixth Plan (1980-85). The Sixth Plan was formulated after taking into account the achievements and shortcomings of the past three decades of planning. For the Sixth Plan actual expenditure stood at Rs. 109,291.7 crore (current prices) as against the envisaged total public sector outlay of Rs. 97,500 crore (1979-80 prices) accounting for a 12 per cent increase in nominal terms. The average annual growth rate for the Sixth Plan worked out to 5.2 per cent, which is equal to the targeted growth rate for the plan period.

Seventh Plan (1985-90). The Seventh Plan envisaged an aggregate outlay of Rs. 348,148 crore with a public sector outlay of Rs. 180,000 crore ended with an average rate of growth of the gross domestic product (GDP) at 5.3 per cent per annum, which was well about the targeted rate of 5 per cent.

The final year of the Seventh Plan (1989-90) saw the growth of national income by 4% largely contributed by the secondary manufacturing and services sector. The annual average growth of the Seventh Plan has been put at 5.3 per cent almost equaling the growth rate of the Sixth Plan.

Eighth Plan (1992-97). The Eighth Plan has recognised the need for a re-orientation of planning in keeping with the process of economic reforms and restructuring of the economy. Though a tangible change in the ongoing development process can be effected only over a period of time, the review of initial experience enables us to discern the direction of change and emerging criticalities with a view to identifying the measures to be adopted. The Eighth Plan emphasises the following:

(a) Human development as the main focus of planning;

(b) A large economic space for private sector;

(c) Physical and social infrastructure development by the public sector (allowing at the same time the private sector to participate); and

(d) A greater role to the market to infuse economic efficiency even in the working of public sector.

The plan proposed a growth rate of 5.6 per cent per annum on the average during the Plan period. An investment of Rs. 798,000 crore at 1992-93 prices was projected for the five year period 1992-97. Out of this, public sector investment was Rs. 361,000 crore (45%). Adding to this the current outlay of Rs. 73,000 crore, the public sector outlay came to Rs. 434,000 crore. Consistent with the expected resource position, the size of the Plans of the states and the union territories was projected at Rs. 1,86,325 crore and the Central Plan at Rs. 2,47,865 crore. This outlay was divided between the Centre and the State in the ratio 58.5 : 41.5.

Ninth Plan (1997-2002). The Ninth Plan (1997-2002) was launched in the 50th year of India's independence. It was developed in the context of four important dimensions of state policy, viz. improving the quality of life of people, generation of productive employment, creating regional balance and self-reliance. The Plan envisaged an average target growth rate of 6.5 per cent per annum in GDP as against the growth rate of 7 per cent approved in its Approach Paper. There was emphasis on the seven identified Basic Minimum Services (BMSs) with additional central assistance earmarked for these services with a view to obtaining a complete coverage of the population in a time-bound manner. These services were: provision of safe drinking water, availability of primary health care facilities, universalisation of primary education, public housing assistance to shelterless poor families, nutritional support to children, connectivity of all villages and habitations and streamlining of public distribution system with a focus on the poor. The Plan also aimed at pursuing a policy of fiscal consolidation, with a focus on sharp reduction in the revenue deficit of the government at the Centre as well as the States through a combination of improved revenue collections and control of inessential expenditure. The specific objectives of the Plan included:

(i) Priority to agriculture and rural development with a view to generating adequate productive employment, and eradication of poverty;

(ii) Accelerating the growth of the economy with stable prices;

(iii) Ensuring food and nutritional security for all, particularly the vulnerable sections of society;

(iv) Providing the basic minimum services;

(v) Containing the growth rate of population;

(vi) Ensuring mobilisation and participation of people at all levels;

(vii) Empowerment of women and socially disadvantaged groups such as Scheduled Castes, Scheduled Tribes, Other Backward Classes and minority communities—as agents of socio-economic change and development;

(viii) Promoting and developing people's participatory institutions like Panchayati Raj, cooperatives and self-help groups; and

(ix) Strengthening efforts to build self-reliance.

The development strategy of the Ninth Plan was directed towards enabling the private sector to reach its full potential for increasing production, creating jobs and raising the income level of the people. It was felt that a vigorous private sector operating under the discipline of competition and free markets would encourage efficient use of scarce resources and ensure rapid growth at less cost. The role of private sector and that of the state were viewed as complementary. Private sector activity needs properly organised markets—and hence the need for economic liberalisation and decontrol. But market forces may lead to undesirable practices which may adversely affect broader national objectives. The Ninth Plan, therefore, accentuates the need for state intervention in the key areas.

Investment needs of the Ninth Plan were estimated at Rs. 2,170 thousand crore, out of which the share of private sector was projected at Rs. 1,119 thousand crore (51.6%) and that of private sector at Rs. 726 thousand crore (33.4%). The additional investment required to fill the gap of Rs. 325 thousand crore was to be met by Foreign Direct Investment (FDI) and disinvestment of PSUs. The public sector outlay for the Ninth Plan was placed at Rs. 8,59,200 crore at 1996-97 prices. Out of this, Rs. 4,92,221 crore was for the Centre and Rs. 3,66,979 crore for States.

A significant shortfall in public sector investment in agriculture was observed in the Eighth Plan—this could not be allowed in the Ninth Plan. The composition of investment had to change from long-gestation to short-gestation projects which required optimal use of existing resources, particularly irrigation potential. The annual targeted growth rate in Agricultural Crops, Livestock and Fishery under the Plan was 3.82 per cent, 6.59 per cent and 6.50 per cent respectively against the compounded growth rate of 2.77 per cent, 4.57 per cent and 6.31 per cent respectively during the period 1980-94.

The demand of electricity in the Ninth Plan was to increase from 289 billion kWh in 1994-95 to 496 billion kWh in 2001-02. The generating capacity to meet the requirement was to be 1,30,763 MW as against the capacity of 85,020 MW.

Critical Appraisal

The rate of GDP growth during the Ninth Plan dropped to 5.35 per cent from 6.7 per cent achieved during the Eighth Plan. Growth in Agriculture and Manufacturing fell for 2.6 per cent and 4.51 per cent respectively from 4.69 per cent and 7.57 per cent in the previous Plan. However, Services registered a growth of 7.78 per cent against 7.54 per cent in the Eighth Plan.

While making an assessment of the Ninth Plan with a view to preparing the basis for the Tenth Plan, the Planning Commission stated:

> Following the Asian crisis in 1997 and subsequent reduction in growth rates in the other parts of the world, there was a slowdown in the Indian economy as well. This, coupled with lower than expected public investment as well as the relatively poor performance in agriculture sector in three of five years of the Ninth Plan, led to a reduced demand for industrial goods and consequent reduction in growth in the industrial sector. Some other developments, e.g. cyclone in Orissa, earthquake in Gujarat, Kargil War, etc. also resulted in diversion of resources from investment and consequent decline in the growth rates.

Apart from above, many other reasons can be traced to the lower growth rate in the Ninth Plan. The rate of saving remained 23.3 per cent of the GDP as against the targeted 36.3 per cent. Actually, there was a dissaving in the public sector to the extent of (–)0.8 per cent. The rate of investment which was targeted at 28.3 per cent, fell short by 4.1 per cent at 24.2 per cent.

The Ninth Plan had projected a resource mobilisation by the Centre and States of Rs. 8,59,200 crore, but actual realisations were to the tune of Rs. 7,05,818 crore or nearly 82 per cent of the projection, which meant a reduction in the size of the public sector plan by 18 per cent.

During the Ninth Plan exports increased by 5.6 per cent against the target of 11.8 per cent, while imports increased by 4.1 per cent as against the target of 10.8 per cent. The trade deficit for the Plan as a whole was US$ 74 billion. The external trade, thus, failed to provide the necessary support for the realisation of 6.5 per cent GDP growth target.

Tenth Plan (2002-2007). The Tenth Five-Year Plan (2002-07) was approved by the National Development Council (NDC) in December 2002. It was prepared against the backdrop of high expectations arising from better growth rate in the post-reforms period—averaging about 6.1 per cent during the 1980s. The Plan has further developed the objectives mandated by NDC, of doubling per capita income in ten years and achieving the annual GDP growth rate of eight per cent. In the past, the growth rates of GDP have been such as to double the per capita income over 20 years or so. However, considering the aspect of steady growth in population, the Planning Commission recognized the need for quantum jump from the past performance.

Since economic growth is not the only objective for national planning, development objectives are being defined not just in terms of increases in GDP growth or per capita income but on broader terms of well-being of people. This includes building an adequate level of consumption of food and other consumer goods, access to basic social services such as education, health care, sanitation, transportation, communication and availability of drinking water.

In order to reflect the importance of these dimensions in development planning, the Tenth Plan envisaged certain specific targets that directly relate to the key indicators of human development. These were:

(i) Achievement of annual GDP growth rate of 8 per cent;

(ii) Reduction in poverty ratio from 26 per cent to 21 per cent by 2007 and to 6 per cent by 2012;

(iii) Reduction in the decadal rate of population growth from 21.3 per cent in 1991-2001 to 16.2 per cent in 2001-11;

(iv) Universal access to primary education by 2007;

(v) Growth in gainful employment to, at least, keep pace with addition to the labour force;

(vi) Reduction in gender gaps in literacy and wage rates by 50 per cent;

(vii) Literacy rate to increase from 65 per cent in 1999-2000 to 75 per cent in 2007;

(viii) Providing potable drinking water in all villages;

(ix) Infant mortality rate to be reduced from 72 in 1999-2000 to 45 in 2007;

(x) Maternal mortality ratio to be reduced from four in 1999-2000 to two in 2007;

(xi) Increase in forest/tree cover from 19 per cent in 1999-2000 to 25 per cent in 2007; and

(xii) Cleaning the major polluted river stretches.

The Tenth Plan had many new features which, *inter alia*, include the following:

The Plan recognized the rapid growth in labour force. Adoption of technology in productive processes is costly and time consuming. Moreover, machinery demands regular supply of power or fuel. At the prevailing rates of growth and labour intensity in production, India faced the possibility of rising unemployment. The Tenth Plan, therefore, aimed at creating 50 million job opportunities during the period. Special emphasis was placed on employment-intensive sectors of agriculture, irrigation, agro-forestry, small and medium enterprises, information and communication technology and other services.

Since national targets do not necessarily translate into balanced regional development, and potential and constraints differ vastly in different states, the Tenth Plan adopted a differential development strategy. For the first time statewise growth and other monitorable targets had been worked out in consultation with the states.

Another feature of this Plan was the recognition that governance is perhaps one of the most important factors for ensuring that policies under the Plan are implemented as envisaged. Considering the present market-oriented economy, the Tenth Plan had taken the well-crafted medium-term macro-economic policy stance, both for the centre and the states, though it laid out the policy and institutional reforms that were required for each sector.

To realise the annual GDP growth rate target of 8 per cent, the Plan estimates revealed that at 2001-02 prices, public sector plan required mobilisation of Rs. 15,92,300 crore. At comparable prices it amounted to an increase of 67.4 per cent over the Ninth Plan realisation of resources. The share of Central Government out of the total resources required was Rs. 9,21,291 crore or 57.9 per cent, and that of States/UTs was Rs. 6,71,009 or 42.1 per cent.

Further, for achieving 8 per cent growth rate, domestic saving rate was targeted to increase from 23.52 per cent to 29.41 per cent of GDP. The investment rate or gross capital formation was targeted to increase from 24.42 per cent in 2001-02 to 23.26 per cent in 2006-07.

The Tenth Plan considers Indian exports primarily to be supply-side determined. Thus, in order to take advantage of international markets, the country has to produce considerable volume of exportable goods. The Plan envisaged that exports would increase from US$ 44,915 million in 2001-02 to US$ 80,419 million by 2006-07, which meant a compound growth rate of 12.4 cent during the Plan period.

The Tenth Plan projections for imports were based on two scenarios. In scenario I, tariff was sought to be reduced from 37.1 per cent in 2001-02 to 15 per cent in 2006-07. In scenario II, gradual tariff reduction was sought from 37.1 per cent in 2001-02 to 18 per cent in 2006-07. On the basis of scenario II, imports were expected to increase from US$ 57,618 million in 2001-02 to US$ 1,22,846 million in 2006-07 showing an average annual growth rate of 16.3 per cent. The trade balance was expected to increase from US$ 12,703 million to US$ 42,427 million during the said period. In percentage terms, the increase was to be from 2.9 in 2001-02 to 6.6 in 2006-07.

According to the Planning Commission, the total inflow of foreign savings in the Indian economy in the capital account was expected to increase from US$ 9,545 million in 2001-02 to US$ 22,222 million in 2006-07. The current account balance was expected to decline from US$ 1,351 million to US$(–) 18,711 million. As a result, accretions to our foreign exchange reserves was expected to decline from US$ 10,896 million to US$ 3,511 million during the said period.

On the basis of Report of the Special Group on creating 10 million employment opportunities per year, the Tenth Plan estimated the backlog of the unemployed to be around 34.85 million in 2001-02. The addition to the labour force during the Plan period was estimated at 35.29 million. Thus, the total employment opportunities needed were 70.14 million. However, on the basis of 8 per cent growth, the Tenth Plan was estimated to generate 29.67 million additional job opportunities on 'business as usual basis'. The additions in jobs were thus not likely to be sufficient to cover the additions in labour force, leave alone the backlog. This called for a development strategy which would boost those sectors which favour labour-intensive production. Following the Report of Special Group, the Tenth Plan identified some labour-intensive sectors which require policy intervention. These sectors included: agriculture and allied activities, food processing, rural non-farm activities including khadi and village industries, small and medium enterprises, and service sectors such as health care, nutrition, education, information technology and communication, etc. According to Planning Commission, the total employment generated from these programme-based policy interventions was likely to be around 19.32 million.

Thus, the total employment generation was likely to rise to 49 million—29.67 million through 8 per cent GDP growth and 19.33 million through policy intervention. Consequently, the rate of unemployment which was estimated at 9.21 per cent in 2001-02 was expected to come down to 5.11 per cent by 2006-07.

Critical Appraisal

The Indian economy made strong progress in several areas during the Tenth Plan period. Growth of Gross Domestic Product at constant prices in excess of 8 per cent has been achieved by the economy in only five years of recorded history, and two out of these five are in the last three years of the Tenth Plan. Many of the key indicators showed a steady growth during the Plan period. Agricultural and allied sector, after dipping below 1 per cent in 2004-05, mostly on account of erratic rainfall, rose to about 3 per cent. The value of industrial production has grown from 176.6 thousand crore in 2002-03 to over 224 thousand crore. Some significant dimensions of the dynamic growth in recent years are: a new industrial resurgence; a pick up in investment; modest inflation; rapid growth in exports and imports with a widening of the current account deficit; laying of some institutional foundations for faster development of physical infrastructure; progress in fiscal consolidation; and the launching of the National Rural Employment Guarantee (NREG) Scheme for inclusive growth and social security. The net FDI flow has also shown a steady increase. India is now one of the most favoured destinations for Foreign Direct Investment.

Growth in manufacturing, exports and GDP is attracting the attention of foreign investors. India has emerged as 10th largest industrialised economy in the world. It is the hub of computer software, information technology, communication, biotechnology, etc. It has made rapid studies in the field of higher education, medicine, health care, hotel industry and business process outsourcing.

However, some chronic problems like regional imbalance, poverty, unemployment, etc. continued to persist. The growth in better off states like Gujarat, Maharashtra and Punjab was higher than the states with lower level of per capita like Bihar, Orissa and Uttar Pradesh. Poverty eradication remained a dream though there was a decline in poverty ratio from 26.1 per cent in 1999-2000 to about 19 per cent in 2006-07. The Tenth Plan also failed to push its pattern of resource allocation to boost agriculture and rural infrastructure. Unemployment has also not witnessed any decline. The economy faced the paradox of rising GDP growth but no commensurate increase in employment, decline in poverty or reduction in regional inequalities.

Eleventh Five-Year Plan (2007-2012). The Indian economy has been growing at an average rate of nearly 6 per cent since the 1980s and at over 8 per cent during the last three years. The Draft Paper to the Eleventh Five-Year Plan (2007-12) suggests that the economy can grow between 8 and 9 per cent per year.

While the performance during the last three years of the Tenth Plan reflects the strength of the economy in many areas, it is also true that large parts of our population are still to experience a decisive improvement in their standard of living. The percentage of the population below the poverty line is declining but at a modest pace. Far too many people still lack access to basic services such as health care, education, transportation, clean drinking water and sanitation without which they cannot be empowered to claim their share in the benefits of growth. These problems are more severe in some states than in others, and in general they are particularly severe in rural areas. There are regional disparities in the level of development.

Strengths of the Indian Economy

The vision of the Eleventh Plan is based on the strengths of the economy and the challenges that lie ahead. The robustness of the Indian economy is reflected in the macro-economic indicators seen through a comparison of Ninth Plan and Tenth Plan. The average annual GDP growth during the Tenth Plan was 7 per cent as against 5.5 per cent during the Ninth Plan. Though Agriculture growth hovered around 2 per cent during both the Plans, Industry and Services grew at 8 per cent and 8.9 per cent during the Tenth Plan as against 4.6 per cent and 8.1 per cent during the Ninth Plan respectively. Gross Domestic Savings and Gross Domestic Investment, both as percentage of the GDP at market prices grew at 28.2 per cent and 27.5 per cent respectively during the Tenth Plan as against 23.1 per cent and 23.8 per cent during the Ninth Plan. The Current Account Balance, which was negative at –0.7 per cent of the GDP during the Ninth Plan became positive at 0.7 per cent of the GDP during the Tenth Plan. The Combined Fiscal Deficit of Centre and States came down though marginally at 8.4 per cent of the GDP during the previous plan. A quantum jump was witnessed in Foreign Exchange Reserves which swelled to over US$ 160 billion during the Tenth Plan as against US$ 54.2 billion during the Ninth Plan. The rate of inflation remained almost constant during the Ninth and Tenth Plans at 4.9 and 4.8 respectively.

The strength of the economy also lies in the fact that it has matured in several respects—responding to the economic reforms implemented by successive governments over the past two decades. The Indian economy is now much more integrated with the world economy. The outstanding success of Information Technology and IT-enabled Services (ITES) has demonstrated what Indian skills and enterprise can do, given the right environment. During the last few years, similar success is witnessed in other sectors too, like pharmaceuticals, auto components, communication, business management and more recently, even textiles. The global integration of the Indian economy has led to an increased inflow of Foreign Direct Investment to the country. The average FDI inflow which was US$ 3.7 billion in the Ninth Plan period rose to over US$ 6 billion during the Tenth Plan period. Another important potential strength arises from our demographic trends. Our dependency rate is falling whereas it is rising in industrialised countries and even in China. Our financial sector has acquired greater strength, efficiency and stability by the combined effect of competition, regulatory measures, policy environment and motivation among the market players including banks.

Major Challenges for Indian Economy

The Approach Paper to the Eleventh Plan recognized the above strengths of the Indian economy but was also aware of certain challenges faced by the economy. Some of the major such challenges are summarized below:

Provision of Essential Public Services

The most important challenge is how to provide essential public services such as education and health care to large parts of our population. Our literacy rate is still below 70 per cent. Though Sarva Shiksha Abhiyan has expanded access to primary schools in terms of enrollment, it has still to provide quality education. The education infrastructure is woefully inadequate in many remote rural areas and tribal belts. In the matter of health care, gross inequalities in the availability of related services in different areas persist.

Lack of Adequate Infrastructure

One of the major reasons for imbalanced growth in our country has been the lack of adequate infrastructure such as transportation, power supply, civil amenities, markets, etc. There is a great divide between urban areas and rural areas in terms of infrastructure. Many far-flung areas still have no road connectivity, access to markets and ensured power supply. Civil and sanitary facilities are non-existent.

Boosting Agricultural Growth

One of the major challenges of the Eleventh Plan is to boost agricultural growth. Between 1980-81 and 1996-97 the average annual growth in agriculture was 3.2 per cent, which fell to 1.5 per cent during the subsequent years. This deceleration is at the root of rural distress and has surfaced in many parts of the country in the form of farmers' suicide. This deceleration is not only affecting small and marginal farmers, landless labour but all farm size classes. The challenge is to bring a Second Green Revolution or to use the words of M.S. Swaminathan an Evergreen Revolution to at least double the rate of agricultural growth.

Increasing Manufacturing Competitiveness

Although the growth rate of manufacturing sector accelerated in the Tenth Plan to reach 8 per cent yet it was below expectations. The challenge is to bring it to around 12 per cent if the GDP growth rate of 8 to 9 per cent is to be achieved. The major constraint in achieving faster growth in manufacturing is the fact that infrastructure, consisting of roads, railways, ports, airports, communication and electric power is not upto the standards prevalent in our competitor countries. This must be substantially rectified within the next 5-10 years if our enterprises are to compete effectively. In the increasingly open trading environment that we face today, our producers must compete aggressively not only to win export market share but even to retain domestic market share against competition from imports.

Developing Human Resources

The emphasis put on quality higher education—setting up IITs and other premier educational institutions—has paid rich dividends. However, the expansion of such institutes has slackened in the past two decades. There are clear signs of an emerging shortage of the high quality skills that are needed in the knowledge-intensive industries. The challenge is to ensure a continuous and growing supply of quality manpower.

Protecting the Environment

Environmental concerns are growing globally as well as within the country. While economic growth and environmental sustainability may appear to be conflicting phenomena in the short run, we must recognize that in the long run, human well-being and environmental sustainability are complementary to each other. For example, neglect of environmental considerations in profligate use of water or deforestation can lead to adverse effects on many industries. The challenge is to preserve the environment and make development environmentally sustainable.

Improving Rehabilitation and Resettlement Practices

Our practices regarding rehabilitation of those displaced from their land because of development projects are seriously deficient and are responsible for a growing perception of exclusion and marginalisation. The costs of displacement, borne by our tribal population, have been unduly high, and compensation has been tardy and inadequate, leading to serious unrest in many tribal regions. The challenge is to ensure that the benefits from forced land acquisition do not accrue to private interests, or even to the state, at the cost of those displaced.

Improving Governance

In order to ensure a rapid and inclusive development, good governance—both in the manner of public programmes and in the way the government interacts with the ordinary citizen, is necessary. Corruption is now seen to be endemic in all spheres, and this problem needs to be addressed urgently. Quick and inexpensive dispensation of justice is an aspect of good governance. The challenge is to rid the system of notorious delays in dispensing justice.

Objectives

Based on the strengths of the Indian economy and the challenges that lie ahead, the Eleventh Plan sets out the following major objectives:

(i) To achieve an annual GDP growth of 8.5 per cent during the plan period with population growing at 1.5 per cent per year. This would ensure that the real income of the average Indian would double in ten years;

(ii) There will be a major effort to provide access to basic facilities such as health care, education, clean drinking water;

(iii) There are many marginalised groups such as primitive tribal groups, adolescent girls, children in the age group 0 to 3, and others who do not have strong lobbies to ensure that their rights are guaranteed. The Eleventh Plan must pay special attention to the needs of these groups;

(iv) The private sector, including farming, small-scale enterprises and the corporate sector has a critical role to play in achieving the objective of faster and more inclusive growth, as this sector accounts for 70 per cent of the total investment in the economy. The policies shall aim at creating an environment in which entrepreneurship can flourish. This will call for a substantial increase in the allocation of public resources for plan programmes in critical areas;

(v) A substantial effort at public financing of essential public services such as education and health care to bring them within the reach of common man;

(vi) To achieve the growth rate of 3.9 per cent of GDP in Agriculture;

(vii) To achieve the growth rate of 9.9 per cent of GDP in Industry;

(viii) In Services, the target of GDP growth is 9.4 per cent;

(ix) The investment rate is targeted to be 33.6 per cent of the GDP—of which 10.4 per cent will be Public and 23.2 per cent Private;

(x) The domestic savings rate will be 31 per cent of the GDP;

(xi) The Plan aims to frame a transparent set of policy rules to address the problem of compensation and rehabilitation of people whose land is acquired for development projects;

(xii) The Plan aims to bring fundamental reforms for bringing speed and affordability in law and justice;

(xiii) The development strategy shall be made sensitive to the growing environmental concerns;

(xiv) In order to maintain our competitive advantage in the knowledge-intensive industries, *i.e.* IT, Software Engineering, Biotechnology, etc. private sector initiatives in higher learning shall be encouraged;

(xv) Keeping in view the need for nationwide connectivity and mobility it is proposed to undertake an expanded programme for highway development going beyond NHDP I and II to include NHDP III to VII;

(xvi) In the energy sector, the Plan aims to address the issues such as: (a) pricing of domestically produced natural gas and its allocation to the power and fertiliser industry; (b) strengthening upstream regulation in the oil and gas sector; and (c) ensuring competition and open access in the proposed pipeline transportation and distribution grid;

(xvii) The Eleventh Plan will make substantial provision of funds under the Jawaharlal Nehru National Urban Renewal Mission to back the momentum of urban reform to infrastructure creation;

(xviii) The Fiscal Responsibility and Budget Management (FRBM) Act requires the Central Government to reduce the fiscal deficit to 3 per cent of GDP by 2009. The combined fiscal deficit of the Centre and the States is to be limited to 6 per cent of GDP from 2008-09 onwards. Thus, far from any increase in fiscal deficit as a means of mobilising resources we are constrained to work with a reduction of fiscal deficit of around 1 percentage point of GDP to be achieved in the first two years of the plan.

Planning in India started as early as 1938 when the National Planning Committee (NPC) was set up under the inspiration of Jawaharlal Nehru. The Committee produced a series of studies on different subjects concerning economic development. The Committee laid down that the state should own or control all key industries, services, mineral resources, railways, shipping and other public utilities. Besides NPC, eight leading Indian industrialists conceived "A Plan of Economic Development", popularly known as the Bombay Plan. There were also a Gandhian Plan and a People's Plan. After the achievement of Independence, Prime Minister Nehru set up the Planning Commission in 1950 to assess the country's needs of material capital and formulate economic plans for more balanced and effective utilisation thereof. The First Five-Year Plan started in 1950-51 which was followed by a series of Five-Year Plans.

Objectives of Economic Planning

According to the Directive Principles of State Policy:

> The state shall, in particular, direct its policy towards securing (a) that citizens, men and women equally, have the right to an adequate means of livelihood; (b) that the ownership and control of the resources of the community are so distributed as best to subserve the common good; (c) that the operation of the economic system does not result in the concentration of wealth and means of production to the common detriment.

The Directive Principles are in the form of directions to the state to provide economic freedom and equality to all the citizens. Based on these Principles, the Government of India adopted planning as a means of achieving fast economic development. The first Planning Commission set out the following four long-term objectives of Planning:

(i) To increase production to the minimum possible extent so as to achieve higher level of national and per capita income;

(ii) To achieve full employment;

(iii) To reduce inequalities of income and wealth; and

(iv) To set up a socialist society based on equality and justice and absence of exploitation.

Thus, securing rapid economic growth and expansion of employment, reduction of disparities in income and wealth, prevention of concentration of economic power, and creation of values and attitudes of a free and equal society have been the objectives of all our plans.

The economic planning can be studied under two main headings—(i) Removal of Poverty and (ii) Social Change.

Removal of Poverty

At the time of achievement of independence, the Indian economy was in a bad shape. The two centuries of exploitative British rule had drained India of her wealth. Large masses lived in abject poverty. The Indian planners aimed at increasing national and per capita income on the assumption that a continuous increase in these incomes would reduce and eventually remove poverty and misery and raise the standard of living of the masses. A rapid growth of the major sectors of the economy, viz. agriculture, industry, transport and power was envisaged.

The first three Five-Year Plans 1951-56, 1956-61 and 1961-66 worked on the theory that expansion in real national income was the basis for increase in per capita income, bring improvement in the quality of life—consisting of life expectancy, infant mortality and literacy—and reduce the number of people living below poverty line. But it was found that increase in national income was not accompanied by alleviation of poverty in the country. The objective of the planning from the Fourth Plan onwards was, therefore, not simply economic growth and raising the standard of living of people living in abject poverty. According to the Fourth Five-Year Plan (1969-74), "The basic goal is a rapid increase in the standard of living of the people.... The emphasis is placed on the common man, the weaker sections and the less privileged." The focus on the problem of poverty is evident from the fact that the slogan of *garibi hatao* (removal of poverty) was coined during the early 1970s.

Removal of unemployment and underemployment has been, from the very beginning, an important objective of economic planning in India since they have been the major causes of poverty in the country. However, the approach to meet this objective has been to increase investment in various sectors—which it was assumed would be accompanied by increase in employment. Separate employment plans for each sector and region to boost employment were not made under any plan. It was in the Janata Party Sixth Plan (1978-83) that the Planning Commission admitted for the first time the possibilities of real conflict between employment and economic growth and accorded employment a pride of place in the plan. But in the finally accepted Sixth Plan (1980-85), the focus shifted back to traditional growth approach—with the old assumption that employment would increase with a rise in investment—irrespective of choice of techniques. This explains why unemployment situation remains grave despite a series of Five-Year Plans. The total employment growth during the last decade has been a little over 1 per cent, much below the population growth. According to an ASSOCHAM study, the organised sector employment was down by 4.14 per cent during the last three years of the Ninth Plan and first two years of the Tenth Plan despite a steady annual GDP growth of over 5 per cent. The National Sample Survey Organisation (NSSO) 60th Round, conducted in 2004, has put unemployment in 2004 at a higher level than in 1993-94, confirming the phenomenon of jobless growth.

Since unemployment and poverty are interrelated the government started many employment schemes like Sampoorna Grameen Rozgar Yojana (SGRY), Jawahar Rozgar Yojana (JRY), Nehru Rozgar Yojana (NRY), Self-Employment Programme for Urban Poor (SEPUP), etc. SGRY was launched in September 2001 with the objective of providing additional wage employment in rural areas as also food security, alongside the creation of durable community assets in the rural areas. The programme is self-targeting in nature in which preference is given to BPL families for providing wage employment, but poor families above poverty line can also be offered employment under SGRY.

Since the above programmes have failed to make much impact on the employment scenario in the country, employment generation needs to be made the major objective of our planning. The Approach Paper to the Eleventh Plan recognizes the need for paying special attention to the growth of employment. Some of the strategies outlined in the Paper in this regard are summarised below:

> As India develops, dependence on agriculture will reduce. This will pose a major challenge not only in terms of generating non-agriculture employment but also managing the resulting livelihood changes. Some concrete measures will be necessary to manage consequences of inevitable reduction in agricultural employment. A shift of labour force out of agriculture into non-agricultural sector can only happen if our growth strategy is a success and the economy as a whole grows at a more rapid rate than in the past and

generates high growth in labour-intensive manufacturing and in productive services sectors.

To increase the employment intensity of economic growth, we must pay special attention to labour-intensive manufacturing sectors such as food processing industry, textiles, small and medium enterprises, tourism and construction, etc.

In the changing economic scenario—global as well as national—labour flexibility is viewed as an essential attribute of competitiveness. There are many aspects of our labour laws where greater flexibility is needed and would be in the interest of labour as a whole in terms of generation of large volumes of employment in the organised sector by encouraging employers to expand employment. This flexibility is especially needed if we want to exploit the enormous opportunities offered by export markets. Other countries, especially China, have been remarkably successful in this area.

The National Rural Employment Guarantee Programme (NREGP), launched in 2006, assured employment for at least 100 days to every rural household and, therefore, provides much needed income security to agricultural workers in lean agricultural season. The Approach Paper to the Eleventh Plan emphasised the need to adequately fund and effectively implement the NREGP.

Social Change

Various types of retrogressive forces such as inequalities of income, poverty, absence of equal opportunities for progress operate in an unplanned society. India's Plans made conscious efforts to remove all these retrogressive forces and bring social change as well as individual development.

Broadly speaking, Indian society is divided into two groups. On one side there are rich landlords in the countryside, merchants, industrialists, bankers and bureaucrats who enjoy all the luxuries and have surplus wealth. On the other hand, there is a vast majority of people who are poor and barely make both ends meet. Some of these live below poverty line—in abject poverty and destitution—and don't have access even to the basic amenities of food, clothing and shelter. It is believed that extreme inequalities of income and wealth in India have their roots in the traditional social formation. Addressing this problem requires abolishing the semifeudal relations of production in our rural areas. The Planning Commission recognized the need to remove these inequalities and outlined measures like removal of all intermediaries and ceiling on landholding. In order to reduce the large disparities between rural and urban incomes, the Planning Commission suggested measures like raising agricultural productivity, development of agro-based industries, fair price to farmers for their products, etc.

Though the reduction of inequalities in income has always been mentioned as one of the objectives in all Plans, it was never given a high priority it deserves. The Five-Year Plans never had a clear and positive strategy to redistribute income and wealth. Jawaharlal Nehru, the architect of Indian Planning, did not believe that the problem of economic equality in India could be solved merely by redistribution. As a matter of fact, the Fourth Plan clearly stated:

> In a rich country, greater equality could be achieved in part by transfer of income through fiscal, pricing and other policies. No significant results can be achieved through such measures in a poor country....

The Approach Paper to the Eleventh Plan points out that data on per capita consumption in the NSSO surveys show a slight increase in the ratio of urban to rural per capita consumption. If the urban-rural comparison is extended to include differences in availability of other essential services, the gap is much larger than in per capita consumption. The Paper suggests that the strategy of accelerated agricultural development combined with infrastructural support for non-agricultural activity in rural areas.

Apart from rural-urban divide there is a divide within urban areas which is growing. Massive problems have emerged as a result of rapid growth of urban population without a corresponding increase in urban infrastructure and provisioning of civic resources. Only a select few have somewhat better access to urban services. The quality of life for the bulk urban population involves many avoidable hardships. Small cities and towns lack facilities of transportation, health care, marketing and employment opportunities. Big cities are crowded and polluted. There are frequent power cuts and water supply constraints. Slum dwellers and squatters multiply all these problems. Cities in backward states do not enjoy the same level of infrastructure and administration as those in other states. The Approach Paper to the Eleventh Plan envisages the backward districts development programme to mobilise growth increase and reduce disparity.

Planning and Socialist Society

The Preamble of the Constitution declares India to be a Sovereign, Socialist, Secular, Democratic, Republic. Accordingly, the Indian planners visualised the establishment of a socialist society in which everyone would get equal opportunities in the matter of education, occupation, and general growth. There would be no exploitation of man by man and the wealth would be fairly distributed. Economic power will not be concentrated in the hands of a few. The first three plans talked of "development along socialist lines" or "socialist pattern of society". The Fourth Plan also talked about "the establishment of a social and economic democracy". It stated:

> The broad objectives of planning could thus be defined as rapid economic development accompanied by continuous progress towards equality and social justice and the establishment of a social and economic democracy.

The definition of economic democracy as given by our planners is the availability of opportunities for education, public health, sanitation and other general amenities, etc. for large masses of people, irrespective of the fact whether they are rich or poor.

Mixed Economy and Planning

The concept of mixed economy accepts the co-existence of private enterprise and public enterprise. In a capitalist or free market economy the private enterprise thrives on profit motive. However, in a mixed economy, private enterprise has to reconcile the element of self-interest with that of social interest. In certain cases, the survival of private enterprise is made conditional to its serving the community at large. Certain sectors are regarded as strategic in which the private sector is not allowed to enter.

India is an excellent example of mixed economy. The state is committed to play a positive economic role and direct its policy to secure a better distribution of ownership and control of the material resources of the country. The Indian Constitution lays down under the Directive Principles that the state shall strive "to promote the welfare of people by securing and protecting as effectively as it may, a social order in which justice, social, economic and political shall govern all the institutions of national life". It would not be possible for state to achieve the goals implied in the directive principles unless it itself enters the fields of production and distribution. This explains the rationale behind the policy of public sector expansion under Five-Year Plans.

In a poor and underdeveloped country like India private sector cannot move into infrastructural development which involves heavy capital investment, long gestation period and low rate of return. As such, state has to promote infrastructural facilities like hydroelectric projects, irrigation, road and railway transport, educational institutions, research centres, heavy industries and banking and insurance networks, etc. This is an important reason for the creation and dominance of public sector in India in the first three decades of planning.

However, India has recognized its vibrant private sector—its dynamism and personal initiative. Agriculture and allied activities such as dairying, animal husbandry and poultry are completely managed by private sector. Under the Five-Year Plans private sector has been given sufficient scope to produce intermediate goods and machines also, and as a consequence, a whole range of industries producing ferrous and non-ferrous metals, chemicals, paints, plastics, and machine tools have come up.

The Industrial Policy Resolution of 1956 clearly demarcated the scope and role of public sector and private sector. In the first category were included the industries whose development would be the exclusive responsibility of the state such as defence, heavy industries. In the second category were included industries which would be progressively state-owned, but the private sector may be permitted to supplement the efforts of the state. The public sector was conceived as a senior partner in the process of economic development. The private sector was to be permitted to exist and supplement the strategies of the public sector within the overall framework for development. According to the Planning Commission, "The distinction between the public sector is one of relative emphasis. The two sectors are and must function as part of a single organism."

During the last two decades, however, the private sector has been encouraged to participate more actively in the economic development of the country. There was privatisation of certain Public Sector Undertakings (PSUs), relaxation in industrial licensing and de-reservation of certain items meant exclusively for public sector. The Industrial Policy of 1991 introduced liberalisation to integrate Indian economy to the world economy. Our planners are recognizing the increasing importance of private sector to usher in an era of rapid economic development.

Financing the Public Sector Plan

The final picture on the size of the Eleventh Plan will emerge after consultation with states and central ministries and taking account of the reports of various working papers. It is felt that the strategies outlined in the Approach Paper will require large increases in plan expenditure in several sectors in both the central and state plans. For example, irrigation and water conservation in rainfed areas are both critical elements of strategy and will require extra expenditure of about 0.5 per cent of the GDP annually above the normal levels. Similarly, in the health sector we need to increase total expenditure by at least 1 percentage point of GDP by the end of the Eleventh Plan. In education we may also need an increase of at least 0.5 per cent of GDP by the end of Plan period to cover the requirements of expanding secondary education, and an additional 0.25 per cent of the GDP for higher education. Large investments are also needed in other infrastructure areas. Some of the demand for increased expenditure could be accommodated by reprioritising and reducing the allocation of public sector funds from existing Plan schemes that do not serve priority objectives, or which have proved to be ineffective.

A detailed estimate of Plan requirements will only be available after the various working groups submit their reports. However, it is assumed that the public sector responsibilities of the strategies outlined in the Approach Paper will require an increase in the Budgetary Resources for the Plan from an average of 7.5 per cent of the GDP (centre and states combined) in the Tenth Plan, to an average of around 9.5 per cent in the Eleventh Plan period.

Critical Analysis

The Approach Paper to the Eleventh Five-Year Plan has avoided many key questions directly related to the balanced growth of the economy. It blindly ignores the declining availability of food and endangered food security. The per capita availability of food has shown no significant improvement since 1991. The paper recommends agro-climatic, zone-specific strategies and packages which some experts call only suicide relief packages—incapable of bringing any perceptible change in the lives of poor farmers. The paper rules out a comprehensive crop insurance system as a Plan scheme. This means that crop insurance would be left to private insurance companies making it unaffordable to ordinary farmers.

According to the Approach Paper, if the economy grows at 9 per cent and agriculture sector at 4 per cent only, the income disparity between agriculture and non-agriculture will increase further unless agricultural workforce reduces absolutely by around 10 million during the Eleventh Plan and non-agricultural employment increases at 5 per cent per annum to absorb not just this shift but also all new entrants into the labour force. This is a gigantic task not only in terms of generating non-agricultural employment but also managing the resulting livelihood changes.

One would expect this Approach Paper to a Five-Year Plan to deal with outline projections of investment in agriculture, which is totally absent in the Approach Paper. According to

Financial Express, the original paper contained something more on employment, land reforms and social welfare schemes. It contained less matter on high speed growth, public-private partnership, labour market reforms and full convertibility of rupee.

The Approach Paper suggests broad objectives and targets and the associated challenges and implications for the policy which need to be considered by the centre and the states in the process of formulating the Eleventh Plan. The major points that emerge from the Paper are briefed up below:

> The previous Plans have made much progress in several areas, but alleviation of poverty has remained a dream. The Paper feels that India's economic fundamentals have improved to the point where we now have the capacity to make a decisive impact on the quality of life of the masses. This can be done by aiming at doubling the real income of an average Indian in less than ten years. The GDP growth target of around 8.5 per cent combined with policies that ensure that growth is broader based than in the past will be a step in the right direction.

The Paper rightly recognizes that lack of infrastructure has been a major constraint in our economic performance and must, therefore, be tackled on a priority basis by both the centre and the states. The development of rural infrastructure is a high priority for ensuring inclusiveness. Bharat Nirman Programme must be reinforced in the Eleventh Plan so that critical targets for irrigation, road connectivity, drinking water, housing, health care and telecom connectivity in the rural areas can be met. The gaps in general infrastructure encompassing power, roads, railways, ports, airports and telecom also need to be plugged.

According to the Approach Paper, the best way to ensure that income growth in the Eleventh Plan is broad-based and extends to rural areas, is to achieve double the growth rate in agriculture—from around 2 per cent in the Tenth Plan to around 4 per cent in the Eleventh Plan period. In this regard, the Paper gives some meaningful suggestions that to increase the rate of public investment in sectors such as irrigation, watershed development in rainfed areas, rural road connectivity and rural electrification a substantial increase in the allocation of Plan funds to these areas is required. The Centre can help through sector-specific programmes such as AIBP, PMGSY, RGVY, NREGS and the Backward Regions Grant Fund (BRGF). Recognizing that the farm is a multi-product system it is necessary to shift focus from productivity of individual crops to productivity enhancement of farm incomes. In order to facilitate agricultural diversification modern marketing and the involvement of corporate entities buying directly from farmers for retail domestic marketing, agro-processing and exports will have to be encouraged.

The Approach Paper also points out some policy distortions. For example, the policy of providing free or highly subsidised power to agriculture, not only leads to excessive drawal of water, wasteful water use and adoption of water-intensive crops at the upper end of canal networks, but also goes against containment of fiscal deficit.

In the industrial sector, the Approach Paper for increase in investment combined with technological upgradation and modernization to increase efficiency levels to survive in the present-day highly competitive world; free entrepreneurs from dysfunctional controls; bring deregulation industries such as fertilizers and sugar which are still subject to controls; cut short the list of items reserved for small-scale industries to allow units in these areas to expand to a competitive size; review the mining policy; and remove rigidity from our labour laws.

The Paper rightly highlights the fact that in order to grow at an average rate of 8.5 per cent during the Eleventh Plan period the domestic investment needs to be increased from 29 per cent to about 34 per cent. Half of this increase is likely to come from private investment and the rest from public investment in critical infrastructure sectors. The high growth of Indian economy during the last three years has built the confidence of Foreign Investors to invest in India. The FDI levels are likely to reach unprecedented heights during the Eleventh Plan period.

Finally, the Approach Paper lays stress on monitoring and evaluation of government programmes to learn lessons about the design and implementation of programmes which can help increase their effectiveness. Such monitoring should not be confined to tracking expenditure levels achieved in relation to outlays as done in the previous plans, as it is not a measure of effectiveness. It is necessary to go from outlays and expenditure to final outcomes.

Thus, the Approach Paper to the Eleventh Plan covers almost all aspects related to Indian economy. The Plan is likely to be prepared on the outlines contained therein. It is hoped that the policies and programmes are implemented in right earnest to achieve the set objectives.

PLANNING MODELS IN INDIAN FIVE-YEAR PLANS

During the last three decades or so a number of growth models have been put forward by the economists of the world. Broadly speaking, these models suggest certain important variables which are supposed to be strategic in the process of economic development. In terms of balancing of various economic factors different variables are put under different assumptions and certain relationships are established on the basis of those different variables. In the light of those limiting conditions, the factors are formulated for particular types of growth, rate of growth, composition of national product and so on.

All plans are based on one or the other model of economic development. This has been the case in India also. In keeping with the progress which has been taking place in the formulation of planning models, Indian planners have tried to use more sophisticated planning models in the successive plans.

First Plan Model

The First Five-Year Plan, though prepared in haste, embodied a projection of an aggregate growth path generated by capital accumulation and financed largely by domestic savings described by a linear saving function. Broadly speaking, it was based on the Harrod-Domar model of economic growth. The sole modification introduced in the Harrod-Domar model was the distinction made between the average and the marginal propensity to save; the linear savings function implied a marginal savings rate higher than the average one. An effort was thereby made to maximise the current rate of growth of the economy through a planned difference between the marginal and the average rate of saving in a general way. It indicated in turn a decreasing reliance on foreign assistance in spite of the higher levels of investment projected. The basic equations underlying the growth process were the following:

(1) $I_t = S_t$ the simple saving investment equality.

(2) $S_t = a\ Y_t - b$ the linear saving function.

(3) $Y_t = a\ K_t$ a is the capital-output ratio.

(4) $I_t = K_t$ all investment leads to increased capacity.

The solution of the above system of equations was

(5) $K_t = (K_o - b/a\ a)^{eadt} + b/a\ a$.

The implication was that an economy which decides to save more on the margin than on the average can hope to do better and better over time in terms of its rate of growth.

At that time Harrod-Domar type of models were being widely used for plan formulation in other countries, *e.g.* Turkey. Soon it was realised that the model is too aggregative to be much useful because it assumed away many of the well-known problems in economic development. It assumed, for instance, that there are no 'structural' difficulties in transforming savings into the desired forms of investment and that there are no real constraints in the economy. Further, the model ignored the fundamental choice problem of planning over time by assuming a constant marginal propensity to save for the economy. The result was that the economists started looking for a better model as framework for the Second Plan.

Second Plan Model

The First Five-Year Plan had considered the overall average productivity of investment and this ratio was used to estimate the amount of new savings and investment required to increase the rate of increase of national income. Professor Mahalanobis showed that the productivity of investment was different in consumer goods and capital goods sector. He pointed out that the productivity was lower in the capital goods sector and higher in the consumer goods sector. A simple conclusion from this would have been that a greater proportion of the available investible resources should be allocated to consumer goods sector and a smaller proportion to the capital goods sector. But Mahalanobis showed that this would not be an appropriate policy in the long run. He pointed out that we should take into consideration not only the immediate results in terms of production but also the effects on future rates of savings and investment. He stressed that though productivity of investment was lower in the capital goods sector, this sector would lead to greater savings and investment. This would happen because the capital goods are meant for savings and investment while the consumer goods are meant for consumption. Thus in order to raise the future rate of saving and investment, our policy should be to allocate more resources to capital goods sector and less to the consumer goods sector.

To determine the strategy of resource allocation between agriculture and industry, Professor Mahalanobis prepared two and four sector models which influenced the formulation of the plan. His model distinguished between investment for production of capital goods and investment for the production of consumer goods. He stressed the importance of allocating the highest possible fraction of investment to the capital goods sector in order to attain the highest possible marginal rate of saving. The Second Plan, therefore, accorded a high priority to the development of basic industry.

Mahalanobis' four-sector model was intended to indicate the investment allocation which would attain prescribed growth rates and employment levels in the course of the Plan. The model was undoubtedly superior to the crude Harrod-Domar approach, but its limitations were soon realised. The model was too limited in scope to indicate the most desirable allocation of resources among interdependent sectors. No effort was made to find out the optimal allocations, dynamic inter-relations were not taken into account, and the targets were defined in highly aggregative terms.

Third Plan Model

Though the Third Plan was based more or less on the same model as was used for the Second Plan, there was a clearer recognition of the definite limit to the fraction of investment which could be allocated to the capital goods sector to the extent the physical composition of investment fund itself determines to a large extent the type of output that could be obtained. The range of choice as to what kind of capital goods might be produced—for instance whether these would be used for producing consumer goods or for producing further capital goods, would highly depend on the type or character of investment goods, which could be produced in a given period of time. It was, therefore, considered important to define the fraction of investment allocated to capital goods sector not merely in broad terms but as capital goods which could be used to produce more capital goods. This to a large extent explains the stress laid in the Third Plan on machine building and such other industries as would help the economy to attain the stage of self-generating or self-sustained growth over the next two or three Plan periods.

An important characteristic of the formation of Plan was that the attainment of inter-industrial consistency was attempted this time in some detail. There was a marked shift from the simple decision models to the multi-sectoral models. This was the result partly of the suggestions Ranger Frisch gave in the course of his lectures at the Indian Statistical Institute and largely of the simple linear programming model constructed by Jan Sandee during his visit to the Indian Statistical Institute in 1957-58. Another analytical improvement made in the Third Plan was the explicit attention given to foreign trade as a bottleneck, to increasing the rate of foreign aid in breaking the bottleneck and on the possible desirability of 'using aid to end aid' so as to attain the stage of self-sustained growth at some foreseeable future time.

Fourth Plan Model

The Third Plan had tried to attain some intersectoral consistency. The method used was that of commodity balances.

An attempt was made to match the demand for and supply of key commodities through supervised discussions of various committees. Professor W.B. Reddaway made systematic supply-demand balance exercises for many industries for the year 1965-66, the last year of the Third Plan. But soon the need was realised for stating carefully the model underlying the investment allocations so that the vague assumptions underlying the simple procedure could be given theoretical elegance and scrutiny. Allan Manne and Ashok Rudra built static multi-sector consistency models while S. Chakravarty, R. Eckaus, L. Lefeber and Kirti Parikh made exercises concerning explicitly dynamic multi-sector models. The Chakravarty-Eckaus-Lefeber-Parikh (CELP) model is a finite horizontal, linear optimization model involving explicit inter-sectoral and intertemporal relationships, which satisfies boundary conditions relating to the initial years as well as to the final year of the Plan. The basic properties of the CELP model are: (i) It formally subsumes the structural features of the preceding models. The preceding models, therefore, became subcases of this more general model; (ii) It provided an optimal path of development over time which brought the economy from the initial situation to the desired terminal situation; (iii) It made a distinction between investment starts, investment in execution and completed investment. When the CELP model was brought to bear on the allocation of resources in the Third Plan, it revealed that the investment figures in the Third Plan represented a serious underestimate. Further, the results pointed to a shift in investment allocations away from the capital goods sectors to the consumer goods sectors—mainly agriculture. This is quite in keeping with the renewed emphasis on the development of agriculture in the Fourth Plan and Approach Paper for the Fifth Plan.

The theoretical elegance and the greater empirical validity of the CELP model should not be taken to mean that it is completely satisfactory for formulating development plans for India. Theoretically it is still rigid construction and is still too simplified to be completely satisfactory. Empirically, it ignores many basic features peculiar to the Indian economy, *e.g.* mass unemployment and underemployment prevailing in India.

Reconciliation of Planning Models

Nehru-Mahalanobis model of development emerged as the driving force of the strategy of development in the 1950s. The strategy continued right upto the 1980s with a short interregnum of about 3 years when Janata Party was in power during 1977-80. The model was based on long-term development strategy which emphasised a high rate of saving so as to boost investment to a higher level; preferred a heavy industry bias to develop industrial base of the economy; opted for the protectionist path to safeguard new industries; and encouraged import substitution to achieve self-reliance. It aimed at the enlargement of opportunities for the marginalised sections of society.

In this model, the state controlled the commanding heights of the economy through public sector. Even Janata Sixth Plan (1977-83) acknowledged the achievements of this strategy, saying: "It is a cause of legitimate national pride that over this period a stagnant economy has been modernised and made more self-reliant."

Mahatma Gandhi was not a professional economist and he had not developed any formal model of economic development. But he advocated certain policies regarding the growth of Indian agriculture and industries. He emphasized the conflict between village-industries and capital-intensive pattern of industrialisation. The Janata Party Government felt that the Nehruvian model, despite all its attributes, gave a step-motherly treatment to small-scale and cottage industries. The large-scale and medium-sized units were allowed in the consumption goods sector to stifle small units. The Janata Sixth Plan was an attempt to rectify this 'mistake'. But, returning to power, the Congress reversed the 1977 industrial policy and continued Nehruvian policy in the Congress Sixth Plan.

It is, however, wrong to criticize the Nehru-Mahalanobis model of growth on the ground that it neglected agriculture and small-scale industry and that all the economic problems faced by the economy were a direct result of such a policy. Ignoring the development of heavy industry and putting all emphasis on agriculture and small-scale sector would confine the economy to a narrow base. As a matter of fact, slow progress of agriculture can be attributed to several factors like irregular monsoons, primitive methods of farming, etc. Small-scale sector itself needs regular power supply and infrastructure which cannot be built without developing heavy industry. What we need, therefore, is a reconciliation of Nehru and Gandhi models of development.

LPG Model of Development

The LPG model of development was introduced in 1991 by the then Finance Minister, Dr Manmohan Singh with emphasis on liberalisation, privatisation and globalisation. The changes made in this model at the domestic level include the following:

(i) Areas hitherto reserved for public sector were opened to private sector. Transfer of loss-making Public Sector Units (PSUs) and disinvestment of some profit-making PSUs were tried.

(ii) Certain shackles that were holding back or delaying the process of private investment were removed by permitting the private sector to set up industrial units without taking a licence.

(iii) The threshold limit of assets in respect of Monopolistic and Restrictive Trade Practices (MRTP) companies and dominant undertakings was abolished. This allowed business houses to invest without any ceiling being imposed by MRTP Commission.

(iv) Cap on Foreign Direct Investment was increased to 51 per cent in high priority sectors.

(v) The chronically sick public sector enterprises were referred to the Board for Industrial and Financial Reconstruction (BIFR).

(vi) Greater autonomy was given to PSU managements and the Boards for public sector companies were made more professional.

(vii) To encourage exports, the economy was opened to other countries. Reduction in import duties was brought to facilitate import of foreign capital and technology.

The LPG model of growth envisaged a bigger role for the private sector. It envisioned a much larger quantum of foreign direct investment to supplement the growth process. It aimed at the export-led growth instead of import substitution, practised earlier.

The critics have pointed out certain fundamental weaknesses in the LPG model of development. It focuses largely on the corporate sector which accounts for only 10 per cent of the GDP. It bypasses agriculture and agro-based industries which are a major source of generation of employment for masses in the rural areas. It is felt that by permitting free entry of multinational corporations in consumer goods sector the model has jeopardised the interests of the small sector engaged in the production of consumer goods. The government has opened the import window too wide and consequently, the benefits of increase in exports have been more than offset by rising imports. The model emphasises the capital-intensive method of development, and there are serious apprehensions about its employment-generation potential.

LPG model has followed the IMF-World Bank prescription of stabilisation and structural adjustment. Ever since the adoption of this model, the Indian economy has been put on a higher GDP growth path. There has been rapid development in services, manufacturing, foreign and local trade, transportation, information technology and communication. The problems of poverty, unemployment and inequality are persisting but there are positive developments in these areas too. It may be argued in this regard that many extraneous factors such as large size of population, low literacy, rampant corruption, etc. are responsible for the said chronic problems. Our economy under the LPG model has shown better results in most of the sectors.

PURA Model of Development

In his address to the Food Security Summit in February 2004, President A.P.J. Abdul Kalam outlined the concept of PURA (Providing Urban Amenities in Rural Areas) as the harbinger of economic upliftment of the villages. The model advocates integrated action in the following five areas:

(i) The country should target food and agricultural production of 360 million tonnes by the year 2020. Allied activities in agriculture and agro-food processing should be given due focus to bring prosperity to rural people and speed up economic growth.

(ii) Reliable and electric power should be supplied in all parts of the country.

(iii) Education and health care should be ensured for all.

(iv) Information and communication technology should be expanded to rural areas to promote education and create national wealth.

(v) Growth in nuclear energy, space technology and defence technology should be given more attention.

PURA model involves four connectivities, *i.e.* physical, electronic, knowledge and economic, to bring prosperity to the clusters of villages. Under physical connectivity, a group of 15 to 25 villages will be linked to each other by road. There will also be provision for electricity and transport facilities. Digital connectivity aims to link villages with modern telecommunication and information technology services, *e.g.* cybercafes and Public Call Offices (PCOs). Knowledge connectivity tries to establish schools, higher education centres and hospitals on every 5 to 7 km of circular ring road around the cluster of villages. Economic connectivity aims to establish good marketing facilities within each group of villages so that all the essential commodities and required services can be procured and the people of rural areas are able to sell their produce in these markets.

In January 2004, the Union Cabinet accorded in principle approval for the execution of PURA within the existing gross budgetary support for bridging the urban-rural divide and achieving balanced socio-economic development. The government envisages development of over 4,000 rural clusters. Rs. 12,000 crore will be spent on these clusters.

CRISIS OF INDIAN PLANNING

Since the Second Plan was launched, Indian Planning has been characterised by a recurrent 'crisis' in the form of failure to attain targets of income and employment growth, rapid rise in prices with their socially undesirable effects on income distribution, heavy strain on balance of payments position. A number of explanations have been offered for this. The official explanation runs in terms of exogeneous factors like poor harvests, inadequate foreign demand for Indian products, failure of foreign aid flows, rapid growth of population, etc. In contrast, the private view is that the formulation and implementation of planning has been very poor in India. Let us examine some of the explanations offered by different quarters.

Failure to Enforce Strategy of Planning

Professor A.K. Bagchi is of the view that the factors responsible for the failure of plans are endogenous. He explains that in the Indian mixed economy "the control over means of production and distribution and over processes of income generation is exercised predominantly by the private sector; while the Government may propose a certain allocation of national income between consumption and saving or of total investment between capital and consumer goods industries, or between essential and non-essential industries, it is the private sector which actually determines the disposition of the resources. In the disposition of the resources it is the saving intention of the richer income groups and the demand pattern thrown up by the initial distribution of incomes and the distribution of the additional income between the different income classes which ultimately count." The Mahalanobis type of 'heavy industry' approach suits well fully centralised economies which can directly influence the distribution of incomes between different occupational groups or the distribution of production between different sectors so as to make them consistent with the strategy of development. The Mahalanobis type strategy which is based on the Russian model involves two basic problems in its execution. In the first place, it requires effective policies to ensure that the supplies of different types of goods mesh together. There should be no imbalances between the outputs of capital goods and the demand for these goods by the consumer-goods sector. Secondly, it requires effective policies to ensure that the distribution of demand for consumer goods is consistent with the distribution of planned supplies of such goods. To take care of these two problems, the mixed economies like India have the cumbersome apparatus of fiscal, monetary and physical controls supplemented by the market mechanism. But the use of this apparatus has serious limitations arising from constitutional and legal difficulties involved in executing these controls in a mixed economy. The imperfections in the application of these measures lead to relative price distortions on the one hand and to inadequate conformity between the intentions of the government and those of the private sector on the other. The direct result of this failure to follow the policy implications of the strategy in full has been the existence of black markets and the consequent malallocation of resources. The private sector has never carried out the intentions of the planners. What is worse is that even the shifting of income in favour of the 'profit-earning' rich classes has not led to a rise in the rate of saving in the private sector. Thus, the gap between the plan targets and plan achievements has been widening.

Inapplicability of Western Economic Models

It is widely believed that the economic models formulated in Western countries are not applicable to underdeveloped countries which have entirely different socio-economic conditions. The Western economists have formulated their models keeping in view the environments and needs of their economies and as such these models are not very relevant to the Indian Planning. The Indian Planning models have been inspired by the Russian model and the execution of the plans is based on the fiscal-monetary measures derived from Western economic theory. It is held that the failure to enforce the Mahalanobis strategy is owing to the misleading assumptions of this strategy in regard to the structure of the Indian economy.

Inadequacy of Planning Technique

According to Professor R.S. Eckaus, the main deficiency in Indian Planning is the lack of a technique that would permit the planners to map out rapidly the implications of alternative sets of social preferences and spell out the merits of alternative paths of development. He has shown that a model of fairly complicated structure can be adopted for computation. He has derived output values for alternative sets of inputs. According to him, the present method of commodity balances followed in India to arrive at consistency of the plan is a static exercise. The model used assumes a linear structure of production and a constant marginal utility of consumption so that future and present consumption would provide the same benefits. No effort has been made to determine optimal allocations; dynamic interrelations have never been taken into consideration; and the targets have been defined in highly aggregative terms. Eckaus points out that Indian Planning has made itself felt on the marginal rather than on the central issues—the issues relating to the questions of welfare, income distribution, time preference and the social control of economic activities. In fact, these issues have not always been adequately identified.

Professor Eckaus, along with Kirit Parikh, has reworked the Third Plan targets through a multisectoral inter-temporal model employing linear programming. He showed that the allocation of resources under that Plan was not even near optimal, given the objective function specifying the goals of the Plan. Professor Edward S. Mason has raised the critical question as to whether one "development path" derived through the optimization techniques can be shown by the exercise to be "better" than alternative paths within any meaning of better that is significant for current planning operations in India. "A judgement on this question rests on the validity of the statistical underpinning, the reasonableness of the very numerous constraints introduced to facilitate computation and the relationship of the assumptions—the implied social preferences—to the social preferences that do and must underlie any realistic planning effort." Eckaus himself admits that the application of linear programming to find an optimum solution to plan allocations requires time-consuming, complicated computerised calculations the data for which may not be immediately available. Further, the assumptions of linearity of objective function and the constraints give a solution in which consumption tends to be concentrated either at the beginning or at the end of the Plan. This is called the 'filip-flop' or 'bang-bang' tendency. No doubt, this tendency can be modified by further constraints on consumption, saving and income growth. But again the question arises whether in such a case contraints do not become more important than the solution. The nature and extent of the data available in India does not permit the use of such complicated models as yet. It is not certain whether the precision in planning obtained through the application of such models is worth the extra costs involved. Professor Mason also observes, "I see no alternative under present circumstances, to the slow alternative procedures now being followed in most effective planning operation."

Peripheral Role of the Planning Commission

Some people trace the recurring crisis of Indian Planning to the marginal role which the Planning Commission plays in the decision-making for the plans. In India, planning is broadly conceived as consisting of technical advice on the totality of government decisions affecting the use of economic resources. Over three quarters of economic activity is in the private sector, where agriculture, commerce and the small industry predominates. The governmental decisions affecting resource use in this part of the economy relate to taxation and subsidies, price controls, licensing, import duties, foreign exchange rates and allocations, etc. In this area, the Planning Commission stands at the periphery of decision-making. The consequence is misdirection and malallocation of resources in the private sector.

So far as the central ministries are concerned, a major portion of the plan investment are in the heavy industrial complex known as the 'core sector'. The industrial complex "provides its own justification for investment funds and grows in an enclave having little connection with the rest of the Indian economy. The steel mills supply engineering installations at Ranchi and, in turn, receive equipments from them. Both the mills and Ranchi require electric power, and thermal plants are built to supply these needs. The thermal plants need equipment and the heavy electrical equipment plant at Bhopal is established and, in turn, secures its supplies from the steel mills. All these enterprises require coal, and the government opens new mines, thus creating a demand for heavy mining equipment from Ranchi. This enclave touches the rest of the economy as a demander of foodstuffs and other consumer goods for its growing labour force. But to date this industrial complex has affected very little the rest of Indian economic activity". The fundamental decision on the development of heavy industry was taken in 1956; now the industrial complex exists and it itself guides the flows of a considerable amount of public investment for a long time to come. These demands for investment now leave no choice to the Planning Commission. The ministries concerned have become the planners within the areas of their responsibilities, looking only to the Ministry of Finance for financial authorization and allocations of foreign exchange.

States are responsible for development heads of agriculture, industry, forests, health, education and local transport. They vie with each other in putting forward inflated plans and in bidding the central resources to their areas. The Planning Commission faces the problem of pruning down these state plans to match the available resources to be allocated to the central ministries on the one hand and states on the other. To cite Edward Mason, "The role of Planning Commission is increasingly that of a negotiator and compromiser rather than of an initiator of development strategy." The economy is cumulatively growing in wrong directions while the Planning Commission watches helplessely and is yet being blamed for the mess that follows.

Inability to Implement Plans

It is widely believed that the failure of Indian plans is primarily because of inability or unwillingness to implement the plans. The problem of implementation is much more complicated than that of formulation. According to Max. F. Milikan, the necessary characteristics of a feasible and implementable plan are: (1) Major target must be fully specified sector by sector. A feasible plan must be detailed enough to make the responsibilities of major decision-making units separately identifiable; (2) The targets must be stated both in capital and current terms; (3) All project and programme activities must be fully specified; (4) All the major activities must have their time dimensions fully specified; (5) The initial conditions in the economy at the time of starting the plan must be fully specified; (6) A careful advance testing of the time phased input-output relations; and (7) For major commodity groups the levels of demand likely to be generated in each period should be reasonably consistent with the levels of supply implicit in the physical (production) targets. If the methods of preparing Indian plans are examined, it would be found that Indian planning seriously lacks in the fourth, sixth and seventh requirements. This obviously leads to serious shortfalls in the attainment of targets.

The failure of Indian plans is largely because of inadequate provision for their implementation. Effective planning requires that every target must be accompanied by policies and measures which have been devised specifically to fulfil it; in the absence of these, it becomes only a forecast or a projection.

Natural Factors

Of the natural factors which hamper economic growth in India special mention may be made of its tropical and sub-tropical climate making economic activity unduly hard both on account of burning heat in summer and severe cold in winter, the type of the soil, some of which is all sand or all hills, the nature of the terrain making construction of road or rail track difficult and expensive, continental dimensions making transport and communications a hazardous, prolonged and an expensive business, and so on. But of all these the most important is the nature of the rainfall which most directly and vitally affects the agricultural production. Both shortage as well as excess of rainfall play havoc with the economy. If the rains are scarce, crops wither away and in case rains are excessive, crops are flooded away. Indian agriculture is said to be a gamble in monsoons. If the rainfall is timely, adequate and well-spread, the crops may be quite rich. Successive years of good rainfall during the First Plan made our agriculture prosperous while unfavourable rain and floods during the Second and Third Plans led to shortages. Slow growth of agriculture has acted as a drag. Rapid economic development would be possible in India only if we can make agriculture move forward.

Demographic Factors

One of the most important factors responsible for slow growth is the rapid growth of population. A major portion of the increased income is required to maintain the increasing people and thus very little remains for stepping up the standard of living of the people. Rapid economic growth would be difficult without taking drastic measures for slowing down the rate of population growth.

Bibliography

I

Adhya, G.L., *Early Indian Economics*, 1966.

Basham, A.L., *The Wonder that was India.*

Basham, A.L., *Aspects of Ancient Indian Culture.*

Basham, A.L., *Studies in Indian History and Culture.*

Chakraborti, H., *Trade and Commerce of Ancient India.*

Majumdar, R.C., *An Advanced History of India.*

Rawlinson, H.G., *India: A Short Cutlural History.*

II

Durant, Will, *Story of Civilisation, Our Oriental Heritage.*

Prasad, Ishwari, *A Short History of Muslim Rule in India.*

Nehru, Jawaharlal, *Discovery of India.*

Sarkar, J.N., *Studies of Mughal India.*

Sarkar, J.N., *Mughal Administration.*

III

Anstey, Vera, *The Economic Development of India.*

Chaudhuri, K.N., *The Economic Development of India under East India Company.*

Dutt, Romesh, *The Economic History of India.*

Gadgil, D.R., *Industrial Evolution in India.*

Gopalakrishnan, *Development of Economic Ideas in India.*

Griffths, Percival, *The British Impact on India.*
Loganathan, P.S., *Industrialisation.*
Misra, B.B., *The Indian Middle Class.*
Thapar, Romila, *A History of India.*
Vakil, C.N., *Economic Consequences of Divided India.*
Varshney, R.L., *India's Foreign Trade.*

Index

D

E

F

G

S

T

U

V

W

X

Y

Z